Li Yong (1627-1705) and
Epistemological Dimensions
of Confucian Philosophy

Li Yong (1627-1705) and
Epistemological Dimensions
of Confucian Philosophy

Anne D. Birdwhistell

Stanford University Press
Stanford, California

Stanford University Press
Stanford, California
© 1996 by the Board of Trustees of the
Leland Stanford Junior University

Printed in the United States of America

CIP data appear at the end of the book

Stanford University Press publications
are distributed exclusively by Stanford
University Press within the United States,
Canada, Mexico, and Central America;
they are distributed exclusively by
Cambridge University Press
throughout the rest of the world.

*In memory of my husband, Ray L. Birdwhistell,
and his "spirit of '76" —*

*inspiring in teaching, exuberant in learning,
passionate in living*

Acknowledgments

I am appreciative of the help I have received from numerous people, too many to name here, over the course of my conceptualizing and writing this study. In particular, I wish to thank David S. Nivison for having first sparked my interest in seventeenth-century thought many years ago and subsequently serving as advisor for my dissertation on Li Yong. I wish to thank my colleagues at Stockton College of New Jersey and the Richard Stockton Foundation for granting me the research support that has helped to make this book possible, and I thank my former student Cheryl Olson for her generous help when my time was consumed by other pressing concerns. I especially want to acknowledge the help and support of Conrad Schirokauer, who read and criticized an early draft of the manuscript. Also, I thank John Ziemer of Stanford University Press for his insightful comments and excellent advice. I further express my appreciation to the University Seminars at Columbia University for assistance in the preparation of the manuscript for publication. The ideas presented here have benefited from discussions in the University Seminar on Neo-Confucian Studies. Above all, I am grateful for the constant support and enthusiastic encouragement of my husband, Ray L. Birdwhistell, whose unsuccessful battle with cancer did not allow him to enjoy the completion of this project. Our years of discussions are inseparable from my development of ideas presented here, and it is no exaggeration to say that he fully embodied his teaching that "nothing never happens." No one I have ever known was more inspiring as a teacher and enthusiastic as a learner.

A.D.B.

Contents

Abbreviations

The following abbreviations are used in the text and notes:

EQQJ Li Yong, *Li Erqu xiansheng quanji* (Complete works of Master Li Erqu), photo-offset reproduction of 1828 ed., 2 vols. (Taibei: Huawen shuju, 1970).

SSFSL Li Yong, *Sishu fanshen lu* (Record of reflections on the Four Books), 1702 ed. Located in the Gest Library, Princeton University. The work is unpaginated; for ease of reference, in citing this work, I have assigned page numbers starting anew with each major section (*Daxue* [Great learning], *Zhongyong* [Doctrine of the mean], *Lunyu* [Analects], *Mengzi* [Mencius], and *Supplement to Mengzi*). Each of the last three sections is subdivided into two parts, and my pagination starts over with each subsection, e.g., *Mengzi*, pt. 1, 2, or *Mengzi*, pt. 2, 3.

Li Yong (1627-1705) and
Epistemological Dimensions
of Confucian Philosophy

1   *Toward a Search Frame*

PERSPECTIVES AND METHODOLOGY

This study has three separate but interrelated aims. One is to develop an analytic perspective that will help establish a field for comparative philosophy. A second is to examine Confucian philosophy as a philosophical system, particularly in respect to its epistemological dimensions. The third is to investigate the thought of a particular thinker as an illustration of how the philosophical system was appropriated. Thus, even though the guiding interests of this study are metaphilosophical, I approach these interests through discussion of specific ideas and concepts.[1] My theoretical concerns lead me, moreover, to focus on certain characteristics of Confucian thinking and to slight others, but I hope my approach is sufficiently explicit to enable the reader to evaluate this reconstruction of Confucian philosophy.

Before I elaborate the aims of this study further, a brief comment regarding the problem of translation is needed, because translation is, on many levels, at the heart of the comparative and cross-cultural enterprise. As a help in gaining perspective, I am reminded of Confucius' teachings, more than two millennia ago, on the "rectification of names" (*Lunyu*, 12.11). We are now, as Confucius was then, faced with a changing world that has brought into question not only familiar terminology and perspectives but even the basic characteristics of the world itself. What were once "facts" are no longer as readily accepted as such, since the questions that gave rise to those "facts" are being displaced by other questions.

Closer to the subject matter of this study, the scholarly understanding of China has changed in the past several decades not only because of new data, especially that of archeological finds, but also because different kinds of questions and analyses have been applied. Changes in methodology have led to alternative perspectives from which to raise new issues. As a result, older interpretations have been challenged, revised, and even rejected. Scholars have come to recognize the limitations both of once standard approaches and of the language used for translating concepts and specific terms. Language and methodological approach are so closely identified that the use of certain words in English is often associated with the use of a particular methodology.

Contemporary discussion questions, for instance, the appropriateness of various terms, including "Confucian" and "neo-Confucian" (or "Neo-Confucian").[2] A difficulty is that certain terms widely used in English, such as "Confucianism," have no exact counterpart in Chinese, which uses terms like *daoxue* (the learning of the Way), *lixue* (the learning of pattern or "principle"), *shengxue* (the learning of the sages), and *ruxue* (the learning of the scholars). Whereas a term such as "Confucianism" may be too vague for the specialist, the Chinese terms have little or no meaning for the many readers who have no scholarly background in Chinese studies. In this study, "philosophy" or "learning" is a translation of *xue*, but it should be recognized that Western conceptions of philosophy and learning do not necessarily encompass the same range of activity as *xue*. In addition, "Confucian philosophy" or "Confucian learning" is a translation of what Li Yong called *ruxue* or *shengxue*, and "philosopher" or "thinker" a translation of *ru*.[3]

In respect to comparative philosophy, my efforts are aimed at searching for productive questions to ask and for methods to evaluate such questions. Since concepts exist within specific cultural contexts, they cannot be adequately compared without also considering the belief systems to which they belong.[4] Comparisons thus need to be made at the level of the system. An appropriate field, or set of issues and ideas, is necessary, if different belief systems are to be compared from a theoretical perspective. Moreover, it is important to make comparisons, because certain issues extend beyond the boundaries of one culture and one time.

My hope is that a perspective that focuses on the systemic level will aid in the efforts to get beyond, or at least to recognize, interpretations that are fundamentally arbitrary. I take it as a given that all views are views "from somewhere."[5] However, the issue of perspective is one not of "objectivity" (however that may be conceived) but of accountability, or how to ensure that one's claims are open to examination and evaluation by others. I am thus proposing to use an explicit perspective in examining Confucian philosophy—what I call a "search frame." A search frame is a methodological approach that provides a specific perspective from which to identify and view data; it is explicit and can be used by other people, and it is not the only possible perspective. A search frame consists of both particular questions and tools of analysis, including issues, concepts, and the language itself.

I am thus interested in devising methods, or offering perspectives, that will allow us to understand the implicit assumptions and patterns that have shaped Chinese philosophical thinking—what I refer to as cultural or epistemological "imperatives." Although this question is related to what contemporary philosophers call "alternative conceptual schemes," I hesitate to embrace this term fully because it seems to place undue emphasis on the conceptual sphere.[6] My search arena (for questions to ask and for epistemological imperatives) deliberately encompasses behavior as well as thought since the Chinese did not make a Cartesian type of bifurcation between a mental sphere and a physical sphere of reality.

My second aim, the task of examining Confucian philosophy as a philosophical system, involves a search for the implicit "rules" that establish the system. Such rules are, in effect, a (binding) social code that philosophers learn but are not necessarily aware they know.[7] Applicable not merely to philosophy, this code for thought and behavior is an aspect of society and of culture itself. The study that I am attempting here differs from many previous studies in that most of them have not emphasized this aspect of Chinese philosophy but have instead focused on the historical development and the historical context of ideas.[8] The epistemological system has frequently been taken implicitly as a kind of cross-temporal or cross-cultural universal. Writers have tended to treat Confucian learning in such a way that the culturally significant characteristics of this theoretical context are assumed to be known, even though they remain unexplored territory.

This tacit assumption of a universal epistemology is reflected in several common approaches. One, for instance, assumes that culturally specific categories, concepts, or standards, such as "mind," "metaphysical," or "truth," fit the Chinese experience as well as they do the modern Western. Categories and concepts are often used with little, if any, definition. Although terms must be translated and concepts must be named, it does not follow that specific terms, such as "truth," have the same referent in different cultures or that a concept in one culture has a match in another culture. Another common approach resembles an ethnographic report in that it aims to describe explicit features and confines its interpretations to that same level of experience.[9]

Although useful, these approaches leave certain critical questions unasked. Despite assumptions of objectivity, the first can present a distorted picture by implicitly shaping ideas in terms of categories and frameworks that are inappropriate because they belong to a different cultural context. The second focuses on "surface" similarities and differences (not mutually exclusive) while offering no measuring instruments that enable one to get beyond the phenotypic descriptions. (In effect, we become familiar with the trees but gain no understanding of the ecological system.) The resulting comparisons exist at a theoretical level that is not significant from a philosophical perspective, although it may be so from another perspective. Thus, if we want to answer such questions as How similar do ideas and practices have to be to be judged similar and how different to be judged different? we must use an approach that addresses the system in which the ideas occur.

My third concern in this study, on yet another level, involves investigating the ideas and system of thinking of a particular person. I assume that one way to uncover the unstated rules of a philosophical system is to examine how a specific thinker appropriates that tradition. Li Yong (1627–1705), a Confucian philosopher and teacher who lived during the tumultuous Ming-Qing transition, seems promising in this regard.[10] Deeply troubled by the social, political, and intellectual conditions of his times, Li was committed to establishing and defending the "proper" content of Confucian philosophy (see Chapter 2). Focusing not only on particular concepts, Li was trying to define the entire Confucian philosophical system. His personal, historically placed concerns thus help reveal tensions and theoretical connections that extend beyond his own position to the system itself. For instance, his views illustrate how Confucian thought contained competing values for what a "genuine" Confucian was expected to think and do. If we knew Confucian thought only from Li Yong's standpoint, however, we would have an impoverished view. Missing most notably from his perspective is evidence of any real appreciation for the role of aesthetic values and objects. Nonetheless, his thinking reflects some of the outstanding cultural strengths of Confucian philosophy, not the least of which was its advocacy of teaching and learning, not just for the present, but for the past and for the future.

In order to integrate these three aims, I organize this study around an analysis of Li's philosophical system from the perspective of educational issues. The reason for this perspective is that Li treated Confucian philosophy as, above all, a tradition of teaching and learning. Ideas and concerns relating to education are thus the focal points of this study. To borrow from Confucius (*Lunyu*, 7.8), Li's conception of Confucian philosophy had four "corners." Interrelated, interdependent, and not truly separable in their actual functioning, these four primary aspects serve as the foundation for my analysis.

The first corner, the subject of Chapter 2, is learning as a body of knowledge and set of values.[11] Li held that Confucian learning, what he called the "learning of the sages," consisted of specific and unquestionable values deriving from the universe itself. Social, political, and personal moral order would prevail if the sages' ideals were realized in society. Since constant change was immanent in the universe, however, it was often difficult to maintain ideals that once obtained. Like nature in both its predictable and its unpredictable aspects, human society also changed over time, and as it did, the ideals of the sages became obscured and not easily implemented.

Teaching specifically by Confucian thinkers became necessary as human behavior strayed from the standards of the sages. Thus teaching as an activity, the subject of Chapter 3, is the second corner of the philosophical system. Since Li held that most people were unable to learn without help, teaching was required if the sages' learning were to be practiced. Li claimed that teaching was as important as governing in maintaining and transmitting the tradition. A primary Confucian responsibility, teaching helped people develop their specifically human capacities.

The set of ideas, the teachings, of particular thinkers constitutes the third corner and subject of Chapter 4. Li viewed the teachings of each philosopher as a response to the problems of a particular time.

All teachings were related to, and inseparable from, specific social and historical contexts. Their purpose was to be corrective and to help people achieve the standards of the sages.

If the teachings were to be effective, people at all levels of society had to learn and to make sustained changes in their behavior. The fourth corner and subject of Chapter 5 is thus learning as an activity. Li discussed several conceptions of the process of learning and various kinds of efforts necessary in order to learn. Successful learners would thereby transform their behavior, making it conform more closely to the ideals of the sages.

Li's interpretation of the Confucian task was founded on the notion of making appropriate (from the Confucian viewpoint) adjustments in a world of constant change. The activities of teaching and learning differed according to what was needed in a particular context. The set of ideas that were taught also changed to fit current conditions. Only the ideals of the sages had an enduring character, since they were the constant standard toward which human beings strived, no matter how far or how often they fell short. Sharing a view with many thinkers of his own time and before, Li assumed that Confucian philosophy consisted of more than an intellectual engagement with ideas. It required their realization in action.

Li's four-cornered system of Confucian philosophy — a specific tradition of values, teaching as an activity, the teaching of the views of specific thinkers, and learning as an activity — is implied in the totality of what he and others wrote and said, but Li never presented these four aspects systematically. Because their relationship is not chronological, the order of my discussion is a matter of my analytic perspective and primarily reflects two concerns. First, this order emphasizes the theoretical system itself, in contrast to particular ideas, and it is the theoretical context that is my foremost interest here.

Second, given the content of Confucian thought, it seems to make more sense to begin with the larger social reality of the tradition itself, rather than the more limited, individual human being who must learn to become a particular type of entity within that broader context. Without the tradition there would be no genuine person in the Confucian sense. My study thus concludes with the learning that must be done by the individual person, whose efforts in turn carry on the tradition. To provide some general information on Li's thought and to help situate Li in a historical sense, the latter half of this chapter consists of a brief account of the historical period and Li Yong's life.

First, however, further discussion is needed concerning my theoretical stance and how it differs from a historical perspective. Although my analysis focuses on Li Yong's thought in terms of questions belonging to a philosophical, and specifically epistemological, framework, I use particulars drawn from historical analysis, and at times I allude to various historical contexts. Such references are necessary and useful, for neither the theoretical context nor the particular ideas exist separately. To borrow from Rorty, I do not accept that ideas can "escape from history."[12] I do insist, however, that different kinds of analyses can be made and must be distinguished.

In brief, a philosophical perspective differs from a historical perspective in terms of the questions asked and the data sought—and so, in particular, the kinds of data that are relevant. For example, the originality of Li's ideas is not relevant to the kind of philosophical analysis I offer here, although it might be to a historical analysis. Although I ground this study in a particular historical person and time, I am not asking questions about such matters as historical development, antecedents, and causes—issues more appropriate to historical narrative and historical analysis. My focus is also not on such aspects of traditional education as the characteristics of the civil service examination system, its promise of social mobility, the difficult writing system, the emphasis on memorization, the high social status accorded scholar-officials, or corruption in such forms as the selling of degrees, the granting of degrees, and the assigning of official posts.[13] Rather, I am concerned with a philosophical analysis that I conceive (here) in epistemological terms, and my aim is to uncover the premises of that thinking. Thus the kinds of questions I am asking are on the order of What shapes do time frames have, What social realities are recognized, What is the conception of a person, What is the nature of responsibility, and How are society and the individual person related? These kinds of issues underlay what philosophers openly talked about.

Said another way, I am attempting an analytic approach that emphasizes a "search for premises" rather than a search for observational descriptions or explanations.[14] What I am attempting to develop I therefore call a "search frame." Such an approach is aimed at producing questions as well as answers—particularly questions that will expand our knowledge of the implicit assumptions, patterns, and rules of thought. This approach finds encouragement, I believe, in the nature of Confucian thought itself. Confucian thought offered a blueprint for social participation, but it had an unwritten code for understanding that blueprint. Although I must examine what thinkers said, the purpose of my investigation is not to yield knowledge about an explicit Confucian doctrine, or the blueprint itself. My interest is in the code, that is, in those beliefs that established the philosophical system and that were held by all Confucians, at some level of awareness.

Analysis of this theoretical context is needed because Confucian thinkers rarely mentioned the principles and issues guiding their thinking. As I suggested in my study on Shao Yong (1012–77), Confucian philosophy had little interest in metaphilosophy and so did not emphasize explicit statements concerning its rules of thinking.[15] Still, it did have scales and standards, known by the initiated, by which it evaluated and judged itself. Not only did these standards belong to the content of thought, but the constant judging and evaluating were themselves an important aspect of Confucian thought. Chinese philosophical thought was a dynamic system, but it left certain critical features unsaid.

In other words, what I am proposing is a way to analyze Chinese thought that consists of a descriptive, rather than an explanatory, analysis. My account is fictive in the sense that it is, like a map, not isomorphic with the territory it represents. Just as other maps can be drawn, my interpretation leaves open the possibility of other interpretations. As a philosophical (or epistemological) description and not an observational description, my account most likely does not reflect how Chinese thinkers themselves understood their thinking. They worked with a field of data quite different from mine. I also am not claiming that the Chinese were either aware or unaware of the kinds of theoretical questions that I raise, for such a matter is beyond the concern of this analysis.

The kind of thought emphasized in this study is educational thought, in contrast to other kinds, but the distinction between Confucian thought and educational thought is often not easy to make. The distinction blurs because Confucian thinkers recognized that ideas had a cultural role and carried imperatives for action.[16] Theirs was thought about action, not merely thought about thought. Moreover, what especially brought Confucian and educational thought together was the Confucian "attitude of living with reference to a larger society."[17]

Although the ideas discussed here are based on those of a Chinese thinker of the seventeenth century, the particular philosophical issues are not comparably confined, temporally or culturally. As anthropologists have long observed, human knowledge and education are critical to human culture; they are essential to its preservation and transmission. Cultures frame educational questions and answers in different ways, but all are concerned with this subject. No highly organized culture with role specialization ignores such questions as Who is qualified to teach, Who is privileged to learn, What kind of knowledge is most valued, and How do people teach and learn? Li Yong and other Confucian philosophers grappled with these issues as they attempted to preserve the kind of society in which they wanted to live.

Historically speaking, Li Yong's ideas about teaching and learning served in a philosophical defense of Confucian culture at a time when profound changes were at work in China (as well as throughout the world). Reshaping every aspect of Chinese culture, these changes turned out to be a prelude to the political and cultural upheavals of modern times. Li's stated intentions were openly conservative—to preserve the Confucian world he believed was threatened by contemporary practices. The theoretical implications of the logic of his thinking were less so, however, as the following comments will suggest.

A first impression of Li is that he offered primarily a continuation of traditional and increasingly lifeless ideas. Many discussions of his thought have contributed to this interpretation by focusing on those aspects that enable (or even force) him to be seen from a particular kind of historical perspective. That is, by implicitly asking questions about the sources of his ideas, writers have described him as a later follower of Wang Yangming (1472–1529), the most prominent philosopher of the Ming (1368–1644); as an eclectic—in drawing from both the Cheng-Zhu and Lu-Wang contemporary branches of neo-Confucianism; and as the last major figure in the Guanxue (learning of Shaanxi) tradition, that is, the Confucian learning of his native region.[18]

In considering the positions Li advocated through his own words and action, we find that he opposed evidential research, one of the major intellectual movements of his time; he had little interest in historical writing, also an important contemporary activity; he refused to participate in government service, the highest calling of a Confucian; and he objected to the writing of poetry, literary prose, and commentaries, all time-honored Confucian occupations. Even though not supporting the newer intellectual activities of his age (especially evidential research), he also condemned the older trend of speculative, abstract thought—of the type attributed to Song and Ming thinkers.

From a positive perspective, Li Yong stressed practical affairs and morality in everyday life, along with a form of self-cultivation that featured rigorous reflective thought and practice (all these characteristics are discussed in the following chapters). He underscored his position through both words and behavior apparently so unusual that no one seemed surprised by the observation, "Strange indeed that in this age there is this person" (EQQJ, 10.24b). Li was praised in his own day as a great teacher (*dashi*) and great Confucian (*daru*). Despite facing a world ambivalent at best about teachers, he claimed that teaching and learning were the core of Confucian learning, and he elevated the teacher's role to a position of critical importance.[19]

There are of course other ways (in addition to the question of sources of ideas) to conceptualize literati activities during Li's time and so also Li's position. For instance, there is Kai-wing Chow's analysis of ritualism, purism, and Classicism as three powerful currents of the period.[20] From this perspective, Li's emphasis on practical morality fits into the current of ritualism, and Li's support of "genuine" Confucian learning into the current of purism. Neither classification, however, touches on the epistemological significance of Li's stance.

Li's opposition to such pursuits as evidential research, the writing of commentaries, and the elite's general emphasis on literary production was based on the theoretical grounds that these activities operated on premises no longer fully appropriate to Confucian philosophy and the times. In evaluating Li's thought from a philosophical perspective, then, the critical issue is not that such newer, Qing (1644–1911) activities as evidential research, historical writing, and lineage organization are different from older, Ming activities, such as discussions of learning, meditation, and speculation, or that the seventeenth-century activities belong to such newer movements as ritualism, purism, and Classicism. On the level of visible behavior these characterizations certainly are legitimate. (This is not to say the early Qing activities did not have historical antecedents.)

From a philosophical perspective, however, the issue involves, instead, the relationship of activities to the system of thought. What were the reasons by which particular ideas and practices were justified? It may be that activities newer in a historical sense are actually based on and support older cultural values. If so, they must still be interpreted, in a philosophical or epistemological sense, as traditional, for they accept and help to maintain an older order. On the other hand, ostensibly older activities, such as the discussion of learning, may have no visibly new characteristics. Still, such activities could be theoretically innovative or even revolutionary if they are justified on the basis of nontraditional premises and so contribute to changing the implicit set of assumptions.

From a historical viewpoint, the shifting focus in the thought and behavior of leading intellectuals from the sixteenth to the eighteenth century can readily be seen. Earlier interests in self-cultivation were gradually augmented by the pursuit of social and political action (in the sixteenth and seventeenth centuries) and then, after the beginning of the Qing, replaced by evidential research and historical scholarship. My proposal here is that these explicit emphases of leading Confucians were accompanied by less obvious but equally important changes in the fundamental premises of thought.

To use a distinction made by Confucius (*Lunyu*, 7.1), Li may be seen as both a transmitter and a creator—the former in a historical sense, the latter in an epistemological sense. Although I do not wish to overstate the innovative aspect of Li's thought, Li's thought does have significant theoretical implications insofar as it belongs to an event at least several hundred years in the making—the changing of certain premises of Confucian philosophical thinking. Such an event is extremely elusive and difficult to locate at any moment in time, however, and contrasts with the tangible and comparatively short-term projects of historians and textual scholars.

Li Yong was of course not alone in his efforts, for his viewpoint was part of a dimension of Confucian philosophy developing since at least the mid-Ming period, if not earlier, that led to thinking in different theoretical terms or, in other words, changing the epistemological framework. Although the following chapters discuss this subject in detail, a few comments here may help clarify what I am referring to. The issue relates to the logical foundations and rules of Chinese philosophical thinking.

Chinese philosophers did not adhere to a single set of assumptions to justify all views, but instead utilized various standards that were expressed by different metaphors. These metaphors—for example, the family, a mirror, or a living plant—established what I variously call a "paradigmatic context," "paradigmatic example," or "theoretical frame." The paradigmatic example played a critical, metaphilosophical role in Chinese philosophy, for it shaped and reflected the fundamental assumptions of philosophical thinking. The paradigmatic example established the theoretical rules for the parameters of a philosophical problem, that is, for how a problem was understood, and for how ideas were evaluated and verified. Different metaphors would establish different premises as the theoretical foundation.

To say this another way, the Chinese philosophical orientation tended to emphasize ideas as they were experienced in the world, not as they might exist in some abstract realm, such as in Platonic thought.[21] Not relying on explicit statements of theory, Chinese philosophers used (whether in awareness or not) the paradigmatic context to provide the theoretical structure of their thought. The paradigmatic example implicitly established a set of assumptions and the relevant patterns of thought and behavior. These assumptions and patterns varied with the example, and different paradigmatic examples existed side by side. They were not mutually exclusive, since there was no requirement for a single perspective (as is often found in Western philosophy).

Philosophical thought proceeded "outward" from the paradigmatic context. That is, the implications of the particular example provided the logic, or the reasoning, of the thinking. For instance, the implications of an example such as medicine entailed thinking in terms of illness and health and established achievement and the solution of problems as relevant standards. In contrast, use of the family as a paradigmatic context meant an emphasis on continuity, with ascription and relatedness to an original source as important criteria.

Thinking in terms of metaphors is of course common in the West as well. William James, for instance, drew on a commercial metaphor with his references to the "cash value" and "credit system" of ideas, and this metaphorical example has in some form continued unabated in American society.[22] Some Western philosophers pursue a further aim, however, one quite alien to Confucian thought, when they attempt to state, as explicitly as possible, the premises establishing the rules of their logic and the parameters of their thought.[23] Who can forget Descartes' rules? (This is not to say, of course, that all Western philosophers make this attempt or that any are completely successful. They do not, and they are not.)

The dominant paradigmatic example of Confucian thought may be termed the "living entity," which in turn is characterized by order and organization.[24] (Indeed, I would argue that any living thing was ultimately seen in terms of order, as opposed to formlessness or disorder.) This theoretical frame entailed a generative or biological metaphor, in that it was based on ideas of birth, growth, patterned development, change, activity, decline, and death. Possessing a set of interrelated assumptions, the theoretical core of the generative metaphor established the foundation for three, more specific and analogically related paradigmatic contexts. These are the plant, the family, and the stream.[25] The plant, with its root and branches, and the stream, with its source, derive from the living world of nature. The human world contributed the family or lineage, which suggests ancestors and descendants.

Although the latter three paradigmatic contexts used different terminology, they shared basic assumptions that philosophers then applied to a variety of situations. For instance, the continuity of life, its ceaseless activity, and its derivation from a single source are critical premises in these three examples. In addition, such relationships as inside and outside, primary and secondary, beginning and completion, and birth and death come into play. Philosophers used these relational ideas as criteria for making judgments in different contexts. For instance, using the metaphor of a plant, with its roots and branches, Li and others judged moral action as primary (the root) and literary production as secondary (the branches).

Other metaphors were important as well. The example of the mirror or still water suggested, among other things, the idea of reflection, and the example of the sun suggested the idea of brightness and an "illuminating power" of its own.[26] The medical metaphor, yet another paradigmatic example, stressed a quite different set of issues and relationships, such as illness and its causes, diagnosis and therapy, health and illness, order and disorder, and actions and effects (see Chapter 2).[27] In other words, the various paradigmatic examples had their own relevant questions and standards, but they were seldom, if ever, used in isolation.

Medicine was the paradigmatic frame that characterized much of Li Yong's thought about the social role of Confucian learning. Using the medical metaphor, Li and others applied medical concepts (such as illness, etiology, diagnosis, treatment, and health) to nonmedical contexts. For example, certain political and social conditions were described as illnesses that needed to be treated.

It is important to recognize that the thought of any one philosopher utilized several, if not all, of the paradigmatic frames available in Chinese culture. Li Yong did not reject, and indeed very much embraced, the generative metaphor, as well as others, such as the "reflective" and "illuminating" metaphors. Apparently, however, the implications of the medical example provided the best solution to the problems that most concerned him. Although the various paradigmatic frames coexisted in his thought, some reflected older philosophical grounds, and at least one represented newer grounds. (By philosophical grounds I am referring to fundamental concerns and how they are formulated and thought about.) Their possible conflict was not an issue for him because there was no necessity to choose among them. Different paradigmatic frames were acceptable alternatives, applicable to varying situations and viewpoints.[28]

From a historical perspective and in contrast to its central importance in Buddhist thought, medicine as a paradigmatic context had never been the primary metaphor to which Confucian thought appealed, although it had been employed in the Chinese tradition since at least the third century B.C.E. and was prevalent in much Han dynasty (206 B.C.E.– 220 C.E.) thought. Prior to the Song (960–1279), the medical metaphor was more central in thought related to the Huang-Lao and Daoist traditions, but during the Song its use broadened among neo-Confucian thinkers. In the Ming, medicine became pervasive as a paradigmatic example. Such a development undoubtedly was due to various factors, including the popularity of Buddhism, whose Four Noble Truths were based on thinking that aimed at diagnosis and treatment; the influence of Wang Yangming, who like the Buddha was called the "great doctor" by his followers; and the spread of medical knowledge and texts as part of a general expansion of literacy that accompanied the increase in printing and publication of books.[29]

In the seventeenth century, with its conflicts over alternative standards and tests for validity, the particular appeal of the medical example lay in its method of confirming ideas. It assumed a pragmatic test of achievement, and the validity of an idea was affirmed (ideally) not by an ascribed relation to a set of starting premises but by the capability of an idea to lead to a satisfactory solution to a problem. This stood in contrast to the standard of an appropriate textual source (assumed by both evidential research scholars and followers of the Cheng-Zhu school).

The difference in criteria for judging validity can be seen, for instance, in Li Yong's exchange with his famous contemporary Gu Yanwu (1613–82), the classical scholar and recognized father of evidential research. When they debated the origin of the bipolar concept *ti* and *yong* (essence and application; discussed further below), Li's final stance was that the source of the concept ultimately did not matter (EQQJ, 16.15a–21a, particularly 17a and 20b–21a). What did matter was the ability of that concept to lead to desired results, in this case, personal moral development and political order. The ability to solve the problem, or to treat the illness, was more important to Li as a standard of evaluation and validity than an origin in the Confucian classics.[30]

Li's position still did not entail a rejection of the classics. Although different paradigmatic examples established and reflected different assumptions and questions, it does not follow that ideas and things (for example, water) were thought about only in one theoretical frame. Rather, depending on the circumstances, ideas were measured against different standards in different theoretical frames. For instance, in contrast to Li's exchange with Gu Yanwu, when Li utilized the familial example as his theoretical frame in summarizing supposedly comparable changes in Confucian, Daoist, and Buddhist learning, the origin of each tradition's essential values and practices (that is, *ti* and *yong*) did matter (EQQJ, 14.5b–6b).

Li's epistemological position in a way challenged the Confucian philosophical system in that his views undermined some traditional values and made moot certain intellectual issues. In terms of the system itself, moreover, as distinct from particular issues, the paradigmatic example was probably the only area in which Li's thought could have this kind of effect. That is, until certain changes occurred in the nineteenth century, neither Li nor any Confucian thinker in late imperial China had a way in his intellectual world of offering genuine alternatives to the process of reasoning and the data used, two other significant areas of potential intellectual disagreement. (That is, the reasoning process utilized paradigmatic examples and correlative thinking. What was recognized as data depended on the questions asked, and older questions remained central concerns.

New particulars in an older theoretical system do not alter the system, nor are they a different type of data.) Even evidential research scholars remained fairly traditional, in a theoretical sense, until the nineteenth century.[31]

I make these comments concerning my theoretical position to emphasize that a number of approaches are possible in philosophical study. I accept that what a thinker says is not the entirety of what she or he thought, for one can communicate in writing only a portion of thought. Ideas recorded in books are merely the footprints of ideas. Since written words are not isomorphic with thought, certain aspects (it is not known how many) of ideas are invariably left unrecorded. Retrieving any of those aspects involves a "reconstruction" of ideas, and reconstructions are of many kinds.[32]

I use the term "reconstruction" because every reader's analysis of an idea always carries with it the imprint of the reader, no matter whether as apologist, critic, or analyst. The analytic or investigative procedure is a filter, acknowledged or not, that conditions where and what kinds of data are looked for, and these data in turn determine what an idea is understood to be. The shaping of that procedure demands explication to ensure as much scholarly reliability as possible and to clarify for others the kind of search engaged in. Thus I assume that as I analyze these ideas, I am also reconstructing them.

The notion of reconstruction can briefly be illustrated with the example of time. Concepts of social and cultural time were important in Confucian thought, and time had many meanings, including the ideas of a situation and of duration. Far more than a calendrical matter, time was not an independent element as it is often popularly conceived in the modern West, even though the philosophers' explicit vocabulary did not reflect the extent of their theoretical distinctions.[33] Although they had no special terms to distinguish them, there was, for instance, something that I call "scholar-time," which differed from "teacher-student time." The former had a duration measured in generations; the latter, one measured in less than a life span. Both were essential to the Confucian system, but different events were relevant in each.

Even when not put in writing, the contributions of the cultural system were critical in making these kinds of distinctions (such as that between scholar-time and teacher-student time) and so in determining meaning. In addition, the reconstruction of ideas extends beyond making explicit certain implicit aspects of ideas. It entails choosing what lens to use and knowing the parameters of the lens chosen. In reconstructing Li Yong's thought in the context of the Confucian tradition, I have attempted to use a social lens as I examine the issues and assumptions giving rise to the ideas.

THE TIMES

Involved with the world in many ways, Li Yong was an active teacher who wanted to be listened to and heard. He was concerned about economic, political, and social problems, about local, regional, and national matters, and about present, past, and future generations. Perhaps more than anything else, the social and political upheavals of the times disturbed Li and captured his attention. His environment was, without doubt, an inseparable aspect of his philosophical thinking.

The seventeenth century was a dynamic and turbulent period, in retrospect as important for China as it was for Europe and the modern world. No area of life escaped change. Starting in the late sixteenth century, China witnessed a series of disastrous events that both contributed to and reflected the decline of the Ming dynasty. Earthquakes, droughts, and floods disrupted the lives of millions of people. Famines and epidemics brought suffering and death to millions more. To compound the problems, rebel groups and bandits roamed the countryside, both attracting and attacking peasants and displaced persons.[34]

The Ming government could and would do little to help. The rulers took minimal interest in governing, their advisors and officials fought among themselves, the military was ineffective, corruption was widespread, and the government retreated from even its limited role in providing certain medical services for the population to help combat periodic epidemics and starvation. The combination of circumstances resulted in the eventual overthrow of the Ming in 1644. The second half of the seventeenth century witnessed the conquest of China by the Qing, a foreign dynasty that brought the Manchus to power over the Chinese, and the building of a new world.

Li was born in 1627 in the midst of increasingly difficult times, and his writings indicate an early awareness of people's suffering. He was not yet fifteen when rebel bands attacked areas in his home province of Shaanxi and the great epidemics of the early 1640's occurred. He grew up knowing from personal experience that the imperial government was not always able to maintain the orderly conditions necessary for life.

Other events and developments reached beyond the political, dynastic framework. Economically, domestic and overseas trade was expanding. Further urbanization, the spread of literacy to new segments of the population, including women and people of the lower classes, and increased economic and social opportunities constituted some of the elements helping to create a different world. With many of the changes focused in the south, in the cities of the lower and middle Yangzi River area, the northern and northwestern regions (where Li Yong lived) were slower to respond. The northern lifestyle came to be seen as conservative and old-fashioned, whereas the southern was considered ostentatious, extravagant, and modern.

Although it is possible that the importance of the medical metaphor in Li's thinking derived primarily from philosophical thought itself, especially the views of Wang Yangming, actual conditions may also have played a significant role. From the mid-Tang (617–907) through the Song and Yuan (1279–1368), the government had taken some responsibility for public health conditions by sponsoring charity infirmaries and charity pharmacies, by publishing pharmaceutical works, and by establishing (in the Yuan) new, medically related government bureaus. By the late Ming, however, the government had mostly withdrawn such interest and support. The government became involved only during epidemics, and even then its efforts were neither consistent nor effective. During the sixteenth and seventeenth centuries, local elites increasingly took responsibility for medical relief by organizing charities, clinics, and dispensaries.

The government distanced itself from medical education as well. The increase in literacy and in publications for all levels of society made medical knowledge more widespread than ever before. Medical texts, from simple handbooks for the relatively uneducated person to highly specialized works for the elite, became available. It is significant that there was no single authority to legitimize and standardize medical knowledge (as well as medical practice and responsibility). This situation was related in part to the ambiguous and widely varying social status of doctors, a phenomenon that made the elite reluctant to pursue (as first choice, before government service) a medical occupation.

There were "doctors" of many kinds, from illiterate healers to those with an education in the classics, and their knowledge and social status were equally disparate. As in other societies, the elite tended to associate illness with immorality and with the lower classes. Nonetheless, the breadth of Confucian responsibility was reflected in Fan Zhongyan's (989–1052) famous saying, "If one cannot be a fine minister, one should be a fine doctor," and Li's thinking suggests his agreement—in principle, if not literally.[35]

Pulled in various directions, scholars and intellectuals exhibited considerable diversity in their interests.[36] Early in the seventeenth century they had been concerned primarily with preventing the Ming dynasty from collapsing. After its overthrow, attention shifted to preserving Chinese culture under Manchu rule. The close tie between, or indeed inseparability of, the intellectual and political worlds led many in the elite to attribute the Ming decline more to intellectual failings than to institutional and social factors, such as economic problems and administrative weaknesses. Some thinkers especially criticized the speculative and reclusive aspects, along with what was judged the moral relativity, of the popular Wang Yangming school of neo-Confucian thought, and even blamed the fall of the Ming on the "emptiness" and lack of practicality of that school.

Meanwhile, other trends that had arisen in the late Ming in association with the Wang school gained strength. Thinkers generally began to favor thought and action that they regarded as concrete, practical, and specific. Some continued to pursue concepts of the individual person and ideas suggesting certain kinds of equality. Others, however, emphasized the web of traditional moral and social obligations based on ancient ideas about *li* (ritual, the code of proper behavior). Inspired by early Confucian thought, some pushed for social and political action even for decades after the Qing victory. Still others, such as Yan Yuan (1635–1704), claimed that there was too much reliance on books, instead of what the books were about, and espoused a practical learning that diminished, and in some cases even rejected, the intellectual role of books and book learning.[37]

The seventeenth century also saw Jesuit missionaries introduce Christianity and Western scientific thought to China, primarily pre-Copernican thought, based on Aristotelian and Christian positions. Although many Chinese held that the Westerners did not comprehend the "whole," that is, their view of the universe was defective, the Chinese did admire the technical skills of the Westerners.[38] Li Yong's comments (see Chapter 5) indicate that he was among those familiar with Western ideas and appreciative of their technical knowledge.

Classical texts were the subject of much attention for their role in the cultural conflict over how best to recover the Way (*dao*) of the past, a conflict seen either as requiring action in society or as utilizing texts or as needing some mixture of the two. Evidential research, a movement largely based on critical and explicit methods of examining classical texts, gathered momentum as scholars reevaluated the classical tradition. Historical studies and concern for practical statecraft thrived, although only the former achieved special prominence in the eighteenth century.

Speculative thought associated with the Song and Ming periods continued to interest a number of Confucian thinkers. Reflecting contemporary preferences for the concrete and practical, such thinking was dominated by a view that espoused a monism of *qi* (matter-energy, the dynamic stuff of the universe, energetic configurations) while rejecting a separate existence for *li* (principles, or patterns of activity and change in the universe).[39] In the midst of diverse and competing positions, there were calls to reaffirm the orthodox, or state-approved, neo-Confucian thought of Zhu Xi (1130–1200) and Cheng Yi (1033–1107). The followers of Wang Yangming had challenged this orthodoxy during the Ming, and many thinkers continued to criticize Cheng-Zhu adherents for an excessive preoccupation with the writing of commentaries. The seventeenth century was thus a time of many cross-currents, a time of ends and of beginnings—for the intellectual sphere as well as for the political, economic, religious, and social.

THE PERSON

The records leave little doubt as to the profound effect the turmoil of dynastic change had on Li Yong.[40] This great event figured centrally in Li's life by leaving him personally without a father, an orphan in the Chinese view, and culturally without a ruler. It conditioned and shaped his social relations, intellectual views, and political stance. Remaining a Ming loyalist like a number of others, Li never accepted the legitimacy of Qing Manchu rule, and all his life he agonized over the social, economic, and political problems surrounding the Ming defeat. The dynastic change also affected his relationship to the Confucian tradition, since he could not help but see current events from the perspective of a concern about the past and the future.

Li Yong was a native of Guanzhong, the modern province of Shaanxi. His home lay in the Zhouzhi district, not far from the provincial capital of Xi'an, formerly called Chang'an. His style-name was Zhongfu (hexagram 61, Inner Truth, of the *Book of Change*), and his scholarly name was Erqu, after the two bends in the river.[41] His life, from 1627 to 1705, spanned the last two decades of the Ming and the first six of the Qing.

Guanzhong (or Shaanxi) and its capital had been an important cultural and political center from ancient times until the Song, when the population and economy began to shift south. It had been the home and capital of kings and emperors, including those of the Zhou (1027–256 B.C.E.), Qin (221–207 B.C.E.), Han, and Tang, and its political and military legacies remained important in people's memories. Ancient tombs and shrines dotted the landscape, reminding people of past glories. By the seventeenth century, however, Shaanxi had become a border area in the northwest, deemed provincial and outside the central cultural area along the Yangzi River.

Li developed a considerable reputation in Guanzhong as a great teacher and as an exemplar of filial piety (EQQJ, 11.7a–13a). It was even claimed that there had been no one like Li in the west for over two hundred years.[42] His contemporaries ranked him with Zhang Zai (1020–77) of the Song and with Lü Nan (1479–1542) and Feng Congwu (1556–1627) of the Ming, the three outstanding past representatives of Confucian philosophical learning in Guanzhong (EQQJ, third original preface to EQQJ, 1a; preface to *juan* 1, 1b; first preface to *juan* 2, 1a; and 9.8b). In addition, Li Yong and two contemporaries, the classical scholar Li Bai (1630–1700) and the poet Li Yindu (1631–92), were together known as the Three Li of Guanzhong.[43]

Li's reputation extended beyond Guanzhong, in part because of a lecture tour he made to Jiangnan, the prosperous region of the lower Yangzi River. Writing from a philosophically sympathetic position, the historian Quan Zuwang (1705–55) classified Li with the philosopher Sun Qifeng (1584–1675) and the historian Huang Zongxi (1610–95) as the "three great Confucians" of the time: Li in the west, Sun in the north, and Huang in the south.[44]

Conventional interpretations of this period do not accept this judgment, however, for Huang had the most influence of the three. Gu Yanwu was, in addition, a much more prominent and important intellectual than Sun or Li during the seventeenth century, and Wang Fuzhi (1619–92) was another great thinker. Still, Wang was virtually unknown during his lifetime, and Gu's reputation as a pioneer in evidential research tended to make people (somewhat mistakenly) think of him as a different kind of intellectual, not truly a supporter of (classical) Confucian values. Sun, Huang, Li, Wang, and Gu were all important in different ways, and late in the Qing, during the nineteenth century, an official request was even made to recognize them as comparable to the five Northern Song masters, regarded as the founders of neo-Confucianism (*daoxue*, the learning of the Way).[45]

Both of Li Yong's parents came from Zhouzhi district, where Li was born. The Li family was neither wealthy nor destitute, but poverty was certainly not absent from their lives. The family apparently was not large, for the records imply that Li was the only son of his generation and thus the only one who could continue the family line. Li did marry, and he had two sons. He was fortunate, moreover, in that both of his parents had some education. Li's father held a minor military post, and his mother provided him with most of his early education, even though the books had to be borrowed. She assumed this responsibility after the local schoolteacher refused to let Li continue attending school because he lacked money for tuition.

When Li Yong was a youth, his father, Li Kecong (1599–1642), joined the Ming forces fighting the rebel Li Zicheng (1605?–45; no relation). Li Kecong subsequently died in battle, along with more than 5,000 others. Although Li Yong was barely fifteen years old at the time, he was old enough to be severely shaken by his father's death. To make matters worse, he was never able to retrieve his father's bones from the battlefield, either at the time or many years later on a trip made expressly for that purpose. Thus he always believed that he did not, and could not, give his father a proper burial. Even his later attempt to "call back his (father's) soul" left Li Yong dissatisfied. Li Kecong had foreseen the possibility of not returning from battle, however. Before going off to war, he had pulled out a tooth and left it behind as a symbol of his whole body, so that he might receive a proper burial. His grave was fittingly called the "tooth grave."

Li's mother, née Peng, raised her son largely by herself, in conditions of unrelenting hardship. Although she wanted to commit suicide out of loyalty to the Ming and her loyalist husband, the Li family would not let her. Still, the villagers could not persuade her to remarry or send her son to work as a lowly clerk in the local magistrate's office. She resolutely held to the Confucian values of chastity and loyalty, further vowing that her son would become educated in the highest ideals of the Confucian tradition. She set for him the goal of becoming a "great Confucian," and the records show that she was given much of the credit for his success.[46]

Li Yong was motivated throughout his life by his determination to be filial and loyal. He refused several recommendations for an official post in the Qing government, and he would not participate in the Qing's special examination in 1679, designed to bring the scholars back into the government. Although a number of his acquaintances obtained degrees, Li never took the regular examinations that led to government office. Reflecting his cultural commitment, he did, however, have close relationships with provincial educational officials and apparently worked with them to revive Guanxue, the tradition of Confucian learning in Guanzhong. His own regional lecture tours, his support of efforts to rebuild local academies, and his cooperation with educational officials to edit and publish the writings of earlier, prominent Guanzhong Confucians were all aspects of his philosophical life.[47]

Li's loyalties to the Ming and to the Confucian tradition were very much related to his filial piety, both to his father, who had died for the Ming, and to his mother, who endured great suffering in order to raise and educate him. He developed such a reputation for filiality that some who were unfamiliar with his renown as an extraordinary Confucian teacher knew him only as "Li, the filial son." Still, Li was apparently never able to overcome his feelings of inadequacy in serving his parents, and he referred to himself as the "ashamed one" (*canren*) or the "wrongdoer" (*zuiren*). Although these epithets were relatively standard, Li's behavior was not so typical. His virtuous behavior garnered tremendous and widespread admiration in a period that was becoming increasingly conservative in emphasizing the preservation of ritual forms and behavior.[48]

Li lived by teaching and by the support of patrons, some of whom were officials, such as Magistrate Luo Zhonglin. Li always insisted that he was a commoner, however, despite his close relations with many provincial government officials. He never sought wealth, and he remained poor throughout his life. Although he claimed not to like travel, he did travel within Guanzhong and he did make one major trip south to Jiangnan. His excursions within his home province involved such activities as lecturing, visiting other Confucian thinkers, paying his respects at various shrines, making pilgrimages to famous sites, and seeing friends off — all important as aspects of Guanxue. The southern trip had three express purposes. One was filial duty, to find his father's bones and to call back his soul. A second was moral obligation, to repay Luo Zhonglin for his kindness to Li when Luo had served in Zhouzhi. And the third was his cultural and educational responsibility, to teach Confucian learning.

In addition to these relationships that linked him to different orders of space (or place) and time, the intellectual shifts he underwent during his life further shaped him as a person.[49] Often following a period of great suffering or illness, the phenomenon of intellectual or "spiritual" transformation, in which one attains a supposedly "greater" or "corrected" state of understanding, was common in the neo-Confucian tradition and is found as well in other great traditions of the world.[50] Such famous thinkers as Zhu Xi and Wang Yangming are well known for their successive stages of insight and comprehension, but numerous other philosophers had transforming experiences as well.

When young, Li Yong was particularly interested in matters relating to the government and the military. He wrote practical treatises on these subjects, made commentaries on the classics, and even employed the methods of evidential research. About the age of thirty, a usual time for this kind of experience, he suffered a serious illness, one that would change his life. Upon recovering, he renounced his previous interests, destroyed his writings, and began to advocate the Confucian position of combining personal cultivation and social action. During this second stage, he emphasized the importance and inseparability of the inner and outer aspects of things, understood by him as knowledge and action, or essential Confucian values and their practical implementation. It would be speculative to say how his illness motivated this change in interests, but the fundamental premises on which the two sets of interests are based do differ in some ways. Most notably and as is discussed below, his second stage of thought emphasized thinking in terms of a medical framework, in contrast to that of a lineage, for example. Also, by the time of Li's early thirties, the restoration of the Ming dynasty was no longer accepted as possible.

Li entered his third and final stage during his early fifties. In 1679, he withdrew from lecturing to large groups, he taught and associated with only a few people, and he increasingly emphasized self-reflection and self-cultivation. Although he became a recluse, he did not completely cut himself off from others, and he never abandoned his commitment to the Confucian ideals of political harmony and personal morality. His major philosophical views had, however, already been expressed.

In sum, the biographical accounts of Li Yong suggest a person intensely involved in his historical period and in his cultural tradition. Like his contemporaries, he exhibited a mixture of characteristics, progressive as well as conservative. Cognizant of some of the strengths and weaknesses of Confucian culture, he held that teaching and learning were critical to the vitality of Confucian learning. He thus stressed these aspects as he defended, embodied, and transmitted that tradition. Recognizing the gravity of the Confucian "burden," he saw himself in the mold of the great teacher, great doctor, and great hero needed to save the age.

2   *The Learning of the Sages*

THE PHILOSOPHICAL SYSTEM

Imperatives and Issues

The learning of the sages is the first of the four corners of Li Yong's philosophical system and is the subject of this chapter. My aim here is to analyze the system of Confucian philosophy in terms of its epistemological and social characteristics and then to discuss four specific philosophical issues that dominated Li's thought. Although my claims about Confucian learning perhaps apply to most of Chinese philosophy, it is beyond the scope of this study to make or document such an assertion. The four particular issues discussed in the latter half of the chapter were certainly addressed by thinkers, Confucian and non-Confucian, other than Li Yong, but treatment of these four issues in other contexts will also have to await further study.

This chapter is divided into two major sections, one on the philosophical system itself and the other on issues of special concern to Li Yong. The first section (on the system itself) is further subdivided into two parts, addressing theoretical aspects of the philosophical system and certain social characteristics of Confucian learning. I identify the theoretical aspects as epistemological imperatives and philosophical issues. The five social characteristics discussed provide evidence for these two theoretical aspects. The analysis of this first section thus constitutes one type of map of Confucian learning.

As a body of knowledge, Confucian learning or philosophy (I use the terms interchangeably) may be studied from various viewpoints. The theoretical perspective offered here aims to describe how Confucian philosophy worked as a system. As pointed out in Chapter 1, I am not asking historical questions, such as how Li Yong differed from, or was similar to, his contemporaries and predecessors. My epistemological concerns lead me, instead, to ask what premises underlie, and so in this sense give significance to, Li's explicit philosophical positions. In answering this question, I have assumed that Chinese thinkers in some way knew (and had learned) the premises, even though they seldom explicitly stated or examined them. For sake of analysis, moreover, I propose that these premises may be placed in three categories—epistemological imperatives of the culture, core philosophical issues, and fundamental social characteristics of the philosophical system.

The records indicate that Confucian learning, taken as a whole, was a systematically organized body of knowledge, possessing fundamental assumptions, concerns, questions, and responses. As an aspect of Chinese culture, it also incorporated the epistemological imperatives of the culture. These imperatives are the culturally based elemental assumptions of thought that members of a culture have no choice but to think in terms of. Embedded in the thinking of the culture, the epistemological imperatives are cultural givens, not necessarily in people's full awareness. A lack of awareness does not, however, prevent thinking and acting in terms of them—any more than the lack of any formal study of grammar prevents one from speaking one's native language.[1]

My claim, to be supported by the following discussion, is that from Li Yong's perspective the dominant epistemological imperatives consisted of the ideas of unity, harmony, continuity, constant and patterned change, and an ethical (as opposed to logical) standard for testing thought. Implicit standards against which ideas are measured, these imperatives are applicable to all levels of experience from the cultural-political to the level of *qi* (matter-energy). The paradigmatic metaphors provide an epistemological foundation and the concept of *qi* provides an ontological foundation that together tie the cultural givens together.

The imperatives identified above are found in the generative metaphor, expressed by such examples as plant, family, and stream. Not coincidentally, paradigmatic examples that do not express these cultural givens so well or that emphasize other assumptions have less persuasive power in Confucian thought. For instance, the example of craftsmen and their products used by Xunzi in reference to the source of moral behavior was not found so compelling by later generations as the plant with its roots and sprouts. From an epistemological perspective, Xunzi's example (of potters and carpenters making vessels and utensils) does not suggest ideas characteristic of a living thing, such as emergence from a single source (root) or constant and patterned change. Contrary to the epistemological imperatives, Xunzi's example suggests that order and pattern (that is, what make a thing what it is) are something "added" and not originally an aspect of a thing (*Xunzi*, "Xing e pian," 291; Watson, *Hsün Tzu*, 160).

The specific problems and general characteristics of the philosophical tradition give clues to the cultural givens. Although philosophers may not always be able to state the epistemological imperatives, they know when particular instances of thought and behavior challenge or somehow clash with these imperatives. The harmony in which all experiences — intellectual, psychological, emotional, aesthetic, social, and political — are integrated is disrupted when such a clash occurs. Such disruptions contribute to philosophical questioning. My thesis is that issues of philosophical thinking emerge when harmony between epistemological imperatives and explicit ideas is disturbed — the issues do not exist beforehand, somehow waiting to appear. Disruption anywhere in the system leads to changes in other places, and the ensuing discord, even if only an ill-defined uneasiness, leads to the development of philosophical issues. Issues arise when behavior "violates" the epistemological imperatives. In other words, from an epistemological perspective, philosophical issues entail a violation (outside of awareness) of cultural givens by one's proposed ideas, whereas from the perspective of social and intellectual life, philosophical issues entail the explicit posing of alternative ideas.

Although I am not proposing an exclusive or one-to-one link, the cultural givens that relate to particular philosophical issues can be identified at least in part. As will be seen below, the issue of the genuine versus the other is, for instance, linked to epistemological imperatives of unity and harmony, whereas the issue of the goodness of human nature is linked to imperatives of unity, continuity, and constant, patterned activity.

Although the ideas suggested by each of the imperatives identified above are addressed in the following discussion, some preliminary comments may be helpful here. The notion of unity holds that everything belongs to one system and that there is nothing outside that system. Harmony refers to the ideal of a cooperative relationship among the parts of the system; the parts help maintain each other and the system itself. The idea of continuity focuses on the ongoing nature of all processes in the universe and the interrelationships among all levels and kinds of reality. The assumptions of constant and patterned change are that change is a given, occurs according to a variety of patterns, and never ceases.

The fifth imperative, the ethical standard that Confucian philosophers ultimately appealed to, needs a little more attention here because of its critical role in thinking. An alternative familiar to everyone in Western society is the logical standard. This is not to say, of course, that the Chinese were illogical or that there is no concept of an ethical standard in Western thought. Rather, the questions and concerns of Confucian thinkers were ultimately related to a kind of order different from, but not in conflict with, one based on a logical standard.[2]

In a system based on a logical standard, there is an implicit order in which ideas are connected in a linear manner, with each idea based on previous reasoning that ultimately leads back to first assumptions. In much of Western philosophy, for example, truths were and are established on the basis of their coherence with premises already accepted (and not always in awareness). Although most Chinese philosophers would probably not disagree with this kind of thinking, the activity of making explicit the logical relations among ideas was not particularly important to them. This is not to say that Chinese philosophers rejected the notion or even authority of logical coherence; rather, it was just not a primary goal.

In the Confucian ethical system, boundaries or parameters were set, and within these limits a range of action was allowed, but the boundaries were not absolutely fixed. Since the entire system depended on adaptation to constantly arising contingencies, the boundaries could be expanded with the contingencies. A thinker may not have been able to say exactly where the boundaries were, but he (Confucian philosophers were men) knew he was "wrong" when he bumped up against the boundaries.[3] Thus there were constant efforts to test and to determine the boundaries. One way the Chinese conceived of this situation was to see it as an opposition between the "standard" (*jing*) and the "adaptive" (*quan*).[4] Moreover, they judged the conflict in terms of an ethical, as opposed to logical, standard. The boundaries of the virtue of loyalty were tested, for example, when there was a change of dynasty or when the ruler's policies made it life-threatening for an official to give advice.

The ethical standard is significant because it enabled notions of social learning to dominate the fundamental premises of thought, rather than such notions as logical argumentation. What appealed to Confucian thinkers was the connection between ideas and action. This focus has some similarities with that of the American pragmatists and perhaps may be clarified by a brief look at them. The pragmatists, too, rejected the idea that truth is to be found in abstract statements. William James, for instance, insisted that there has to be a difference in practice between two metaphysical claims if one is to be judged true and the other false. Therefore he emphasized the importance of method. If there were no practical difference, then two ideas meant the same thing. James therefore favored the particulars of experience and practical results, while opposing, among other things, verbal solutions, abstractions, categories, fixed principles, absolutes, and origins.[5]

Claiming that knowledge is the outcome of action and that action validates knowledge, John Dewey advocated similar ideas. For him, the importance of thought was that it enabled a person to do something. Thus he opposed classical educational methods that were authoritarian in approach and aimed more at "the ability to talk about things rather than to do things."[6] Even though the pragmatists and the Confucians differed in many ways, both regarded the realization of ideas and the actual experiences of life as important to the testing of thought. For Confucian thinkers, however, an ethical, as opposed to a logical, standard for testing thought was a critical epistemological imperative.

Along with a foundation in the cultural givens noted above, Confucian learning had a structure, much as languages and behavior have. It had its own grammar, one based on perennial issues. Despite differences over time in questions, answers, and stated claims, continued attention to particular issues provided an implicit, and sometimes explicit, organization to Confucian thought. From Mencius and Xunzi in the fourth and third centuries B.C.E., texts both by one author and by more than one author display similarities in structure, usually in their organization around particular topics.[7]

The existence of core issues (structuring the philosophical system) is seen not only in repeatedly raised topics of discussion, but also in the Chinese terms used in reference to Confucian learning. Although the various terms (older ones remained in use even as new ones were invented) had political and historical as well as philosophical significance, few writers attempted to provide systematic statements of the ideas they represented. (Nuances important to the Chinese are, of course, not retained in such broad English words as "Confucianism" and "neo-Confucianism.")

To give a few examples, in the Southern Song Zhu Xi and his followers used the term *daoxue* (the learning of the Way) for their own thought and claimed to be following the Way (*dao*) of Confucius and Mencius, which had been recovered from obscurity by Zhou Dunyi, the Cheng brothers, and Zhang Zai of the Northern Song. For them, "Way" referred to their Way, not that of Mozi or Yang Zhu, both rivals of Mencius, and certainly not that of Wang Anshi or Su Shi, prominent Northern Song literati. By the seventeenth century, however, Li Yong dismissed the idea that the term *daoxue* had any special philosophical significance and equated it with *ruxue* (the learning of the scholars, Confucian learning) — for him, it was not something outside *ruxue* (EQQJ, 14.3a).

From the Song to the Qing, various terms for Confucian learning reflected other issues. The learning of emperors (*dixue*) pointed to the political arena, whereas the learning of the heart-mind (*xinxue*), the learning of principle or pattern (*lixue*), and the learning of human nature and principle (*xinglixue*) indicated moral, theoretical, and ontological interests. The transmission or tradition of the sages (*sheng-chuan* or *shengzhuan*) and the learning of the sage or sages (*shengren zhi xue* and *shengxue*) emphasized historical origins, the authority of the past, ostensibly unchanging ideals, and an orientation stressing practical action in society. Reflecting ongoing tensions relating to intellectual and social change, "genuine learning" (*zhengxue*) was used in contrast with "other" learning (*yiduan*).[8]

Signifying an opposition to ontological and theoretical speculation, "real" or "solid learning" (*shixue*) was a common term in the seventeenth century. "Learning of the sages"(*shengxue*) and "learning of the Confucians" (*ruxue*) became popular terms as well, the latter reflecting a renewed interest in early Confucian thought as well as differences with Daoism and Buddhism. The last two terms had been in the philosophical vocabulary for centuries, but their new currency suggests thinkers were attempting to come to grips with disruptive ideas by focusing on aspects of the Confucian tradition that were not so much in dispute.

Li used all these terms, most of them only rarely, however. The two most prevalent in his vocabulary were *shengxue* and *ruxue*. For Li, the "learning of the sages" implied learning that included practical social and political action (along with a set of values), and "learning of the Confucians" suggested the learning of the teachers, those who had transmitted the tradition. In other words, particular terms for different aspects of Confucian learning suggested emphases that were, in turn, linked to core philosophical issues, epistemological imperatives, and historical realities.

From the time of Confucius, philosophers were drawn to certain issues that emerged from the continual disturbance of the cultural givens. Although others may perhaps be identified, five issues stand out as particularly important in shaping the epistemological aspects of the thought of Li Yong and his late Ming, early Qing contemporaries. Overlapping and interdependent, these perennial issues established an implicit, but systematic, organization of Confucian thought.

The first issue is the question of the origin of beliefs. According to tradition, Confucian truths were first apprehended by the ancient sages, recorded in the classics, and subsequently transmitted by the philosophers, teachers, and scholars. Since the source of an idea served as a primary (but not exclusive) authority, the identity of the source as well as questions about the transmission were important.

Second is the vision of the ideal society. As the foundation of Chinese Confucian culture, the sages' learning defined the culture by specific kinds of social and political relationships. It was believed that these relationships were neither arbitrary nor contrived, but originated in the capacities that human beings had by virtue of being human (and the relationships often had a theoretical equivalent in the cosmos). If these relationships were not realized, it was thought that human beings would be reduced to the level of animals or barbarians, who did not exhibit social order and harmony. There was no acceptable alternative social system.

The third issue is the aim and purpose of knowledge. Although the sages' learning incorporated several kinds of knowledge for different social groups and for different purposes, its central focus was on ways to bring about harmonious order in the world and the moral cultivation of individual persons. Although once restricted to the ruling group and its ways of ordering the world, the sages' learning expanded over time as ordering became more complex in its activities and ideas. It broadened from the elite's concern with activities of government to a way that potentially applied to everyone. On the social-political level, the sages' learning included specific ideas about governmental policies and the actions appropriate for the ruler, bureaucratic officials, and the masses. On the personal level, it offered ideas on social roles, behavior in personal relationships, and moral action. It offered flexibility within order and stability in the midst of change.

Fourth is the issue of the conditions that best facilitate the goals of Confucian learning. Here questions arise concerning the relative emphasis on, and content of, different activities, such as participation in government, efforts of self-cultivation, and classical scholarship. Also important is the question of whether there is an ordering process with successive steps, from self to society to the whole world, or whether the process is a whole entity not open to segmentation. Zhu Xi stressed the former view, and Wang Yangming the latter, but the difference between these two views is more a question of emphasis and focus than a matter of fundamental disagreement.

The fifth issue is the question of how knowledge is best communicated, that is, in what state or form philosophical knowledge is best presented so as to achieve its aims. Among those philosophers who presented their ideas as teachings in question-and-answer sessions, knowledge was kept alive not so much in abstracted formulations as in a form that was thought to represent how people think and learn. The distinction between these two states of knowledge was an important one, and it was of concern to Li Yong.

In sum, I suggest that the Confucian philosophical system was founded on epistemological imperatives of unity, harmony, continuity, constant and patterned change, and an ethical (not logical) standard for testing the validity of ideas. Arising from implicit challenges to these cultural givens, philosophical issues gave structure to the system, and the five issues noted above were particularly significant in defining Confucian learning in Li's world. This implicit theoretical dimension of the philosophical system was seldom, if ever, the subject of explicit or sustained examination, but it can be uncovered by analysis of observable characteristics. Presented here as a philosophical (not observational) description, the imperatives and the issues were preserved in particular conflicts and positions rather than in abstract theory.

Social Characteristics

The epistemological imperatives and philosophical issues become apparent through the characteristics of the philosophical tradition. For the present analysis, five social characteristics of the philosophical system are especially helpful in providing data for establishing this theoretical aspect. The five discussed below are not meant to be a full account of the Confucian system, nor do they have a one-to-one correspondence with the imperatives. They do, however, reflect assumptions about the conception and aim of knowledge, as well as the arena of relevance and the mission of Confucian thought.

Learning as patterns of thought and action. From early times, Confucian philosophers identified themselves, and were identified by others, with particular subtraditions of Confucian learning.[9] The subtraditions were based primarily on teacher-student relationships and seen in genealogical terms. There was also a geographical component, for regions gave their names to the learning of the thinkers who lived there. "Luoxue" thus came to be a term for the learning of the Cheng brothers and their followers in Luoyang, "Minxue" for the learning of Zhu Xi and his followers in Fujian, and "Guanxue" for the learning of Zhang Zai and his followers in Guanzhong (Li Yong's home). This is not to say, however, that the followers were necessarily faithful to the philosophical stance of the founder of their tradition. The link could depend as much on geographical and social factors as on intellectual ones. In addition, thinkers outside the region could join a subtradition by becoming identified with its ideas, as Xue Xuan (1389–1464, from Shanxi) did with Guanxue.

Not only did subtraditions represent the Confucian tradition in particular regions in a geographical sense, but they also developed historical affinities that helped to distinguish them from each other. Over time, the shared experiences of participants, the "accidents" of history, and various environmental factors worked together to produce separate traditions of learning. The Confucian emphasis on concrete, lived experience, as opposed to abstract formulations, gave support to the importance of the subtraditions and to the three facets identified above. Confucian learning hence cannot be reduced to a body of abstract ideas and issues. The specific social and historical contexts do matter and are part of the ideas themselves.

I suggest, however, that along with the differences of historical particulars, the subtraditions shared certain patterns of thought and behavior. That is, in some respects, they had a similar theoretical structure. Like ideas, the philosophical traditions (or subtraditions) emerged from implicit patterns of belief and behavior that shaped Confucian culture and that structured thought and behavior. Although these implicit patterns did not necessarily need to be discussed, no one became a Confucian philosopher unless he participated in them. My claim for their existence derives, therefore, not from explicit statements about them, but indirectly from writings concerning what people thought and did.

In the specific case of Li Yong, it appears that his philosophical tradition of Guanxue was organized around (at least) three major elements: particular people, specific concerns, and an awareness of itself as a community with historical continuity. Ideas were linked to contexts, and the behavior of past and present people was important. Stressing the inseparability of thought and action, Li claimed, for instance, "With genuine knowledge there is real action, and real action is genuine knowledge" (EQQJ, 5th preface, 1b, by Wang Xinjing [1656–1738]). Reflective thought about the tradition and one's place in it was critical, for in this way present behavior and ideas were linked to those of the past and the future.

Particular people were important because they became in some way a realization of Confucian ideas. Reflecting a pragmatic view of validity, the actual embodiment of an idea made the idea. Second, specific concerns formed another kind of continuity that was maintained along with the conditions that helped generate the concerns. Some concerns focused on social-political conditions, others on Confucian learning itself. Third, the sense of community with ties to the past and future was an important aspect of the specific value of tradition. Participation in the multi-generational and multi-level Confucian community validated that community and the person as a philosopher.

Although Li's writings indicate he was familiar with numerous Guanxue philosophers, he singled out only a few for special praise. Those he mentioned most often were Zhang Zai from the Song and Lü Nan, Nan Daji, Zhou Hui, Feng Congwu, and Zhang Shundian from the Ming.[10] Li's standard for judging whom to include in Guanxue was how well they exhibited, in his view, the full range of Confucian learning, including its "inner" and "outer" aspects. Like Confucian learning, Guanxue was both a descriptive and a prescriptive term for Li, and it is highly unlikely that he regarded these two aspects as separate.[11]

The intellectual emphases of Guanxue stressed those ideas characteristic of early Confucianism, especially those found in the Four Books, rather than such popular late seventeenth-century activities as evidential research and historical writing. Guanxue adherents maintained an interest in social, moral, and political issues and action and tended to approach philosophical issues from a pragmatic viewpoint within a moral framework. They had little patience for ideas that had become separated from their social functions and often viewed aesthetic interests like painting and poetry from a somewhat derogatory perspective. None of these emphases in itself was unique to Guanxue, but together they formed a certain style, especially in contrast to other contemporary and more fashionable subtraditions.

Occupying an ever-expanding time frame, the Guanxue sense of community consisted of a network of people and a range of customary practices linking present cultural-political traditions to the past and future. The practices included visits to famous pilgrimage sites, graves, and shrines; the support of academies; the exchange of letters; the writing of biographies and epitaphs; and the editing and publication of the writings of others. These kinds of activities formed and maintained the social ties that were part of Guanxue as a community. By deliberately engaging in these activities, a philosopher became part of and continued that tradition.[12]

In sum, Guanxue was Confucian learning in one region in China, a region of ancient cultural and political importance that had become a peripheral area by the seventeenth century. Although other regional traditions differed in terms of the particulars of experience and aspects of their social relationships, I suggest that, as philosophical systems, they shared these theoretical similarities in their patterns of organization. Deriving from cultural givens, the three important aspects of Guanxue identified here did not form a pattern of behavior unique to this tradition, although the particulars of how the pattern was manifested were its own.

Guanxue may further be seen as reflecting the paradigmatic example of the family in its theoretical structure. It was made up of people, it had ancestors and potential descendants, it was multigenerational, it distinguished itself from other, similar groups, it had a genealogical record (Feng Congwu's *Guanxue bian* [A Guanxue register]), it had an informal body of ritual behavior or customary practices, and it existed within a larger social and intellectual context. In addition, its sense of identity was based on descriptive and prescriptive characteristics. Guanxue, a particular instance of neo-Confucian learning, was composed of patterns of both thought and action.

The discussion of philosophical issues. A second characteristic of the philosophical system was the type of approach that thinkers used in the discussion of philosophical issues and the presentation of their positions. From the earliest Confucians, the social and "concrete" aspects of the approach are especially noteworthy.

The most popular forms of philosophical writing were commentaries on the classics, essays, reading notes, and recorded conversations (not necessarily actual) in the form of questions and answers. The style was more documentary than rhetorical.[13] Although none of these forms was exclusively a philosophical genre, the form itself is not my primary concern here. What is important is that these forms (with the possible exception of the essay) reflect an assumption that the social aspect of philosophical thinking was critical. Said another way, these forms suggest that Confucian thinkers were involved with past and future thinkers in an open-ended engagement.

The conversation was a particularly important philosophical form from the Song to the early Qing.[14] Perhaps more clearly than the other forms, conversation implied and reinforced the view that philosophical thinking was a shared activity, not a solitary one. Rather than aiming at a victory of one position over another, the participants often engaged in an exchange in which each successively adapted his position to that of the other. To borrow from Whitehead, they participated in an "enlargement of thought."[15] Confucian philosophical thought was shared thinking, involving relationships with various kinds of behavior and ideas, and not the exclusive property of one person. Thought arose and developed in a social context, and the conversational form made this clear.

The social aspect of thought may be seen even in commentaries and reading notes, in that the philosopher-writer was responding to the ideas of others. Although in these cases the writer was not answered immediately (and who would answer was not known), there was no expectation that he would be or needed to be. In other words, I am suggesting that the relationship among ideas was a major feature of the thought itself. A thinker knew that he entered an already established world of ideas. He did not present his ideas as somehow standing alone, without reference to other ideas and situations. Ideas were presented, and indeed existed, as part of a context that in turn provided instructions on how to understand them. Readers had to learn how to "read" the context. In considering an idea, they were also considering its connections with other ideas.

Confucian thinkers typically engaged in philosophical issues by focusing on specific topics rather than on general theoretical concerns or general rules for thinking about ideas. And, as we shall see, Li was no exception. Like their counterparts in literary, art, or historical criticism, neo-Confucian philosophers discussed particular texts and ideas. Their explicit focus on a particular idea in a specific context or text does not mean, however, that they did not have concerns about theoretical issues or that they did not make philosophical claims. Rather, the form of their claims was such that the "point" invoked and represented the "pattern." Claims about particular, individual ideas carried unspoken, but known, theoretical implications, indicated by the context. Within Confucian philosophical culture, the implicit rules for establishing a claim involved generalizing from the particular to the general.

In other words, philosophers often used an oral rhetorical device in writing. In the oral presentation of ideas, previous examples of an event are cited as a mnemonic device to arouse appropriate memories. The act of linking several examples makes a particular event have meaning beyond itself. This meaning extends to another theoretical level, in that the particular event becomes part of a class of meta-facts. Membership in a class gives the particular an authority it does not have in itself. The particular event stands not only for itself, but for a class of events. The use of examples thus strengthened the philosopher's position.

The kind of data accepted as confirming a claim had similar, concrete, and particular characteristics. Since an unstated part of many philosophical claims was the desired social behavior that was to follow from the ideas, Confucian philosophers often presented data that spoke to that part of the claim, namely, the resulting action. Discussed further below, Li Yong's *Guan'gan lu* (Record of observations and impressions, EQQJ, 22) is such an example. Although it appears at first to be a biographical work, containing accounts of some unusual thinkers, Li Yong actually was using particular cases to advocate certain philosophical ideas and provide data that justified those ideas.

A further consideration relevant to the philosophical approach is the state in which philosophical knowledge was preserved and transmitted. A brief look at what two Western philosophers have said may help clarify the nature of states of knowledge. I turn to them first because they were more explicit about this matter than Confucian thinkers. Not by coincidence, they tended to be most concerned about this topic when discussing ideas about teaching and learning.

Both Jean-Jacques Rousseau and John Dewey claimed that effective teaching required one to make a distinction between knowledge in its final, systematized form and knowledge in its earlier, fluid state, as it was in the process of being learned. To be effective, teaching has to incorporate how knowledge is acquired, that is, a person learns things first in relation to his or her own experience and only later begins to organize this knowledge within a general framework. Thus, teaching should emphasize the process of learning rather than knowledge in the codified form that the teacher knows it. Dewey thus said:

> The subject matter of the learner is not, therefore, it cannot be, identical with the formulated, the crystallized, and systematized subject matter of the adult; the material as found in books and in works of art, etc. . . . [The instructor's knowledge] involves principles which are beyond the immature pupil's understanding and interest. In and of itself, it may no more represent the living world of the pupil's experience than the astronomer's knowledge of Mars represents a baby's acquaintance with the room in which he stays. In the second place, the method of organization of the material of achieved scholarship differs from that of the beginner. It is not true that the experience of the young is unorganized — that it consists of isolated scraps. But it is organized in connection with direct practical centers of interest. The child's home is, for example, the organizing center of his geographical knowledge. . . . To the one who is learned, subject matter is extensive, accurately defined, and logically interrelated. To the one who is learning, it is fluid, partial, and connected through his personal occupations.[16]

Earlier, Rousseau took a similar position:

> You wish to teach this child geography and you provide him with globes, spheres, and maps. What elaborate preparations! What is the

use of all these symbols; why not begin by showing him the real thing so that he may at least know what you are talking about? . . . As a general rule—never substitute the symbol for the thing signified, unless it is impossible to show the thing itself. . . . His geography will begin with the town he lives in and his father's country house, then the places between them.[17]

There is a series of abstract truths by means of which all the sciences are related to common principles and are developed each in its turn. This relationship is the method of the philosophers. We are not concerned with it at present. There is quite another method by which every concrete example suggests another and always points to the next in the series. This succession, which stimulates the curiosity and so arouses the attention required by every object in turn, is the order followed by most men, and it is the right order for all children.[18]

Although Confucian philosophers did not talk about knowledge in these words and their advanced teachings were not directed to children, the conflict between those supporting textual scholarship and those dubious of it was very much related, in a theoretical sense, to this distinction between these two states of knowledge. Li Yong's position implied that knowledge of the sages' learning should be preserved in a state closer to the process of learning recommended by Dewey and Rousseau than to a finished, codified statement. With his strong interests in teaching, Li took an approach that openly did not involve a finished presentation of a fixed position. This is not to say, however, that Li's writings and recorded sayings were not systematic and organized or that his thought itself had no guiding theoretical organization.

In sum, discussion of philosophical ideas focused on particulars. The particular point invoked and represented the pattern or class of events. Furthermore, the social aspect was a critical element of ideas. Ideas were seen not as somehow freestanding but as belonging to particular contexts of ideas and as finding realization in actual human experience. They belonged to an ongoing, ever-changing discussion.

Social time. A third characteristic of the Confucian philosophical system was its arena of relevance, which consisted of a framework of social space-time. While not denying calendrical (or chronological) time, Confucian philosophers thought in terms of social time.[19] Establishing the conditions and conventions of the philosophical system, this kind of temporal framework made the criteria for marking time different from that of calendrical time.

Time according to the clock and calendar is measured in terms of such abstract units as years, months, days, and hours. These numerical categories are commonly seen as abstract, but they derive from events having astronomical significance, that is, from the movements of the sun, moon, and earth. Social time, in contrast, is measured in terms of events having social and political significance. For instance, dynasties, generations, persons, ideas, certain sociocultural events, and even classical texts could be and were markers of social time in the Chinese world. Appealing to human events, social time functions without reference to quantification as the critical standard for segmentation. Social time stresses continuities, moreover, rather than discontinuities.

The framework of social space-time implies that Confucian philosophers lived in a present that included the historical past and the future. Theirs was an "insistent present," to borrow a term from Whitehead, with continually expanding boundaries.[20] Their present consisted of ideas and events drawn from all historical periods existing together in viable relationships. It was not a punctiform present, for past and future generations were, or could be, equally part of it.

Ideas and events that had occurred years before in a historical sense belonged to the social present as long as they remained relevant to the sociocultural concerns. Such events were, in effect, still "happening." Events were not "over" when their punctiform moment passed, because their duration (known by their boundaries) was not measured by categories of calendrical time. Thus, for instance, no one objected, or even thought of objecting, to a philosopher's quoting the words of Confucius even after a hundred, five hundred, or a thousand years. Ideas belonged to the present as long as they retained cultural significance. In other words, the framework of social time entailed an expanded present.

The notion of social time and its expanded present is implied, for instance, in the nature of the responsibilities assumed by Confucians. A phrase from the writings of the Song philosopher Zhang Zai often quoted by Li Yong illustrates the scope of Confucian responsibility. Li instructed people to "establish their aim on behalf of heaven and earth; establish the Heavenly derived standards of morality on behalf of the people now alive; continue the interrupted learning on behalf of those in the past; and begin the era of great peace on behalf of the myriad generations of the future."[21] Also reflecting the Confucian conception of social time is the comment of one writer who said that Li "regarded the myriad generations as one generation."[22] These quotations indicate that "heaven and earth" (the universe) and "generations" (those of the living, the dead, and the future) were relevant markers of time, even though they were not calendrical categories. Confucian philosophers focused on human experience, and this experience was measured in terms of categories relevant to itself rather than to the sun and moon.

The framework of social time means that Confucian philosophers perceived the world and measured the duration of events against a standard of values, an ethical standard as opposed to a numerical standard. Openly promoting a particular conception of the culture, they looked for the sociopolitical relations of events. Their expanded present was, of course, as selective as it was broad. The historical past was often condensed — from a contemporary viewpoint — into a highly restricted grouping of rulers, advisors, thinkers, texts, and events. For the Confucian thinkers, however, these were the things that "mattered." These were the things relevant to their criteria of judgment.

It is not that Confucians did not acknowledge other kinds of time. Rather, calendrical time was simply not the relevant measuring frame for Confucian responsibilities. The calendrical frame of the modern world is no less biased, of course, than the ethical frame used by Confucian philosophers, and the modern claim of its neutrality is certainly fictive. Calendrical time simply measures relationships among events by another standard, one that was not relevant to the Confucian purpose.

Social space-time offers a perspective that seems to make temporal movement more like a "spreading out" than a linear or cyclical pattern of movement. (This is not to deny the importance of the cyclical pattern in Chinese culture — from other perspectives.) In spread-out time, relevance to certain values rather than chronological sequence is the critical criterion of measurement. For instance, on those occasions when Li Yong regarded Zhu Xi as belonging to the past, it was not because Zhu lived five centuries before Li, but because in those contexts Zhu's ideas did not speak to the problem at hand (and so were "dead"). This conception of time thus differs from that commonly utilized by historians. What is past in terms of chronological time may easily be, or not be, part of the expanded present of the Confucian philosopher.

Assuming value-based markers, Li (and many other thinkers) constructed the past on more than one occasion with the "events" of "Kong, Yan, Si, Meng; Lian, Luo, Guan, Min of the Song; and He, Hui, Yao, Jing of the Ming" (EQQJ, 3.9a). Thinking in terms of a medical metaphor, Li claimed that these philosophers (Confucius or Kongzi, Yan Hui, Zisi, Mencius or Mengzi, Zhou Dunyi, the brothers Cheng Hao and Cheng Yi, Zhang Zai, Zhu Xi, Xue Xuan, Chen Xian-zhang, Wang Yangming, and Lü Nan) were the "doctors" who had the "prescriptions." However, "Yin, Zhou, Kong, Meng" (i.e., the achievements of Yi Yin, the Duke of Zhou, Confucius, and Mencius) were the noteworthy events of the past when meritorious fame was Li's concern (EQQJ, 3.4b).

A conception of social time is assumed, moreover, in the ontological understanding of the universe inherited from classical Confucianism. This view recognized situations or events as the fundamental entities.[23] Situations were not frozen, moreover; they had constantly shifting boundaries. Any situation from the historical past could be part of the expanded present because of its relevance to certain ideas and values.

I emphasize this Confucian philosophical perspective on time because it differs so radically from the numerical conception used in the modern world (which is related to modern science). We live in a period in which the reality of social time is commonly denied or denigrated as merely "qualitative"; even when social time is accepted, chronological time is still seen as "objective" and quantitative, and so more "real." An understanding of the Confucian conception of social time forces us to consider that units of time, like other units of experience, are a matter of conceiving as well as perceiving.[24] That is, the units in which things are distinguished and measured are not somehow objectively present, waiting to be per-ceived, as a mirror seems to wait for objects to appear before it. Rather, human beings formulate units of perception in reference to specific interests and aims.

In sum, taking social entities as their arena of relevance (given their responsibility to preserve the Way), Confucian philosophers assumed an ethical standard, as opposed to a numerical standard, for measuring time. Their thought is thus premised on a concept of social time.

A search for the Way. A fourth characteristic of the philosophical system pertains to the fundamental Confucian aim. In contrast to Western philosophers' pursuit of truth and certainty (widely seen as fixed entities tied to a logical standard of testing), Chinese thinkers engaged in a search for the Way (*dao*), a path of action and knowledge tied to an ethical standard.[25] Their focus was based on the assumption that the primary task of philosophers was to serve in government and to preserve and transmit the Confucian tradition. Like leadership groups in other cultures, the Confucians took as their responsibility the preservation of their culture. Thus they attended to certain activities while ignoring or denigrating others.

The search for the Way was a dominant theme occupying all kinds of thinkers during all periods. Since there was no single opinion on how one should search for or embody the Way, this question remained a continual, and often sharp, source of conflict among Chinese thinkers. Although varied and superficially unrelated, the activities of philosophers were not unstructured. They were "organized forms of . . . social activity."[26] As such, they were social institutions, contributing to the shape of society and culture.

From the classical period to the time of Li Yong, the search for the Way involved activities as diverse as the writing of textual commentaries, the struggle for political and social reform, self-cultivation and ritual action, the farming of small plots of land, literary creativity, and landscape painting. Moreover, the variation within each of these kinds of behavior was almost as great as that among them. For instance, the writers of commentaries in the Han dynasty emphasized the explication of the historical meanings of particular words in the classics, whereas Song commentators were more likely to express speculative and ontological views. Although Qing evidential research scholars returned to a stress on the supposedly original meanings of the classical texts, they further worked to expose passages that were forgeries and later additions.

The question of the nature of the Way also lacked a single answer. Like many important cultural terms, the Way was subject to "semantic slippage." That is, the same word was used in different ways in different contexts, not necessarily with the full awareness of those employing the term. Thus, disagreement about the "meaning" of a term like "Way" often reflected the fact that different subjects were being discussed.

Although the Way was generally accepted as a path of ethical action and knowledge, some philosophers saw it as a fixed standard not dependent on human culture and society, whereas others emphasized its inseparability from the contingencies of human society and history. For the latter, the Way implied a set of ideals that humans sought to achieve in various ways depending on the circumstances. Conceived broadly as cultural knowledge, behavior, and values, the Way was seen as expanding over time, with new conditions providing new issues as well as new examples of appropriate action. From this perspective, the flexibility of the Way did not imply expediency or opportunism, as some Chinese philosophers claimed, and various thinkers took pains to point this out.[27]

Accepted by Li Yong and Guanxue more generally, this broad conception of the Way consisted of the cultural tradition first defended and taught by Confucius.[28] Seen as deriving from the culture of the early Zhou dynasty, the Way was closely associated with the early Zhou rulers, Kings Wen and Wu and the Duke of Zhou. It continued to be defended by later philosophers despite profound historical changes. Over time, the Way incorporated elements not found in ancient Zhou culture, and because some of the new elements derived in part from Buddhist formulations, a foreign source, the acceptability or even the possibility of these additions was fiercely debated. (A non-Chinese source violated the epistemological imperatives expressed in the generative metaphor.)

In contrast to this sociohistorical perspective, the Way was also conceived in ontological terms, as coexisting with, deriving from, or giving rise to the universe. In these senses, the emphasis was on the Way as cosmic pattern or process; human society participated in it, but it was greater than human society. Moreover, just as the natural world did not always exhibit its patterns in fully predictable ways, so the human world could also experience periods in which the Way was not fulfilled or not fulfilled well. Zhu Xi is thought by Western scholars, for instance, to have argued for this "cosmic principle" position, as against the sociohistorical conception of some contemporaries, such as Chen Liang.[29] In Zhu's view, the Way was an unchanging set of values expressed in the classics and was equivalent to the patterns or principles (*li*) of the universe.

Although many Western scholars use the term "metaphysical" to describe the Way in the sense of cosmic pattern or principle(s) of heaven, I find this description misleading. The Chinese did not think of the physical world as composed of inert matter. They made the distinction of "above (or before) forms" (*xing er shang*) and "below (or within) forms" (*xing er xia*). This distinction is not equivalent to the Western one between material and spiritual substances. That which is non-corporeal or without form is not necessarily metaphysical in the sense of being a spiritual (or mental) substance.

Although Confucian philosophers advocated many variations of these two positions concerning the Way, the difference between the ontological and the social conceptions of the Way tended to be reduced to a crude dichotomy between the Way as unchanging moral-political-cosmic pattern and the Way as culture (*wen*), especially in the sense of literary and artistic endeavors. Although some thinkers interpreted the separation of the Way and culture as a failure of those engaged in Confucian learning, other factors were seen as relevant.[30] The epistemological framework, particularly the paradigmatic example of the plant, led literary and artistic achievements to be understood as the branches or secondary aspects of learning, and moral values, the Way, as the root.[31] Buddhist ontological distinctions between principle (*li*) and reality (*shi*) and neo-Confucian distinctions between principle (*li*) and energy-matter (*qi*) also reinforced a separation of the Way and culture. Both the Buddhist and neo-Confucian concepts of principle encouraged (but did not necessitate) an ontological, in contrast to a sociohistorical, status for the Way.

The disagreements among Confucian philosophers concerning the meaning of the Way and how to search for it led to controversies over moral, social, and political issues, as well as over concepts of reality, culture, and genuine learning.[32] Although the Way occupied a central place in Confucian thought for many reasons, one particular reason deserves mention here because of its relevance to fundamental epistemological premises. I suggest that the "religious," that is, the social, function was of critical importance.

Here I use the term "religious" in the sense of Durkheim, as a social matter and as a matter involving beliefs and ritualized action. According to Durkheim, "If religion has given birth to all that is essential in society, it is because the idea of society is the soul of religion."[33] For the "soul of religion," we can substitute "core of the Confucian Way." To quote Durkheim further, "The real function of religion is not to make us think, to enrich our knowledge, nor to add to the conceptions which we owe to science . . . but rather, it is to make us act, to aid us to live."[34] Confucian thinkers would have agreed — after having substituted their "Way" for his "religion." As a primary characteristic of Confucian philosophy, a search for the Way ensured that philosophical thought would remain closely tied to the sphere of action.

Teaching and learning. A fifth characteristic was the assumption of the central importance of teaching and learning. Established by Confucius and reaffirmed by later thinkers, this responsibility involved two kinds of teaching: teaching matters of content concerning such things as the Way and how to be a superior person, and teaching about teaching. Confucius was a teacher of teachers. As a result, in addition to matters of content, questions such as who may be taught and who is qualified to teach were philosophically important.

Confucius' claim that he was a transmitter, not a creator, points directly to this central task of Confucian learning (*Lunyu*, 7.1).[35] Although other interpretations are possible, this statement is often taken to reflect Confucius' attitude toward the past. Presenting a view widely accepted by Guanxue thinkers, including Li, Zhang Zai reconfirmed that the ancient sages created the culture and later sages transmitted it. Commenting on the claim of Confucius, Zhang Zai said that there were seven creators — Fu Xi, Shen Nong, Huang Di, Yao, Shun, Yu, and Tang. Zhang defined a creator as one who makes something that previous generations did not have. From Fu Xi, who is given credit for beginning the practice of harnessing oxen and riding horses, to Tang, who first changed the mandate of Heaven (from the Xia to the Shang dynasty), each of the seven began a new kind of activity. Zhang said that, although greatly esteemed, other sages such as King Wu, Yi Yin, and Confucius were not creators. King Wu, for instance, transmitted the affairs of King Tang, and Yi Yin should have reprimanded the Duke of Zhou. Although there has been no one like Confucius since antiquity, Confucius himself said that he was a transmitter, not a creator.[36] In other words, Confucius recognized that his role differed from that of the earliest sages. Theirs was to create; his was to teach.

Attacking hereditary privilege, Confucius stated that his teaching should be extended to everyone, regardless of social class and ability to pay (*Lunyu*, 7.7 and 15.38). An eagerness to learn, rather than family and class background, should be primary in determining access to education. Access was critical, of course, given that the educational concerns of Confucius applied to the leadership class, not to the common people. Although social realities limited the availability of a Confucian education throughout history, the ideal of access remained.[37]

In addressing the question of who may teach, Confucius insisted that it had to be someone able to use his knowledge of the past in acquiring new knowledge (*Lunyu*, 2.11). The good teacher did not simply possess great erudition or traffic in "inert ideas."[38] The good teacher taught people how to learn, and he emphasized using, rather than accumulating, knowledge. Although others elaborated further, Confucius established the philosophically important idea that the teacher is not simply a conduit but actually embodies what is taught.

The question of when a person should be taught was a further issue, and here Confucius stressed the readiness of the learner. Neither teaching nor learning can occur if the student is not prepared to learn and does not actively participate. As a learner, Confucius was always alert for someone who could teach him, and as a teacher, he was adamant that he would only teach those willing to learn (*Lunyu*, 7.21 and 7.8). This approach has some interesting parallels to the educational ideas of John Dewey and Rousseau, who claimed that teaching must begin with the personal experience of the student. All three insisted that the instruction fit the level of the student, and all were concerned with the reference, or use, of knowledge as well as its content.[39]

Following Confucius' emphasis on teaching, the early Confucians established the view that it was the government's duty "to instruct the people."[40] Ming and Qing philosophers still maintained this view, even claiming that the ruler should also be a teacher.[41] They held that the lack of such a ruler had foisted this responsibility on the Confucians, however, and thus Feng Congwu was led to describe Lü Nan as one who took the "teacher's way" as his responsibility.[42] A further belief, and one accepted by Li Yong, was that, in editing the classics, Confucius had "established an instruction to hang through the ages."[43] Believing themselves to be following in the path of Confucius, the Song philosophers especially saw themselves as "teachers to the world."[44] Confucians of all periods, however, took "the ages" as their responsibility, not just individual students, and in this way their teaching had reference to that time span that I above call "scholar-time."

From the Song period on, great teachers were given special recognition. There was the fame, for instance, of the Five Masters of the Qingli period (1041–48) and the Four Masters of Siming (1160's).[45] Despite considerable differences in their philosophical orientation, many of the leading Song thinkers were regarded as great teachers, including Shao Yong, Zhu Xi, and Lu Jiuyuan.[46] Some had large followings and others did not, but greatness was not measured in numbers.

To be called a great teacher, as Li Yong was, was a genuine compliment, and it put one in the company of the great philosopher-teachers of the past. Although the content and methods of teaching changed over time, the classical formulation of the teacher's importance was never forgotten or dismissed. It was accompanied, moreover, by an ambivalence toward self-teaching. Although Confucians stressed the importance of having a teacher and carrying on the instruction of one's teacher, they also could not help but admire those who succeeded without one. Li Yong was such a person.

The acceptance of the ancient sages as sources of authority also reinforced the central importance of teaching and learning. Representing the ideals of Heaven, the ultimate authority (whether conceived in anthropomorphic terms or as given patterns of nature), the sages were active teachers, not rigid possessors of a static body of abstract truths. They were seen as human beings who had to struggle in situations that posed difficulties, from the floods that confronted Yu to the oppressive familial relations faced by Shun. Offering realistic examples of good behavior in everyday life, the sages derived their authoritative force from their roles as creators, teachers, and exemplars. Viewing the sages as teachers reinforced the philosophical assumption that the validity of ideas is found in experience itself. The sages as exemplars showed people how to live morally in a constantly changing world that often provoked the more destructive capabilities of human beings.[47] Good behavior required learning — learning not only appropriate ways to behave but also how to achieve that kind of behavior. Intentions alone were not sufficient.

In sum, teaching and learning were central to the philosophical system and derived from the challenge of preserving and transmitting the cultural tradition, as the Confucians interpreted it. Teaching and learning were also inseparable from the fundamental premises that Confucian philosophy was a matter of action as well as knowledge and that the best way to achieve social order and well-being was to help human beings develop their human capacities, just as one waters and feeds a plant to encourage its best development.

ISSUES FOR LI YONG

With these three aspects of the philosophical system in mind — the epistemological imperatives of the culture, philosophical issues arising from discord around the imperatives, and fundamental social characteristics of the philosophical system — I now turn to four issues of the Confucian tradition that especially concerned Li Yong. His concerns are those of a particular person in a specific sociohistorical context, and an examination of his concerns will help reveal how a thinker appropriated the philosophical tradition. Alhough related to the problems of the times, his ideas were also directed toward a much larger audience than his seventeenth-century contemporaries.

Philosophical Discontinuity and Social Disorder

Like many others, Li addressed the issue of the discontinuity of Confucian culture, or the Way. Referred to as an interruption (in the transmission and realization) of the sages' learning and implied by the Song claim of having recovered the Way, the issue of discontinuity was important for its relation to social order. Confucian philosophers believed that their learning was the carrier of their culture, which in turn was the foundation of all social order.[48] This view had been voiced by Mencius (*Mencius*, 3B.9, 7B.38, and 2B.13) and was reinforced by implicit cultural givens, particularly those inherent in the generative metaphor. That is, the flourishing of the branches (actions leading to social order) depends upon the care of the root (the sages' learning). How to maintain the sages' learning and Confucian culture (the Way) was the problem. Along with others, Li believed that some activities, such as textual studies, mistook means for ends.

To analyze the theoretical aspects of Li's position, a brief look at what Li Yong and his predecessors said is needed. With his suggestion that he bore a great responsibility for society, Confucius led the way with his claim that he was carrying on the lost culture of King Wen and the early Zhou (*Lunyu*, 9.5). Mencius saw himself as continuing this special mission, and his positing of a historical pattern of alternating periods of five centuries of order and disorder emphasized the conditions (disorder following order) that made this concern urgent (*Mencius*, 3B.9, 7B.38, and 2B.13).[49]

Han Yu (768–824) of the Tang is most widely recognized as the person who next raised this theme (some thinkers credited a slightly earlier Confucian, Wang Tong [584–617], with resurrecting this cultural transmission),[50] and his account of the transmission of the Way and its loss after Mencius set the stage for the Song thinkers. Extremely critical of certain aspects of Buddhism, Han Yu expressed a position that clearly had reference to a philosophical and cultural context.[51]

The recovery of the Way became a central topic of the Song philosophers, with thinkers such as Zhou Dunyi, Cheng Hao, Cheng Yi, Zhang Zai, and Zhu Xi (who "wrote the history"—the *daotong*, the transmission of the Way) regarded as principal transmitters. Ming philosophers continued to devote attention to the matter of transmission, and during the late Ming the content of the Way was challenged and expanded.[52] The focus of philosophers varied over time, of course, as they addressed the interrelated aspects of discontinuity, recovery, and transmission.

Often allowing the words of others to speak for his own view, Li Yong mentioned discontinuity in the learning of the sages in several contexts. Li quoted, for instance, an extensive passage on this topic from the writings of Wu Cheng (1249–1333), a Confucian of the Yuan period (EQQJ, 1.10b). Discussing the Mencian concept of the virtuous nature, or moral heart-mind, as the essential characteristic of being human, Wu noted that Confucian learning had had no teaching to follow after the sages' transmission had been cut off. This situation prevailed during the Han and Tang, that is, for more than a thousand years after Mencius. The two masters during that period, Dong Zhongshu (179?–104? B.C.E.) of the Han and Han Yu of the Tang, were able to "get close to it [the Way], but the original source was still obscured from them. Only with the flourishing of the Song philosophers Zhou [Dunyi], Cheng [Yi and Cheng Hao], Zhang [Zai], and Shao [Yong, who was often excluded from such accounts] were people again able to comprehend thoroughly the thought of Mencius" (EQQJ, 1.10b). This revival then reached its peak with Zhu Xi.[53]

Li followed Wu's remarks with the comment that people now "consider the contemporary Confucian practices of memorizing and reciting phrases and chapters as vulgar learning, but such practices are not separate from the branches [secondary activities] consisting of words and writing. These practices simply reflect the deficiencies that arose after the Jiading period [1324–28] among the later followers of Zhu Xi when they did not have any means by which to save genuine learning" (EQQJ, 1.10b).

Elsewhere, in quoting from the writings of Feng Congwu, Li emphasized that it was important to discuss learning in order to clarify it, for only then could it contribute to good government. Li quoted from a memorial in which Feng linked the Way and order (good rule) with Confucian learning (here called *lixue*) and its practice of discussing learning. Feng said that this practice began with Confucius and flourished with Mencius. Although attempts were made to expose the errors of Yang Zhu and Mozi, other ways (*yiduan*) arose after Mencius died. The various states fought against each other, and political turmoil lasted a long time. After more than a thousand years, the Song Confucians emerged and revived the tradition of Mencius. It flourished in the Song, but it also was proscribed in the Song (EQQJ, 12.7a–b).[54]

In a lecture, Li gave his own account of how the sages' learning was interrupted and then later recovered.

When the former sages [those who apprehended first, *xianjue*] advocated a way, it always was to provide help according to the times, just as when one is sick, the medicine that one takes varies according to one's illness.[55] After Mencius, learning degenerated into commentary and exegesis. The Song Confucians emerged and saved it with [the prescription of] "residing in reverence and thoroughly investigating principles." After Hui'an [Zhu Xi], it again degenerated into a concern with petty details. Thus, [Wang] Yangming emerged and saved it by advocating the application of moral knowledge. This teaching enabled people to have some success quickly, without long periods of work and discipline, but eventually people just talked about basic substance and ignored practical effort. Thereupon, Gu [Xiancheng, 1550–1612] and Gao [Panlong, 1562–1626] of the Donglin [Academy] and Feng Shaoxu [Congwu] of the Guanzhong [Academy] appeared and saved it by advocating the cultivation of reverence and resting in the highest good. Now again, there are many illnesses. People do not know what their duties are, they have no sense of shame, and the primary virtues of ritual action, rightness, modesty, and shame have lost their meaning. (EQQJ, 10.7a–b)

Like others, Li spoke about the issue of discontinuity and disorder in terms of the heart-mind (*xin*) and its transmission. In referring to Li's ideas, one of Li's contemporary followers, Lu Shikai, emphasized the sequence of first receiving a transmission, then learning, then realizing the heart-mind: "Learning can be talked about only after there is a transmission. The heart-mind can be talked about only after there is learning" (EQQJ, 6.1a, 1671 preface by Lu Shikai). Lu further said that although it was not easy to define learning, it is concerned with completing the "four sprouts" and not obscuring one's "luminous source" (both terms refer to the root, or heart-mind, from different paradigmatic contexts).

Directly connecting the heart-mind and the sages' learning, Li said, "That which makes humans what they are is the one heart-mind, and its preservation [i.e., realization] depends completely on learning" (EQQJ, *fu* 15.2a). For support, Li quoted Confucius, "[Is it not a pleasure] to learn and at the appropriate time to practice what one has learned?" (*Lunyu*, 1.1), and Mencius, "The way of learning is nothing other than to seek for the lost heart-mind" (*Mencius*, 6A.11). For Li, learning without reference to the heart-mind is not genuine learning. It is either common and ordinary learning aimed at fame and profit or the confused and superficial learning of perverted Confucians who follow the branches and forget the root. These two inferior kinds of learning "have no relationship to the effort to become a genuine person, and they are certainly not what Confucius and Mencius called learning" (EQQJ, *fu* 15.2a). Li held that the learning of the former sages was genuine and pure, as was the learning of Zhou Dunyi, the two Chengs, Zhang Zai, and Zhu Xi in the Song, and Xue Xuan, Hu Juren, Luo Qinshun, Lü Nan, Gu Xiancheng, Gao Panlong, Feng Congwu, and Xin Quan in the Ming (EQQJ, *fu* 15.2a). And, "if one rejects the constant and delights in the new and strange, that is madness or perversion, and both are what learners should take precaution against" (EQQJ, *fu* 15.2b).

Statements like these enabled Li to frame the problem of cultural preservation and transmission in such a way that he could easily criticize the positions to which he objected. All Confucians agreed on the necessity of social order and its dependence on Confucian learning, but they disagreed on what to do. From Li's perspective this disagreement derived from others' failure to understand what had been interrupted. The textual focus of his contemporaries indicated to him that they saw the interruption as a matter of accuracy in the texts that transmitted the words of the sages. That is, what the sages had said had been corrupted or not understood. For Li, what had been lost was moral knowledge, understood as wisdom or moral understanding. This was not a matter of words, although words (and actions) were used to convey it. In Li's view, moral knowledge could not be gained from texts, as some seemed to think, but only from one's heart-mind. Textual commentators thus focused on the wrong activities to maintain the Way.

In Li's view, Confucian philosophers had a critical role in preventing a discontinuity of the Way. His primary claim was that the role of philosophers is to correct Confucian thought so that appropriate social behavior can follow. This claim was linked with several others. Li held that people's frequent failure to act morally is due to ignorance. People lack moral knowledge despite the presence of the values and teachings of the ancient sages and past philosophers in various writings as well as in other institutions of the Confucian elite.

For Li, moral ignorance was not simply an individual failing. Rather, the nature of human beings and of their environment made moral knowledge and behavior difficult. Like many other Confucians, Li saw humans as morally frail, easily subject to error. Immoral behavior was thus more likely than moral behavior. The sixteen-character phrase, popular among neo-Confucians, from "The Counsels of Yu the Great" in the *Book of Documents* served as a constant reminder of human fragility. "The human mind is precarious: the mind of the Way is subtle. Be refined and single-minded. Hold fast the Mean."[56] The surrounding world was also a contributing factor in that it was constantly changing. Since different actions were needed at different times, appropriate teachings and actions did not have a fixed content. The words of the sages (contained in the classics) were thus not always applicable.

Li further claimed that moral (that is, appropriate) behavior depends on first having correct thoughts. People cannot do what is right without first knowing what to do. For Li, moral behavior entailed doing the right things for the right reasons. Moral behavior was that which was done in awareness and with intention. The right thing done for the wrong reason or done unintentionally was not moral behavior. Since "right thinking" came before "right acting," the first problem was how to attain moral knowledge. Attacking the focus on texts as an inappropriate method for gaining such knowledge, Li emphasized instead the heart-mind. Two senses of this concept were critical in Li's thinking here.

One sense was the Mencian concept of the heart-mind as consisting of the four sprouts (the senses of compassion, shame, courtesy, and right and wrong) common to all humans that provided the foundation for moral behavior and social order (*Mencius*, 2A.6 and 6A.6). Confucian culture (the Way) was seen as based on what the ancient sages had taught people to do, and the sages' teachings ultimately were grounded on the four sprouts. When developed, the four sprouts formed the basic characteristics defining social order. Thus, the heart-mind referred to those human capacities whose development led to Confucian culture and society, and consequently, the "transmission of Confucian culture" and "transmission of the heart-mind" were interchangeable phrases. Transmitting the heart-mind meant transmitting the Way (Confucian culture). Moreover, the heart-mind was the site of such activities as thinking, feeling, desiring, and willing. In this sense, "heart-mind" was thus occasionally a substitute term for thoughts, emotions, desires, or aims.

Criticizing the emphasis on texts and the written tradition was a difficult, although not impossible, position. The very notion of civilization for the Chinese was inseparable from writing, and it was widely accepted that the written tradition was a central aspect of Confucian culture. Words, as well as actions and institutions, were important for conveying what was necessary to be known. Li himself acknowledged the necessity of reading the classics, the words of the sages. On the other hand, no amount of textual study could help a person gain real understanding, for it was the wrong method.

From Li's perspective, the philosophical difference between his position and that of those engaged in evidential research and writing commentaries was more than a matter of rhetoric. Although Li held that moral knowledge could never fully be expressed in words, he assumed that textual scholars believed that the sages' words did embody wisdom, or the "truth." For Li, the actual words were not the critical point. As he said on one occasion, the "great root and extended Way are different names for the same thing" (EQQJ, 4.10b). Li's position echoed the view of many others, such as Xue Xuan, who earlier had said, "The 'extreme good' of the *Great Learning*, the 'one thread' of the *Analects*, the 'goodness of nature' of the *Mencius*, the 'sincerity' of the *Doctrine of the Mean*, the 'Supreme Ultimate' of Master Zhou Dunyi—although the words are different, they all have the same meaning."[57]

Li acknowledged that words were necessary to communicate moral knowledge, but held that actual understanding constantly changed with the circumstances. Although the sages spoke the truth, their words reflected an understanding appropriate only for their times. Understanding itself cannot be transmitted; it must be grasped by the individual person. Thus the search for what the sages had actually said was, at best, a peripheral activity in the search for moral knowledge. Li's assumption that the discontinuity of the Way referred to a break in moral understanding laid the groundwork for his view of the philosopher-teacher's role.

As a cross-cultural concern, this philosophical issue is significant for education. Both Chinese and Western thinkers have questioned not only the relationship between words and their referents and the adequacy of words to communicate and express, but also our ability to represent some forms of knowledge by words. To take one example from Western thought, Augustine argued that words do not convey knowledge, but are only signs. Knowledge requires a personal confrontation with the reality signified by the words.[58] Although not everyone has agreed with Augustine's definition of knowledge, many Confucian philosophers would have been sympathetic with it.

From a broader perspective, the concern about the interruption of the Way is an issue of cultural change and of cultural memory and transmission. The Song recovery of the Way implies a theoretical rejection of those concepts (mostly associated with Buddhism and Daoism) challenging the cultural given of unity and the generative metaphor. However, a theoretical rejection does not necessarily, and did not, entail a rejection of all content. Consisting of a reaffirmation of certain aspects of classical Confucianism, the Song "recovery" of the Way allowed, in effect, a reintegration of ideas and values that had strayed too close to the permissible boundaries. The recovery confirmed the validity of the sages' ideas and values even as it demonstrated the flexibility of the tradition. By affirming the pattern of recurring order and disorder, the recovery of the Way helped to preserve tradition by allowing the entry of new ideas and practices that could not be accepted for their own sake. Without their acceptance being related to exigencies, foreign ideas and practices might have to be rejected because they were branches that did not develop out of "this root."

Although Chinese philosophers did not offer an analysis of how a culture stores necessary information, their actions suggest a realization that a culture preserves and transmits its memory in various ways, using alternative and overlapping methods. The Song three-part conception of fundamental values, applications, and the written tradition implies a recognition that methods of storing cultural memory include recognized types of knowledge, patterns of behavior, social and political institutions, and literary and artistic works.[59]

Confucian philosophers recognized that what people do not only reflects cultural values but also embodies and transmits them, and they openly talked about this behavioral aspect. For instance, the Qing scholar Liu Guyu commented that Li's learning was *shenxue* (learning of the self), not *xinxue* (learning of the heart-mind), and Wang Yangming claimed to be talking about the *shen* and *xin*, or *shenxin zhi xue*, translated by Tu Wei-ming as "the study of body and mind."[60] The emphasis on ritual action and various types of social interaction and relationships indicates that the Chinese knew that cultural memory is maintained by patterns of behavior as well as by patterns of rhetoric.

Li's (and others') objection to the preoccupation with texts was theoretically related to the belief that a concern with writing (of all kinds) as well as painting did not fulfill the Confucian imperative to act. Moreover, since philosophical texts appeared to state fundamental values in a more direct way than behavior, institutions, and other kinds of texts, they could more easily be mistaken for the wisdom that they represented. Texts survived over long periods of time, but they could not enable a person to turn values into action. Only a person's understanding could do that. Thus, rejecting knowledge of words as a test of comprehension, Li emphasized that "discussing books" was not the same as "discussing learning" (EQQJ, 3.9b–10a). Moreover, the early sages did not concentrate their attention primarily on texts (EQQJ, 16.5a). Great teachers were the critical storage sites for the culture, for they alone achieved the necessary wisdom.

In sum, I suggest that the issue of philosophical discontinuity concerned the preservation of cultural memory so as to ensure social order. The problems of cultural change and transmission were also relevant. Failed efforts were not seen as offering the possibility of another system of learning, for given the epistemological imperative of unity, there was no alternative. Order and turmoil were thus appropriate opposites, located within a natural pattern of alternation in which human beings had the power to intervene but not to control.

Philosophy, History, and the Medical Metaphor

A second concern important to Li Yong was the "proper" conception of Confucian learning and, as a corollary, the purpose of specific philosophical teachings. That is, what were Confucian philosophers trying to do? This issue further related to the question of how ideas are legitimated. As the following discussion indicates, in Li's view Confucian philosophy (learning) and specific teachings required both appropriate ideas and actions and judged the validity of ideas by the results of acting on them. A primary goal was order at all levels, from the person to the universe, along with the continuity of the culture that could achieve this order. By emphasizing effective action, Li made a sharp separation between the tasks of philosophy and those of history, for the latter in his view involved only "literary" action.

If a genealogical link between the successive teachings of Confucian learning were the critical key to cultural continuity, then the legitimation of the teachings would be a matter of attesting the historical sources of the ideas — as the familial or genealogical metaphor implies. If, however, continuity depended on a process more like that of medicine, in which illnesses are treated in order to regain health, then legitimation becomes a matter of the effectiveness of prescriptions. Li challenged the former, more traditional view. By providing an example of epistemological change, Li Yong's thought illustrates the process by which the premises of thought, and hence the cultural significance of ideas based on those premises, can be altered.

Confucian philosophers typically (although not exclusively) appealed to historical sources to legitimate their teachings. "Explaining" an idea entailed uncovering its antecedents. The "family background" served both as a legitimizing method and as an explanatory device. Because it was grounded in this generative metaphor, the conception of Confucian learning and of specific teachings became based on a pattern of thinking associated with the family, and, like a family, learning came to have a founding ancestor and descendants.

Li Yong was concerned about the goals of cultural continuity and social order, and he knew that ideas had historical backgrounds. In order to attain these goals, however, he rejected the view that the critical relationship among ideas was a familial relationship involving ancestors and descendants. He did not deny the importance of source and antecedents, and he often cited philosophical texts and persons, but he also held that there was another way to understand the sages' learning. Believing that too much emphasis on questions about antecedents hindered the actual realization of Confucian learning (such questions were more appropriate to the sphere of history, which in Li's view worked on premises especially derived from the generative metaphor), Li Yong was in effect raising questions about method — the method used to produce a teaching that would aid the world. His approach thus entailed use of a different theoretical frame, one with assumptions and questions different from those of the generative frame.

In addressing the issue of order, Li's thinking (as noted above) drew on the paradigmatic context of medicine, a social context involving a pattern of thinking concerned with questions about complaints, diagnoses, prescriptions, and treatment. The aim in medicine was, in brief, to diagnose and treat illnesses, while considering the complaints and appropriate prescriptions. The medical context and its relevant questions contrasted to a mode of thought emphasizing a source and its subsequent developments, exemplified in the family, the plant, and the river. In following out the implications of the medical frame, Li approached intellectual conflicts somewhat differently from those who thought in genealogical terms. His treatment of the conflict between the Cheng-Zhu and Lu-Wang schools, for instance, indicates that he was thinking more like a doctor than like a father. That is, he was thinking in terms of treatment rather than genealogy.

Although there were many kinds of doctors in traditional China with widely varying positions in society and associated with different kinds of knowledge, the important point here involves a more general issue — namely, how a doctor's role and responsibilities (to treat illnesses) differed from the role and responsibilities of a father (to continue the family). Emphasizing a curative and corrective conception of Confucian learning, Li maintained that the philosophers' teachings, like prescriptions, served to help restore a state of health, which (he believed) declined into illness without constant vigilance.

In traditional Chinese medicine illness and health were complicated matters and, unlike modern Western medicine, involved more than the body of a sick person. Although there was no single word for health, health was seen as a positive state, not merely as the lack of illness, and it involved a balance among physiological, emotional, and moral factors.[61] Or, to expand this point slightly further, health and illness "can be evaluated as change on any or all of four levels: physiological processes, psychological processes, social relationships, [and] cultural norms and meanings."[62] Health and illness thus involved the person and all the contexts in which people are situated (see, e.g., EQQJ, 1.3b).

Associated with disorder, the pathological situation was often referred to as *bing* (illness, medical disorder), a concept opposed both to *zhi* (to cure, treat, order) and to *he* (harmony, balance). Illnesses were largely understood as imbalances in *qi* in specific persons and in broader social settings. Based on the *Huangdi neijing* (Inner classic of the Yellow Sovereign), a Han dynasty work, traditional medicine shared the same fundamental concepts and assumptions as the wider culture, that is, such concepts as *yin* and *yang*, *qi*, the five phases, and correlative thinking (often involving correlations between the macrocosm and microcosm).[63] In addition, there were beliefs, especially associated with (but not limited to) the masses, that attributed illnesses to unpredictable actions of demons and ghosts.

For Li, the patient was the sociopolitical order itself as well as individual persons, who possessed moral and social dimensions. In applying medical thinking to the society, Li regarded health as a balance among essential values (*ti*), practical actions based on the philosophers' teachings (*yong*), and the constantly changing conditions of the times. Illness, then, was an imbalance and disorder. He conceived of philosophical teachings as analogous to medical prescriptions and alchemical elixirs. Just as the alchemist's elixirs could slow or hasten cosmic processes, so the teachings of the Confucian philosopher could bring desired change to sociopolitical processes.[64] Recovering social and moral health was, moreover, a process not too much different from that of "restoring the primary vitalities" of physiological alchemy.[65]

Li drew the analogy to medicine quite explicitly. He said, for instance, that Confucius, Yan Hui, Zisi, and Mencius in antiquity, Zhou Dunyi, the Cheng brothers, Zhang Zai, and Zhu Xi of the Song,

and Xue Xuan, Chen Xianzhang, Wang Yangming, and Lü Nan of
the Ming were "famous doctors among doctors. The Five Classics,
the Four Books, and the recorded sayings of the Confucians are the
efficacious prescriptions [*liangfang*] of the doctors" (EQQJ, 3.9a). He
also claimed that all the teachings of the classics and ancient philosophers were aimed at enabling people to recover their faultless essence and abide in the way of daily renewal, just as the *Suwen* (Basic
questions) and *Qingnang* [*aozhi*] (Mysterious principles of the blue
bag) were the "efficacious prescriptions of the former sages and were
transmitted to treat the illnesses of ten thousand generations" (EQQJ,
1.3a–b).[66] (Given Li's analogies between philosophy and medicine, it
is clear that he did not regard these two texts as prescription manu-
als. Rather, he used the term *fang* [translated here as "prescriptions"]
to mean ideas and teachings, just as he conceived of the philosophers' teachings as "prescriptions.") Li held that philosophical teachings did not add anything not originally present, and such teachings
were of use only when there were defects (EQQJ, 1.3b and 11.5b). He
further stressed that inappropriate medications were not efficacious
no matter what quantities one consumed (EQQJ, 13.8b–9a).

On the personal level, errors in thought and action were the
equivalent of illnesses.[67] When asked, for instance, whether Zhu Xi
was the "only person among those whose words fill the world who
had no verbal faults," Li answered by appealing to a curative standard rather than to the authority of the past and the classics. Mr.
Gao, the questioner, pointed out that Lu Jiuyuan's verbal fault was to
say, "The Six Classics are all my footnotes," and Wang Yangming's
was, "Everyone in the street is a sage." Li responded:

> The words of Ciyang [Zhu Xi] were lofty and true, and so the great
> mean and extreme uprightness were pure and unblemished. And
> yet the teachings of Lu and Wang of the Confucian school corrected
> errors and saved the world from abuses [that had developed from
> Zhu's teachings], and their words were like the great yellow croton-
> oil bean in medicine. It clears out the accumulated obstructions in a
> person's chest, but truly one cannot give it in general to people with
> imaginary pulmonary consumption. (EQQJ, 11.5b)[68]

Teachings, like prescriptions, were not socially isolated entities,
and their worth was based on their appropriateness to conditions.
Since conditions constantly changed, teachings and prescriptions
also had to change. Past philosophical positions (teachings) were

historical matters in Li's view, and conflicts between them should be evaluated by philosophers in terms of how those teachings responded to their (past) surrounding circumstances.

> When Yaojiang [Wang Yangming] faced the confused and obscured remnants of learning, he advocated [his theories of] extending moral knowledge, directly pointing to the human mind, and the subtlety of the one mind alone knowing. He regarded these teachings as concerned with the Confucian issues of king versus hegemon, rightness versus selfish profit, and humans versus ghosts. After he saw his own essence, he immediately helped others to comprehend their basic natures. [His learning was] simple and direct, and he contributed greatly to the teachings of the times. And yet the later followers [of his teachings] mostly just trifled with practical affairs. They constantly rejected practical studies and concentrated on rarefied speculation. When their obscurations and constant emptiness hindered their few practical efforts, then they were lost. Confused and empty, they mixed with Chan [Buddhism]. Therefore, it was necessary to aid [Wang's learning] with the learning of Kaoting [Zhu Xi]. And yet most of those in the world who followed Kaoting only exposed the fallacies of Yaojiang's learning. And in the end they reached the point of forbidding anyone to talk about the learning of rarefied speculation. When they regarded only "hearing and seeing the deep and broad" and "distinguishing and discriminating between the fine and the subtle" as the ultimate of learning, then they also in reforming the crooked lost the straight and labored in vain their whole lives. And in the end their learning had no relationship with their fundamental luminosity [*xingling*] and did not help them to learn Kaoting well. Even those who knew a little bit to look inward also regarded only the lack of pride and lust as ultimately the great root and great source, and so they, too, mostly were confused. It is necessary to regard extending one's moral knowledge as comprehending the basic essence and to regard abiding in reverential seriousness and thoroughly investigating principle and nourishing and examining as their application. From the subtlety of one idea to cautiously following after what one has seen, heard, said, and done, one adds [to those things] one's efforts at cultivation, so that inner and outer are completed together, and the teachings of Yaojiang and Kaoting do not end up unilaterally discarding practical studies and rarefied speculation. One thread runs through it all. Therefore, in learning when the two aid each other, then the two complete each other. When the two reject each other, then the two are both sick. (EQQJ, 15.8b–9a)[69]

Li thus held that the teachings of the former worthies were of aid according to the times and conditions, just as the medicine that one takes varies according to the illness (EQQJ, 10.7a–b, 16.18b, and 1.3a–b). This perspective led Li Yong to criticize certain activities, such as the study of ancient writings and texts, as irrelevant for solving the problems of the times (EQQJ, 7.10a). Such activities were the wrong medicine for the illness. In condemning this inappropriate "medicine," Li also maintained, "The Confucian school regarded virtuous action as basic and literary learning as ancillary. Later generations then solely regarded literary learning as their occupation. One can see the changes in the times" (SSFSL, *Lunyu*, pt. 2, 2).

As noted above, in Chinese medical thinking it was accepted that illnesses were complex and varied widely, from the personal level to the sociopolitical level, and Li concurred. He claimed that each person's illness was different and ranged from sensual lust to a striving for selfish gain or fame. Since Li assumed that thought preceded moral action, he generally spoke about illnesses as faults of the mind. Among the illnesses he identified were having an arrogant mind, a jealous mind, a stingy mind, a miserly mind, a selfish mind, and an immoral mind (EQQJ, 3.8b). Although he spoke of the mind, his point was that such faults lead to immoral behavior. The "mind" here is not the heart-mind, but rather a person's thoughts, aims, and feelings.

Not only did the medicine have to vary to match the illness (EQQJ, 3.8b–9a), but it was also up to each person to diagnose his or her own illness and to treat it, even though additional help was available from the philosophers' teachings. One could not take medicine for someone else. Moreover, just as individual people could benefit from the philosophers' teachings, society, too, needed a great doctor or hero to diagnose and treat the illnesses of social disorder.

Although Li certainly did not originate the application of the medical context to sociopolitical thought, as the positions of Zhu Xi and Lu Jiuyuan of the Song and Xue Xuan, Wang Yangming, and Liu Zongzhou of the Ming indicate, Li seems to have emphasized more than most thinkers the necessity of finding a great doctor (Confucian teacher). Although, as noted above, the medical metaphor had long been important in non-Confucian thought and texts, it gained an importance in Wang Yangming's thought that it had not had in the thought of previous Confucian thinkers, and Li continued the emphasis. For instance, much as in Li Yong's thought, the *Lüshi chunqiu* (Spring and autumn annals of Mr. Lü), a compilation of the third century B.C.E., explicitly compared sociopolitical problems and conditions to illnesses, and laws (rather than teachings, as Li did) to medicine.[70]

Medical ideas had been incorporated into most aspects of Chinese culture and society from ancient times. Shen Nong, an early sage and culture hero, was the patron deity and supposed inventor of the biological arts, including medicine and pharmacy.[71] And Yi, the mythological archer who shot down the extra suns, was thought to have obtained the medicine of immortality from the Queen Mother of the West.[72] Although the evidence is not firm for the Shang, the first historical period, shamans at that time may have been a link between the sociopolitical world and some form of medical thinking.[73] During the Zhou, philosophers of the different schools made occasional use of the metaphor of medicine, and from the late Zhou and Warring States period on, thinkers began more consistently to make physiological-political correlations. The five senses, for instance, were called the five officials, and analogies were drawn involving medicine, military troops, the state, the body, and illnesses.[74] By Han times the development of correlative thinking and scientific advances contributed to extensive systematic correlations between political and medical thought. The human body, for instance, was correlated with the universe as macrocosm and with the state.[75]

In addition, popular beliefs and practices, often associated (first) with Daoism and (eventually with) Buddhism, tied illness together with such things as sins, faults, demonic possession, disorder, and crime.[76] Buddhist thinking added further to the medical metaphor, in that its Four Noble Truths were theoretically comparable to the medical concepts of diagnosis, etiology (cause), remedy or prescription, and treatment.

The experience of pain and suffering became critical in Song and Ming neo-Confucian thought.[77] Indeed, by the Ming, the medical metaphor was used widely throughout society, on the popular and elite levels, and can be seen in such cultural elements as vernacular literature, religious language, and neo-Confucian thought. Medicine was associated both with Buddhism and with the thought of Wang Yangming, and Wang Yangming and the Buddha were both called great doctors.[78]

Since correlations are multi-directional in a system of correspondence, as long as the body and the state, for example, are correlates, either can be discussed in terms of the other. Whereas medical thinking used the image of the state as a way to describe the structures and functions of the human body, Li and certain others reversed the direction of this correspondence and used medical assumptions and imagery to discuss sociopolitical conditions and moral affairs.

Although Li's thinking entailed theoretical reformulations in Confucian philosophy, his concern was not theory. Rather, he wanted to clarify what Confucian learning "properly" was and to criticize erroneous views. Thus his medical assumptions become apparent only as he discusses actual problems. His teaching of criticizing and removing one's faults and renewing oneself (*huiguo zixin*; see Chapter 4) and his comments on the Zhu-Lu controversy are two contexts that particularly illustrate assumptions characteristic of a medical framework. A discussion of Li's comments on the Zhu-Lu controversy will indicate further how Li's thinking was grounded in a medical metaphor and the philosophical significance of this stance.

Li did not take sides. He did not favor the teachings of either Zhu Xi or Lu Jiuyuan because he regarded their philosophical positions as past teachings for past situations. As historical matters, their differences were only of historical interest, not of present philosophical concern. For Li, approval or disapproval of past teachings was an aspect of historical thinking, but not philosophical thinking. He even held that the judgments of historians were useless for philosophical thinking (SSFSL, *Mengzi*, pt. 2, 9). The reason was that, in Li's view, the primary philosophical question was not the source or the historical relations of ideas, but methods—specifically, how to restore the health of society and persons. (History, in contrast, was concerned with sources in his view.) As Li said, "To speak constantly about the Supreme Ultimate, to talk about principle and nature, to argue over the differences and similarities of Zhu and Lu, and to point out that Wang Yangming is close to Chan Buddhism—all these things are like tangled masses of creeping plants and are only unruly gossip. Such discussion is a sickness of learning" (EQQJ, 3.10a).

Reflecting his view that the source of ideas is not the primary philosophical question, Li also said, in a letter to Gu Yanwu:

> Now, it does not matter whether the concepts of essence [*ti*] and application [*yong*] came from Buddhist or Confucian works. It only matters what essence it is and what application it is. If comprehending the Way and preserving the heart-mind are regarded as the essence, and ruling the world and governing things are regarded as the application, then the essence is the true essence and the applica-

tion is the real application. If these two words came from Confucian works, naturally it is all right. Even if they came from Buddhist works, there is also nothing wrong in that. (EQQJ, 16.17a)

Effective action in maintaining the health of society and its members was more important than the source of the prescription in both medicine and philosophy.

When asked about the differences between Zhu and Lu, Li's response was analytic and ostensibly descriptive, rather than obviously judgmental. Li said that Lu taught people to wash out the irrelevant and obscuring vulgarities, and so Lu's ideas served as an extreme warning among Confucians. Lu further helped people attain a joyful awakening and have that which they themselves obtained. Zhu taught people to be methodical in faithfully preserving the Confucian teachings. For Zhu the teachings of centrality and uprightness were important. Both thinkers were equally great, Li claimed, and both had lessons for the world (EQQJ, 4.7b–8a).

For Li, learning (or philosophy) was not a matter of selectively choosing from the ideas of others, as some people seemed to think. Li admitted that arguing over the similarities and differences of Zhu and Lu may have been an extremely urgent matter for the ancients, but held that this was no longer a necessity.

> One must first discuss the differences and similarities within oneself, examine within oneself, and investigate by oneself—[to determine] whether one's daily intentions and thoughts, and one's words and actions, are similar to or different from the words in the books that one reads. If they are similar, then one is on the road of learning, and one may either respect Zhu and reject Lu or select Lu and discard Zhu. But if they are different, then one may not either respect Zhu and reject Lu or select Lu and discard Zhu. One should only pay attention to [the faults of] oneself and not be concerned about [the faults of] others. (EQQJ, 4.8a–b)

Although Li viewed philosophical teachings as comparable to medical prescriptions, he did not stop thinking according to the logic of the generative metaphor, which placed the authoritative source in the root, father, or ancestor. He continued to use the family and the plant as analogies for that part of the sages' learning that consisted of unchanging, given values. Philosophical engagement was, however, another matter and involved a different question. Since the purpose of teachings was (like that of medicine) to treat illnesses, the authority of philosophical teachings was related to their appropriateness and effectiveness in action. The authority of fundamental values, in contrast, was traditionally based on their source—in the sages, the classics, and the universe.

Li broadened the basis of the authority of fundamental values by suggesting that appropriateness and effectiveness in action were also relevant. That is, truths come both from the sages and from their effectiveness in self-cultivation, even the self-cultivation of a common person (EQQJ, 1.4a). Although Li deemed the generative frame inappropriate for evaluating philosophical engagement, he applied it to the constant values. The authority of tradition helped set the boundaries, moreover, for the range of appropriate action (EQQJ, 11.3a).

Although Li saw the notion of the genuine transmission of the Way (an aspect of the Zhu-Lu controversy) as having more historical than philosophical significance, he used this concept as a departure point for criticizing contemporary practices and for presenting his ideas about philosophical engagement. When asked what should be believed, given the scholars' incessant arguing over the impurities of Zhu's and Lu's thought, Li answered:

> From the time when Confucius, with his teaching of broad learning and restraint by ritual action, followed the pure tradition of Shun to a thousand years later, the origin has been continued and truly preserved without change. Only Master Zhu obtained the teachings. He encouraged himself and others throughout his life, and he completely regarded as primary abiding in reverential seriousness and thoroughly investigating principles. Thoroughly investigating principles was the broad learning of the Confucian school, and abiding in reverential seriousness was the restraint by ritual action of the Confucian school. Inner and outer, root and branches, together they become complete. This is genuine learning. Therefore, to respect Zhu is that whereby one respects Confucius. (EQQJ, 15.4a–b)[79]

In other words, although Zhu offered a different teaching from that of Confucius, he still continued the original values. In Li's view, Zhu's was not a new learning (with different fundamental values), but a new teaching that spoke to the conditions of his time.

> And yet today, people also know to expose the fallacies of [Lu] Xiangshan and to respect Master Zhu. But if one examines their so-called respect, it is nothing more than making commentaries. It is only "literary morality" [*wenyi*]. I doubt that they arrive at Master Zhu's combined teaching of inner and outer, and root and branches, and the real cultivation of abiding in reverential seriousness and repose, much less at any achievement in the pursuit of practical stud-

ies. Xiangshan cut through the obstructions of Zhu Xi and taught "first establish its [the heart-mind's] greatness." A defense of rightness over personal profit, this teaching also naturally had things that obscured it. Are those who today respect Zhu able to be [unbiased] like this? If they are not able to be like this, and they expose the fallacies of Lu and respect Zhu only with the branches of petty words and writing, it is easily seen that they do not know the measure of things. (EQQJ, 15.4b–5a)

Li criticized the followers, but not Zhu or Lu themselves, for not understanding what Zhu and Lu were doing. Unlike some of his contemporaries, Li was not troubled by the claim that Zhu and Lu had changed the original ideas of Confucius. In Li's view, they had no choice but to do so. Despite his respect for Zhu, Li attacked Zhu's contemporary supporters for their preoccupation with commentaries and "superficial" matters. That is, they did not fulfill Zhu's teachings about either the inner or outer aspects. Offering words but no moral and political action, theirs was only a "literary morality." Although they professed to follow Zhu, they did not understand Zhu's full teaching. Neither did Li's respect for Zhu imply opposition to Lu, or vice versa, for Li praised Lu while attacking contemporary followers of Lu who did not embody his full teaching.

Li's treatment of the differences between Zhu Xi and Lu Jiuyuan (or Wang Yangming) as unimportant in a philosophical sense does not mean that he did not understand their ideas. Rather, since philosophy necessarily entailed an engagement with one's times, Li saw no philosophical conflict between Zhu and Lu, for both were responding to the needs of the times. Wang was correcting abuses that arose from deficiencies in the thought of Zhu Xi's followers and deficiencies in society that Zhu's thought had not corrected.

Past philosophical differences failed to remain relevant in the present, because Confucian learning and philosophical engagement involved a relationship among ideas, behavior, and characteristics of the times, and these three elements were constantly changing as they interrelated with each other. The relationship between rival sets of ideas abstracted from specific and different contexts was not critical. The fact that Zhu and Lu were contemporaries did not detract from Li's position, moreover, for sociopolitical conditions overlap in complex ways and do not march along in strict chronological time, each neatly succeeding the last. Because constant change in the world led to a constant need for new teachings, Li as well as others thus claimed that even the sages did not say everything (EQQJ, 1.4a and 16.16b). Just as disorderly conditions in society, in Confucian thinking, and in individual people were regarded as illnesses, so also were teachings that had lost their appropriateness, if people continued to apply those teachings.

Li's view thus was that Zhu had attained the true Way, derived from the teachings of Confucius, Lu had offered appropriate and needed corrections, and Ming philosophers had further corrected the biases of the later followers of the Zhu school (EQQJ, 15.8b). The context was necessarily part of the thought, because all philosophers' positions were based on particular historical conditions. The "meaning" of a teaching and of its related behavior was inseparable from both the more immediate sociopolitical context and the broader context of the Confucian tradition.

Li's interpretation of the Zhu-Lu antagonism as one of historical rather than philosophical importance is further seen in comments like the following.

> Zhou, the Chengs, Zhang, Zhu, and Xue, Hu, Luo, Lü, and Gu, Gao, Feng, and Xin are the branch flowing from Zengzi of the Confucian school. Their learning consisted of imitating the ancients, praising the former worthies, and sincerely believing in the sages. Lu, Wu, Chen, Wang, and Xinzhai [Wang Gen], Longxi [Wang Ji], Jinxi [Luo Rufang], and Haimen [Zhou Rudeng] are the branch flowing from Mencius of Zou. Their learning consisted of reflection on the self and self-knowledge. It did not emphasize textual knowledge [literally, the seen and heard], but it was not separate from it. The fact that our Confucian learning has these two branches is like the Chan [Buddhist] school's having the Southern [Hui] Neng and the Northern [Shen] Xiu [branches]. Each has what it sees. Each has what it attains. If you harmonize them and return them to a unity, then learning will not have biases. Like a split gate or divided door, it will be firm and unbreakable. (EQQJ, *fu* 15.3b)

Li held that his contemporaries who supported the position of one historical philosopher over another were attempting to participate in the controversies of the past. This kind of involvement with past conflicts was not a concern of philosophy, and attempts to participate in former debates indicated a confusion about the nature of Confucian philosophy. Moreover, this confusion was extremely dangerous, because it prevented philosophy from flourishing and consequently led to social and political turmoil. Philosophy, but not history, was knowledge that demanded moral behavior, and because of the real social and political consequences, it was essential to distinguish the two endeavors.

Philosophical engagement with Confucian learning meant that one applied the learning of the sages to the times in which one lived. Although the teachings of the early sages pointed to the standards, philosophers had to use concepts appropriate to their own periods. Thus, like Zhu Xi's and Wang Yangming's teachings earlier, Li's own teaching of *huiguo zixin* used terms that made classical ideals relevant to contemporary problems. Yang Shen, an eighteenth-century follower of Li Yong, went even further, restating classical ideas in the popular language of his time.[80] And, where others saw Song thought as tainted with Buddhism and Daoism, Li regarded the new Song ontological ideas as appropriate responses to changed circumstances. Li's emphasis on appropriateness and timeliness was a characteristic of the Confucian tradition (and other traditions of Chinese thought) that fit into the medical frame quite well.[81]

Focusing more on recent rather than ancient history, Li held that philosophical positions from the late Song to his own period reflected the constant efforts of philosophers to adjust their teachings to the times. Li further detected a recurring tendency among philosophers to overcorrect biases, thereby establishing the need for further correction. The views of Song and Ming philosophers thus were views of and for particular situations and were fundamentally different from the universal givens upon which Confucian learning rested. To approve or disapprove of past teachings was not relevant to the philosophical task.

In defending the learning of the sages, Li thus addressed the issue of how to conceptualize the task of the Confucian philosopher. What paradigmatic context most reflected the philosopher's thinking? Li departed from the dominant view in holding that the context of medicine provided a more appropriate conceptual framework than that of the family. For Li, the philosopher, like the doctor, was concerned primarily with curing illness and restoring health rather than continuing the family line.

Since the purpose of the sages' learning was to treat illnesses, knowledge was a prescription as opposed to an appeal to classical sources, and its validity was affirmed by its appropriateness and effectiveness in treating illness. Understanding the context was critical. The complaint, diagnosis, prescription, and treatment all were important, and it made no sense to prefer one medicine over another without regard to the illness. Li applied this reasoning to Confucian learning and the positions of individual philosophers, and thus he relegated disputes between past philosophical positions to the sphere of history.

In sum, Li's conception of Confucian learning required the appropriate fit of three elements — constant values, the particular conditions of society and of individual persons, and implementation of the teachings of the philosophers. The last were prescriptions designed to treat specific illnesses of society, of individual persons, and of Confucian thought itself, and their authority derived from their effectiveness as forms of treatment. Given this view, which made genuine Confucian learning analogous to medicine in its function, Li then utilized the Confucian construction of the past to show that history did indeed confirm his position. Li's position implicitly made a sharp distinction between the methods and aims of philosophy and those of history.

The Genuine and the Other

A third concern for Li was the tension between the "genuine" and the "other." Although the Chinese terms *zheng* and *yi*, or *zhengxue* and *yiduan*, are often translated "orthodox(y)" and "heterodox(y)," the English terms suggest ideas not completely appropriate to the Confucian philosophical system. Thus, I substitute the "genuine" and the "other" for the more common translations. This choice is influenced by the content and terminology of Confucian thought. For Li, the sages' learning was genuine learning, *zhenzheng xuewen* (EQQJ, 3.5a).

The concepts of orthodoxy and heterodoxy are inappropriate for Confucian thought in part because Western and Confucian thinking exhibit different patterns of organization. From a theoretical perspective, much of Western thinking has traditionally assumed the existence of an absolute standard, conceived as external to the world and to thought, against which thought is measured. Confucian thinking has proceeded under a standard of harmony internal to the world and maintained by constant adjustments, and it has assumed nothing outside the system. Adaptation to contingencies, including the use of multiple paradigmatic frames, has enabled Confucians to maintain the tradition.

The Confucian system thus had no theoretical equivalent to orthodoxy and heterodoxy, in the common Western sense. Orthodoxy and heterodoxy oppose each other. Heterodoxies are outside the system of orthodoxy, and the latter has no theoretical need for the continued existence of the former. The same cannot be said, however, for Chinese thought that is called *zheng* (proper, correct, genuine, orthodox, true) and *yi* (other, deviant, strange, heterodox). With a relationship analogous to that of health and illness, the genuine and the other worked together in a single system. No matter how unacceptable, the other never completely disappeared. Although it may be the object of criticism, it remained an alternative within the system.

A further theoretical difference is the Western emphasis on the individual thinker, in contrast to the Chinese emphasis on the stream of thought. In the West, ideas "come out of" the minds of thinkers, and originality is important. Chinese thinkers, in contrast, emphasize participation in a stream of thought and action. Their focus is on preserving and transmitting the cultural tradition—keeping to a true or straight course. Confucian thinkers became important through their participation in maintaining the tradition rather than through unusual originality. The "I" of Descartes' *cogito ergo sum*, for example, did not exist in the Confucian philosophical world.[82]

The tension between the genuine and the other was tied to the theoretical patterning of Confucian thought in additional ways. Because Chinese philosophers tended to discuss theoretical matters in a non-theoretical manner, conflicts over the acceptability of a particular idea (as genuine or other) served implicitly as a discussion of broader, often fundamental issues. A specific conflict provided a concrete context in which thinkers could consider and debate more far-reaching concerns, such as the aim and purpose of knowledge and the fundamental standards of Confucian culture. For instance, Mencius' opposition to the thought of Mozi and Yang Zhu did not concern only these two thinkers, but evoked questions about larger issues, such as fundamental values. Or, to give another example, the perennial opposition to the emphasis on texts and commentaries stood for the broader issue of what the Confucian social role was or should be.

The tension between the genuine and the other persisted because of its epistemological grounding in the generative metaphor and the cultural imperative of unity. As an aspect of the theoretical pattern-ing of Confucian thought, the conflict between the genuine and the other continued in tandem with the development of philosophical thought itself. In ancient times, for instance, Confucius had advised people not to study the strange or the deviant, which he saw mani-fested in such matters as music, colors, and rites (*Lunyu*, 2.16, 15.11, and 17.16; SSFSL, *Lunyu*, pt. 1, 14–16). The clash was still an impor-tant issue to Li, not in a doctrinal or historical sense, but in a philo-sophical sense. Li's concern, like that of Mencius (*Mencius*, 7B.37), was sociopolitical engagement and the proper fit of ideas and actions to the times, not arguments over which beliefs or which schools of thought were "correct" or more faithful to the teachings of previous philosophers.

For Li, the relationship between the genuine and the other in-volved two kinds of tensions, those within Confucian learning and those between Confucian learning and other traditions of thought. Within Confucian learning, activities incorporating both the "inner" and "outer" aspects were approved, as opposed to those regarded as one-sided and hence harmful. Li thus attacked contemporaries who "only read the words" but did not realize the teachings in their be-havior (SSFSL, *Lunyu*, pt. 1, 9). The conflict with other traditions in-volved the recognition that other traditions of learning differed from the Confucian in their interests and standards. Their concerns were outside the sphere of Confucian concerns. Following Confucius in suggesting their harm to people and society, Mencius earlier had called them "perverse" doctrines (*Mencius*, 3B.9; SSFSL, *Mengzi*, pt. 1, 12). The struggle to preserve Confucian knowledge and its social and cultural institutions from problems within and without was seen as never ending.

Implicitly accepting the generative paradigm, Confucian thinkers linked the question of the genuine versus the other to discussions about the source and subsequent development of particular views. Knowledge of the source would supposedly settle doubts about the acceptability of an idea. Strange or other ideas also helped mark the limits of what was genuine, in that other views were not abandoned positions but positions not taken within Confucian learning. As a consequence, certain ideas served as the boundary criteria, separat-ing what was within and without. Ideas "within" and "without" the boundaries were related, for both belonged to the larger theoretical context. For the Confucian philosopher, the "without" consisted of conceivable, but not acceptable, alternatives within the Confucian framework.

Li Yong used the medical metaphor to approach this topic. He agreed that the sages' learning had to be preserved, not because the sages' learning was the source of authority for Confucian culture, but because the sages' learning was the only system that dealt with the critical problems concerning order and harmony in the world. For Li, only Confucian learning could lead to the realization of social and political goals. Genuine learning was important because of the activities it encompassed and their effectiveness, not because of its origin in the sages.

Although he used only one term (*yiduan*), Li made a distinction among the different kinds of "other paths." Buddhism, Daoism, and the thought of Yang Zhu and Mozi were non-Confucian, other paths. Deficient positions within Confucian learning were also other paths. When asked, for instance, about Zhu Xi's instruction in the teaching of inner and outer, root and branches, together completing each other, Li replied:

> If one thoroughly investigates principle and yet does not reside in reverential seriousness, in the end one will have no way to complete one's nature and preserve oneself even though one's intellectual knowledge is great. And that is vulgar learning [*suxue*]. If one resides in reverential seriousness and yet does not thoroughly investigate principle, then one's learning is empty and useless, and in the end one is not capable of managing the world and ruling things. And then one is a pedant [*furu*]. . . . The activities of virtue and the activities of learning advance together. Knowledge and action are one. (EQQJ, 15.5a)

Li also stated that if one did not pursue "comprehending the essential values" (*mingti*) or their practical application (*shiyong*), but only pursued superficial, clever talk, then that was an "other path" (EQQJ, 14.3b). Like Confucius and Mencius, Li regarded those paths that closely resembled the learning of the sages as more harmful than those that were clearly different.

Although all were outside Confucian learning, Li described the learning of Yang Zhu and Mozi as other paths and those of the Buddhists and the Daoists as "the other paths of the other paths" (EQQJ, 14.4a). Yang and Mo were more dangerous than Buddhism and Daoism, but even more dangerous were the other paths within Confucian learning. Li criticized those within Confucian teaching who "followed the flower [appearance] and discarded the fruit [reality]" (EQQJ, 14.4a; see *Mencius*, 7B.37). Striving for success in the exams for the wrong reasons—for wealth and fame rather than to help bring order to the world—exemplified such behavior, which emphasized superficial characteristics, not matters of virtue. Following Cheng Yi, Li claimed that the harm of other paths outside Confucian teaching was superficial and easy to expose, but the harm of other paths within Confucian teaching was serious and difficult to oppose (EQQJ, 14.4a; SSFSL, *Lunyu*, pt. 1, 15). Since Confucianism, or "our teaching," concerned the matters of greatest importance, the harm resulting from subverting it was greatest.

Li called upon "history" in presenting his view of other paths within Confucian learning and offered the following "review."

In antiquity, the Way and virtue were unified, and people had similar customs. The teachers did not have other teachings, and learning did not have other methods. There were no farfetched and abstruse theories. All were able to develop their moral capacities and to follow the constant moral distinctions. The people were in agreement, and they attained the highest principles in their behavior.

After the decline of the Three Dynasties, the Way and the methods of learning were no longer unified, and learning began to have many divergent paths. These paths gradually became customs by destroying virtue and rightness. An alarmed Confucius is thus thought to have said, "To study other doctrines is harmful indeed" [*Lunyu*, 2.16]. Confucius acted with urgency to protect the Way of the world and the human heart-mind. Although he had not yet clearly determined who would spread his ideas, he hated how the "good, careful people of the villages" confounded genuine virtue, and three times he condemned their deceitful behavior [*Lunyu*, 17.13–19]. The other paths of the time of Confucius consisted of behavior that superficially resembled, but actually confounded, genuine virtue.

The other paths during the Warring States period belonged to the followers of Gaozi, Xu Xing, Zhuang Zhou, Zou Yan, Deng Xi, and Gongsun Longzi. The "calls to battle" were numerous and confusing, but Yang Zhu's theory of acting for oneself and Mo Di's theory of universal love were especially valued by the world. Mencius attacked their abuses, which arose in their minds and harmed the government [*Mencius*, 3B.9 and 2A.2]. Fiercer than flooding waters, Mencius' words exposed their errors, and only then did their theories begin to be extinguished.

The other paths since the Han and Tang looked to Laozi. Those like Wei Boyang's techniques for the immortals and Zhang Daoling's magical charms were sufficient to poison the aims of people. The five sects of Buddhism, especially the Chan sect, also flourished. Lowly commoners were deluded by Buddhist ideas about sins and blessings, and high-ranking people were intoxicated with its cleverness. Buddhism led the people to reject reality and to esteem emptiness, and the central way was lost. It is impossible to overstate the harm that Buddhism did.

Cheng Yi and Zhu Xi subsequently exposed the harms of Buddhism, and as people began to have some understanding, they returned to the standards of right over wrong. Now although the theories of Daoism and Buddhism are not completely extinguished, they generally do not reach the point of arising in people's minds and harming the government. What arises, however, are the other paths among us Confucians. The sprouts of our Confucian learning originated with Confucius; [Zi]si and Mencius continued them; Cheng [Yi] and Zhu [Xi] made them widely known; and the Four Books recorded and completed them. No one does not desire that people complete the good capacities that they naturally have, fully develop themselves and others, and regulate the world and pacify the people. (SSFSL, *Lunyu*, pt. 1, 14–15).

Li summarized in additional statements how Mencius attacked the ideas of Yang and Mo because they were the other paths harming the people during the Warring States period (SSFSL, *Mengzi*, pt. 1, 12–13; *Mencius*, 3B.9). Similarly, Buddhist and Daoist ideas had been harming the people ever since the Han and Tang periods, and so Cheng Yi and Zhu Xi attacked them. Li also mentioned Lu Jiuyuan and Xin Fuyuan, both of whom were concerned about the other paths within Confucian learning. Lu saw contemporary prose writing as particularly harmful, and Xin attacked the practices of memorization and recitation, and the striving for wealth and rank. They claimed that aid should be offered where it was directly needed, according to the situation and the times, and thus there was no point in attacking Yang and Mo or Buddhism and Daoism, which were the harmful other paths of another time. Li claimed that the paths attacked by Lu and Xin remained within Confucian learning, and so the situation was all the more dangerous. The shallow, hypocritical practices of memorization and recitation within Confucian learning were more harmful than the teachings of Yang Zhu and Mozi or Buddhism and Daoism.

Implicitly relying on the logic of the generative metaphor, Li pointed to the transformation in meaning of certain concepts to help clarify his position. Whereas for Li and most philosophers since the Han the concepts of genuine, correct (*zheng*) and other, deviant (*yi*) were regarded as an appropriate polarity, for thinkers of the Warring States period (who were attempting to advance the learning of the sages in a decadent environment) the appropriate complementary pair consisted of the concepts of similar (*tong*) and different (*yi*) (EQQJ, 14.4a). *Yi* is the same word in both cases, but the complementary idea in each pair suggests a slightly different meaning for *yi*.

Li argued that the early followers of Confucius attacked other paths because they resulted in behavior harmful to society and asked what these paths were, since Buddhism had not yet entered China and the ideas of Laozi had not yet spread in the time of Confucius. His own answer was that one must think of *yi* as antithetically paired with *tong* (similar) and so having the meaning of "different." That is, the early Confucians regarded the ideas of their rivals as different from their own and hence deviant. The early Confucian position toward other or deviant paths was not phrased in terms of the question of *zheng* (correctness, genuineness), but in terms of the question of *tong* (similarity). The notion of similarity was not applied to the source of the ideas, but to how the ideas were understood. The ideas early Confucians judged as different or deviant (*yi*) dealt with the same social and political problems that concerned the Confucians but offered different analyses and solutions. All positions, whether Confucian or other, were thought to be based on similar assumptions about the world and society, and they all had their source in the sages' ideas.

Eventually, however, the concept of similar (*tong*) came to mean correct and genuine. The assumptions and standards of the discourse of similar and different were not the same as those of the discourse of correct and other (or incorrect). The earlier polarity emphasized description, whereas the later one added a value judgment. Li said that all the early philosophers had the same teachers, the sages Yao and Shun, but that the philosophers learned different things. Those ideas that differed from the sages' teachings were called "other paths." Li claimed that the situation in his time was comparable. The Confucians read the same books, but ended up with different results in understanding and in behavior (EQQJ, 14.4a).

The paths of Mozi and Yang Zhu were similar in many respects to those of the Confucians, but the differences were crucial. It was their apparent identity, a superficial similarity, that made the learning of Mozi and Yang Zhu so dangerous. Buddhist and Daoist learning, in contrast, clearly derived from other sources, and so there was no question of similarity. The ideas themselves were obviously different and, in the case of Buddhism, even came from beyond China's borders.

Li noted that Confucians often argued that only learning from within China could be genuine, because only it was descended from the sages' learning. Having different roots from Confucianism, Buddhism and Daoism were manifestly different, and their differences made it impossible to confuse them with, or to substitute them for, Confucian views. Li held, however, that although the matter of a similar or different source was important, the source was not the final standard of authority. Since foreign things were acceptable under certain circumstances, the more important criterion was the capability of the ideas to bring about the desired results (EQQJ, 16.16b–17a).

According to Li, genuine Confucian ideas consisted of the set of beliefs faithfully derived from the teachings of Yao and Shun. Defining what was genuine in this way raised problems, however, because many claimed these sages as their teachers. Holding positions not compatible with those of the sages, some falsely represented the sages' views. These other schools of learning were dangerous because their specious views led to confusion and disorder in society. Other paths within the learning of the sages thus posed a far greater danger than those from outside.

Most thinkers seemed to accept that a teaching or path was genuine if it was related to the sages' values in a way comparable to the relationship of the branches to the root. For Li, who was struggling with the logic of the generative metaphor, however, other standards applied. Perhaps not even in awareness, he knew that the generative paradigm did not offer the appropriate theoretical stance from which to address the conflict regarding the genuine and the other. It was clear to him that identity in the root or source did not guarantee identity in the branches or streams, and vice versa. Still, his thinking was in many respects shaped by the generative metaphor.

Li's view here was connected with further concerns—the relationship among particular ideas, the texts in which the ideas appear, and the readers and interpreters of those texts. Many factors influenced those who read and interpreted the texts. Not only did commentarial traditions offer particular ways of understanding, but conditions of time, place, and person varied. For Li, a critical question was how fixed was the meaning of an idea. Li saw that people received the same teaching and read the same books but ended up with different interpretations of fundamental beliefs and necessary practices. He specifically referred to the excessive emphasis on the examinations and the kinds of narrow skills and knowledge required for them. People with this emphasis regarded themselves as Confucians and as followers of the learning of the sages, but in Li's view they were mistaken. He compared this situation to the relationship between being asleep and awake (EQQJ, 14.4a). While sleeping, one can be convinced of the reality of the events in one's dreams, but upon awakening, the deception becomes clear. Since vulgar Confucians were like those asleep, those who followed other paths were even more so.

Li claimed that the issue of other paths centered on the notion of *duan*, a beginning, a sprout, an incipient capacity (EQQJ, 3.5b). Human moral potential was based on the four sprouts articulated by Mencius, which, when developed, became benevolence, rightness, ritual action, and wisdom. When the four sprouts were first aroused and thoughts began to emerge, the four sprouts could (but did not necessarily) lead to these four virtues. If the four sprouts were developed properly, however, then one's thoughts were genuine thoughts, and the developed sprouts were seen as derived from the practices or cultivation of the heart-mind.

Someone whose thoughts did not result in a development of the four virtues had depraved thoughts, and the practices of that person's heart-mind did not derive from the four sprouts. That is, the sprouts that developed were not moral capacities, but other capacities. Other paths thus entailed more than following the learning of such people as Yang Zhu or Mozi, or even Buddhism or Daoism. They began before that, with perverse thoughts and behavior not grounded in the four sprouts.

Not able to reject the matter of origin completely, Li noted two kinds of origins. One was the learning of the sages, known from classical texts and their accompanying traditions of interpretation. The other was the moral heart-mind (the four sprouts) with which all humans were born but which was easily obscured and needed to be developed. Although distinguishable in the sense that texts were contrasted to the minds of individual persons, ultimately the two origins had the same ontological source. The learning of the sages was an expression of the sages' minds, which, like the moral minds of all humans, were congruent with heavenly principles. This reality was also known by other terms, including moral knowledge, the luminous origin (*lingyuan*), and the Way, but everyone had "this mind" (SSFSL, *Mengzi*, pt. 2, 9, and *Lunyu*, pt. 1, 15–16).[83]

Confucians opposed other paths because they were harmful and disruptive to society as they envisioned it, but the fact that not all disruptive beliefs and behavior were classified as "other" indicates the epistemological importance of the source. Faults (*guo*), whether verbal or behavioral, fell into a separate category. Faults were a characteristic of behavior originally based on the Way or the moral mind. They referred to biased behavior that could be corrected and so become genuine. Seen as virtually inevitable, the faults arising from a philosopher's teachings usually began as a corrective for previous biases within the sages' learning (EQQJ, 11.5b). That is, a teaching served in part to correct the biases of previous teachings. Biases inevitably arose, because the conditions that teachings addressed constantly changed. As circumstances changed, teachings that had been appropriate became biased. A new teaching was then needed for the new situation.

Li treated the dangers of Buddhism and Daoism more leniently than the dangers of vulgar Confucian learning because their teachings did not concern issues within Confucian learning. To have had the same concerns as Confucian learning, Buddhism and Daoism would have had to originate in the four sprouts of the moral heart-mind. Li reasoned that since the moral heart-mind was ultimately congruent with the source of all things (the universe), the teachings derived from the heart-mind were the only true teachings. There was only one reality, and so there could only be one Way. "The Way is one and that is all. How can there be three teachings? If you make the teachings into three, then the Way also is three" (EQQJ, 14.5b).

Rejecting the possibility of parallel truths, Li denounced the contemporary view that the three teachings of Confucianism, Buddhism, and Daoism were equally valid and simply provided different ways of reaching ultimate truth. Li objected to the so-called unity of the three teachings because actions were just as much a part of the Way as verbal teachings.[84] To support his position, Li briefly summarized the major ideas and transformations in each of the three traditions. Although a superficial account if viewed from a critical historical perspective, the phenomena that he singled out are from a theoretical viewpoint cultural markers of Confucian philosophical issues.

Li said that Confucian teaching had its source in the ideas and practices of statecraft. After this original focus became obscured and depraved theories appeared in the world, Confucian teaching was transformed into practices for obtaining merit and private profit. These were the practices connected with obtaining an official post. Li claimed that the original reason for wanting an official post was lost. It changed from being an opportunity to help bring order to society to a chance for personal gain. Confucian teaching further changed into the practices of commentary and exegesis. Immersed in false beliefs and practices, Confucian teaching presently consisted of the skills of writing and memorization, and the sages' teachings had become obscured by the desire for office and the related emphasis on literary and verbal skills necessary for success in the examinations. Li said that contemporary Confucians were such in name only, for examinations and exegesis retained only the appearance of genuine learning. Li thus held that Confucian teachings stood for a specific content, involving ideas and actions morally and socially useful to a Confucian society. Although the ideals had become obscured, they did not fundamentally change (EQQJ, 14.5b–6a).

On the other hand, one cannot restore something not initially present. Just as a brick cannot be polished and made to reflect like a mirror, so Buddhism and Daoism cannot be accepted as alternatives for realizing the one Way (EQQJ, 12.7a). Like Confucianism, however, these two teachings were also subject to processes of change and had experienced distortions over time. The teaching of Laozi (Daoism) was originally based on the concept of non-action. After that concept became obscured, Daoism was transformed into a teaching of immortality. Subsequent changes led first to its becoming a teaching of magic and then to the practices of chanting the classics, fasting, and praying. Although its original teaching, its Way, was no longer followed, its name still survived. Thus Daoist teachings represented a specific content (although presently lost) that differed from that of Confucianism (EQQJ, 14.6a). Buddhism had suffered equally extreme distortions. From a teaching based on extinction or complete stillness, it was transformed into a teaching of "dried up" meditation. Later it became a teaching of causation and then turned into the practices of publishing classics, making images, and giving liberally.

These were practices for obtaining merit. Its original teaching was lost, but the same name was still used (EQQJ, 14.6a–b).

Although the practices of these two traditions were socially harmful, Li claimed that their harm could be stopped if their teachings were destroyed (EQQJ, 14.6b). The same was not true for Confucian learning, however. If it were destroyed, current abuses would cause even greater harm because there would then be no teachings about statecraft. Without Confucian teachings, there would be no essence, no core of values, on which to base political activities. Political leaders would become as ruthless as opportunistic Confucians and hegemons, who supposedly lacked moral standards for guidance. The only hope lay in comprehending and making clear genuine learning.

In sum, from an epistemological viewpoint, the problems concerning genuine learning and other paths derive from several cultural assumptions about the nature of the universe. Ontologically, everything was one reality, called by various terms depending on the emphasis and subject, and that reality had a specific socio-politico-moral content that developed from the four sprouts. Although the world of nature and the phenomenal world of human experience were seen as constantly changing, the results of those changes were not predetermined. Humans had the potential to help shape events. Constant change in the universe required constant efforts to maintain, or to regain, a state of affairs close to the original wholeness. If followed correctly, genuine learning would help achieve that goal. Other paths within Confucian learning would harm that goal because they would appear to be helping when in fact they were not. Other paths both within and without Confucianism provided no help in achieving that goal, and since no progress was made by following them, harm and turmoil would ensue.

Li's position reflects thinking consonant with both the generative and medical metaphors. Li was bound to the generative paradigmatic context in that all teachings had to be situated in the framework of the sages' learning. This learning set up the framework because it alone was concerned with the critical problem of social order. This learning was the root. On the other hand, Li utilized a standard of appropriateness and effectiveness for specific teachings proposed as solutions to problems. Like medicines, these ideas could come from anywhere. The critical criterion was that they treat the illness. Given that future social illnesses were as yet unknown, other paths remained within the broader theoretical system as possible sources for new teachings and as boundary markers for what was genuine learning.

Exemplars and Heroes

Knowledge that is not in words is an important aspect of all cultures, and how it is preserved and transmitted is a problem that has been addressed from a variety of perspectives and by many thinkers, Chinese and Western. With their emphasis on implemented, as opposed to theoretical, knowledge, Confucian philosophers were concerned with this problem too, particularly in terms of storing and teaching this knowledge in ways that did not require texts. One widespread answer, utilized by all philosophers from ancient times to the present, was the concept of the extraordinary person. Li Yong's search for a hero who would save the age implicitly related to this cultural problem even as it was a direct call for political action.

Called by a range of terms with different denotations, including sage, superior person, great man, and hero, the outstanding person served as an exemplar who embodied the ideals and virtues of the culture.[85] I use the term "exemplar" rather than the more commonly used "model" because I take it to be a stronger term and to convey better the dynamic characteristics of this unusual type of person. The term "model" (as a noun) suggests something rather static, without the critical relational aspect that the Chinese concept embodies, that is, the relation between the person and the context giving rise to the exemplar's extraordinary actions.

The use of exemplars in both teaching and learning was popular for various reasons. Exemplars seemed particularly appropriate for teaching moral behavior because they illustrated the realization of values in realistic situations of life. Li's references to historical examples, often of recent times, certainly brought to life this practical dimension of Confucian thought. In addition, the suspicion of many philosophers about the adequacy of words to convey knowledge helped empower exemplars with an importance they might not have had if language had been regarded as more trustworthy and more relevant to what was being taught.

The specific ideals represented by exemplars varied with the context; women and men, for example, often looked to different exemplary figures for guidance.[86] A central ideal applying to everyone, however, was that of becoming a genuine human being, a real person—*zuo ren* (EQQJ, 1.4a). For Li Yong, this was a primary goal in Confucian learning. To achieve this goal, a person's efforts had to focus on the social and psychological aspects of the self (to use Western terms), not on one's physical aspects or some extra-physical entity. The genuine person was morally cultivated and virtuous, distinguished from the masses by his or her acts. Based on the Mencian concept of morality, Li's views continued certain emphases prominent during the Ming with thinkers like Wang Yangming and Wang Gen, a "radical" follower of Wang.[87]

Like other philosophers, Li recognized a hierarchy in the various levels of personal development. In general, the highest aim was to become a sage, next came the worthy, then the superior person, and fourth the true Confucian (*zhen ru*). Even becoming just a good person was considered a worthy aim for those at the lower social levels (EQQJ, 3.4a). The distinctions between these levels were seen as gradual, not absolute, and this made it possible for anyone to strive for self-cultivation, as Li's philosophical-biographical work, *Record of Observations and Impressions (Guan'gan lu)*, attempts to demonstrate.

Chinese culture admitted bad exemplars, as well as good, to instruct people what not to do. The bad last ruler of each dynasty fit into this category, and fictional stories were full of wicked characters. Li Yong and Confucian philosophers in general did not make great use of the evil types, however. Although many people (high and low) believed in demons and ghosts as sources of evil, Confucian philosophical thinking did not formally conceive of evil as an independent entity that constantly had to be fought. Rather, it was most often a behavioral characteristic arising from imbalances in *qi* or from insufficient efforts to develop moral capacities.

Although also an exemplar, the hero was an exceptional type, close to the sage in ranking. The hero embodied cultural ideals, but his social position was special, possibly even outside the established order of the social system. A hero was one who could or did save society in times of distress, but he did not necessarily need to act through a government position. His specific acts varied with the circumstances. For instance, Shao Yong, who never held office, was called a hero by some of his contemporaries, and Li Yong regarded Wang Yangming, who was active in numerous posts, as the last hero (EQQJ, 12.6a).

To help distinguish the hero from the "more ordinary" exemplar, it is useful to consider the concept of charisma as discussed by Max Weber.[88] Developing further the ideas of Rudolf Sohm, Weber applied the concept of charisma, as creative power, to the hero. Such a person was a self-appointed leader of people in distress. Through their ability to perform "miracles" or heroic feats of valor, charismatic leaders became military and political heroes, prophets, and even founders of world religions. They provided a kind of enthusiastic leadership that often resulted in the breakdown of the social barriers of class and status. They thus were revolutionary forces in history.

Weber further claimed that the hero or charismatic leader was especially important in social dynamics because he provided a counterbalancing force to the "rationalization process of bureaucracy." A bureaucracy symbolized stability and the lack of change. It had permanence, it represented tradition, and it was an "institution of daily routine." Opposed to it were those "natural" leaders who appeared in times of distress. They derived their authority not from their office, even if they were officeholders, but from the creative powers that enabled them to do great things. The people Li described in his *Record of Observations and Impressions* had this gift of a creative power, and they used it to lead others.

Although Confucians, including Li Yong, typically regarded a person's occupation as an important means of distinguishing those who followed the great Way from those who followed the lesser ways, this distinction was less relevant for the hero. The critical factor was that person's effect on others in helping to bring about a moral transformation of society. Although the methods used to accomplish such a goal varied with the circumstances, the ideal was embodied in the early sage-kings, who both taught and governed. In Li Yong's time (if ever), this ideal of a sagely ruler was not considered realistic, and consequently teaching gained in importance.[89]

The search for a hero was a critical matter to Li Yong. Although he spoke of the ideal characteristics in terms that seem rather lofty now, he was using accepted philosophical vocabulary, and his concerns were practical, not speculative. When questioned about the ideal Confucian, for instance, Li replied with characteristics applicable to the hero: a genuine Confucian was someone whose virtuous power (*de*) achieved cosmic proportions. Following an idea found in the *Book of Change*, Li said that a Confucian's virtuous power harmonizes the "three powers" of heaven, earth, and humans.

The virtuous power of heaven lies in giving birth to the myriad kinds of things, and that of earth lies in assisting them. A scholar [*shi*] reaches his head to heaven and treads on the earth, and on behalf of others, he values the means by which he regulates the myriad things. If he in fact is able to comprehend the essential values and put them into practice and so regulate the myriad kinds of things, he then succeeds in harmonizing with the virtuous powers of producing and of nurturing that belong to heaven and earth. (EQQJ, 14.2b)

In typically Confucian manner, Li further defined a Confucian as a person able to govern and keep order among the myriad kinds of things and thereby participate with heaven and earth in the activities of the universe. To be engaged in ordering and regulating things and to desire to participate with heaven and earth was the goal of learning. Someone who pursued other goals was merely a vulgar Confucian, and other types of learning were simply vulgar learning. If a person learned but his learning was not like this, then it was simply vulgar learning. The superior person was ashamed of such vulgar behavior (EQQJ, 14.2b). Here it can be seen that Li's notion of a Confucian is close to that of a hero.

Certainly the duties of a Confucian to undertake responsibilities on behalf of heaven and earth, and on behalf of the people in the past, present, and future, suggest heroic qualities. Li stressed this association by claiming that a hero is one concerned about the world and whose actions lead to Confucian learning being made clear to the world and to everyone's mind being awakened to his or her moral duties (EQQJ, 12.3a). Furthermore, a hero was able to flourish without depending on others (EQQJ, 12.6a). He derived his authority from his own creative power.

For the hero, society and the world were aspects of the self, or to say this in another way, they were the levels of reality in terms of which the hero acted. Such a person had to act and learn in reference to all of society. Concerned with the ordering of society, the hero knew that the importance of this task ranked equally with the creative and nourishing activities of heaven and earth in the natural world. Li held that even when not in a position of political power, the Confucian teacher could still become a hero by teaching moral behavior.

Even if most people did not actually attain high levels of moral achievement, Li wanted them to know that they could learn from heroes and exemplars. Although the sage and the common person had different duties in particular social contexts, Li Yong insisted (like Wang Yangming and others) that the sage and the commoner began with the same human capacities. The moral principles were the same in everyone, from the sage to the "ignorant husband and wife." Everyone had this same "original brightness," and people did not differ in their original endowment of *qi*, their heart-mind, or their essence (*ti*) (EQQJ, 3.3b [drawing from *Zhongyong*, ch. 12], 1.1a–b, 9.5a–b, and *passim*). For Li, the difference between the sage and the commoner was the person's learning. The sage learns and so manifests his moral heart-mind. The commoner does not learn and so "loses" it. The moral heart-mind was not lost permanently, however; rather, it becomes clouded over. Just as the sun retains its brightness even when hidden behind clouds, so everyone's original brightness remains, no matter how much obscured (EQQJ, 1.2b–3a, 10.11a–b).

Li Yong was concerned that the common people did not have sufficient confidence in themselves to exert the effort to learn and to develop their moral capacities (EQQJ, 1.1b). He postulated that the philosophers' slogans seemed unrealistic for the masses because the slogans were aimed, or at least had been aimed, at an audience of highly educated people. And many philosophers themselves believed that the common people were so far from the Way that the slogans were not really appropriate for them (EQQJ, 1.2b–3a). But Li disagreed and sided with those who followed Wang Gen and those who emphasized the authority of the individual person's moral heart-mind in contrast to the classical texts. If common people could get rid of the obscuring clouds, they, too, could become sages. Like Wang Yangming and Wang Gen, Li made the hero and the sage, the highest types of exemplars, ideals for all classes of people.

Li still acknowledged a difference between the affairs and responsibilities of the literati class and the commoners, a difference that followed the Mencian distinction between those who ruled and those who were ruled.[90] Hence, Confucian learning (in a restricted sense) was for the literati, whereas the community compact was for the common people. Moreover, only when the literati paid attention to their reputations would there be good customs throughout the country (SSFSL, *Mengzi*, pt. 1, 11).

Despite the difference in the details of self-cultivation between the literati and the commoners, Li held that even common people could achieve something (EQQJ, 1.8a). Utilizing a view as ancient as

Confucius, Li claimed that all people could begin by attempting to correct their own faults, particularly their behavioral faults, or faults of the self (*shenguo*), those seen by others. Some people would go on to correcting their faults of the mind (*xinguo*), those seen only by oneself. Successful effort could enable a person eventually to reach the sages' level. Li thus stressed what all people had in common as humans, and regarding himself as a common person, he urged the elite not to have pretenses (EQQJ, 1.5b–6a, 1.4a).

To demonstrate that the sages' teachings applied to everyone, Li compiled a record of heroic and exemplary persons from the Ming period. Compilation of such records was a recognized practice in Confucian learning and served both to instruct and to confirm the validity of the instruction. We should recognize, moreover, that the exhortations to become a genuine person incorporated in these accounts were as much a part of this system of knowledge as the exemplars themselves.

Li's account, compiled in his thirties, just after his own realization of what genuine learning was, and called *Record of Observations and Impressions* (EQQJ, 22), consists of biographical sketches, drawn from other writings and edited, of nine men who transformed their own lives and then taught others. These men overcame lower-class backgrounds to become widely recognized as exemplary figures. Li did not regard the nine figures in his account as "ordinary" exemplars. Their self-reliance and personal determination made them heroes who, Li claimed, were needed to save the age. With the way of the teacher neglected by the ruler, they were the teachers who enabled the Way to be known.

Li stated that his record was intended as an aid for teaching about the moral knowledge possessed by everyone. He pointed out that possession of moral knowledge did not constitute the difference between a sage and a commoner, or a high-ranking and a lowly person, since such knowledge was the same in everyone and neither increased nor decreased. What made people different was whether they established their aim and acted on it.[91] Even a lowly person could through personal effort rise to become a sage, a worthy, or a good person. This teaching was thus directed to everyone, not only to educated and high-ranking people. Li purposefully recorded cases of commoners who elevated themselves by developing their human moral capacities so that people would know that it was possible for everyone to fulfill his or her moral potential (EQQJ, 22.1a–2a, self-preface).

Li also used this work to support his position that the Way did not have to be learned from books, but could be learned from one's own moral nature. Confucian learning thus should not be a preserve only of the literati and those engaged in examination learning. Like Wang Gen, Li supported Wang Yangming's concept of extending the moral knowledge as an alternative to the textual approach to the Way.

Li selected nine people as heroic figures: Wang Gen (Xinzhai), a salt merchant; Zhu Shu (Guangxin), a woodcutter; Li Zhu, a yamen clerk, registered as a farmer; Han Zhen (Lewu), a potter; Lin Na, a merchant; Xia Tingmei (Yunfeng), a farmer; Zhou Hui (Xiaoquan), a frontier soldier; Chen Zhensheng (Shengfu), an oil seller; and Zhu Yunqi, a weaver. Li described the changes that each experienced and their effects on others. Although most did not have writings that made them widely known, Zhou Hui and Wang Gen became famous Ming philosophers.

Wang Gen has been widely portrayed as the founder of the so-called Taizhou school, an intellectual affiliation whose very existence is now questioned by scholars. A charismatic figure, he attracted large crowds and many followers. He emphasized that everyone could understand and practice the sages' learning, not just the educated class. He claimed that the Way was to be found in oneself, in one's own heart-mind, in one's own moral knowledge. Others in Li's account were transformed by Wang Gen's teachings either directly, like Zhu Shu, Li Zhu, and Han Zhen, or indirectly, like Lin Na and Xia Tingmei. Xia apparently was a particularly forceful person, emphasizing self-reliance. He belittled dependence on others because, to use a concept of Mencius, it was the "way of the concubine." Like another well-known contemporary, He Xinyin, Xia advocated the notion, radical to some, that there was no distinction between moral principles and human desires. This distinction had been favored by many neo-Confucians, including Zhu Xi. Although he lived his adult life in Taizhou, Zhou Hui often visited Xi'an and was a prominent figure in Guanxue, with numerous followers. Finally, there was Zhu Yunqi, who learned from Feng Congwu, Li Yong's eminent Guanxue predecessor.

These nine people came from the lower levels of society, worked hard on their own to gain knowledge of Confucian learning, experienced a personal transformation (to realize that their own moral heart-mind was identical to the Way), and then taught others, often large crowds. Since many taught themselves to read when they were adults, it cannot be said that they rejected reading in itself. Rather, they focused on the personal source of morality and hence were not interested in textual knowledge as a goal. Despite their rejection of "outside" authority, they clearly were not anarchists, in a Western political sense.

The lowly status and lower-class occupations of these exemplars conflicted with traditional Confucian notions about the occupation of the Confucian and the audience to whom Confucian learning was addressed. The sages' learning was not concerned with teaching manual and technical skills, and manual workers were not occupied with governing the country. Li, moreover, accepted the occupationally based class system with the literati at the top, and he recognized that social and political responsibilities were the concern of the sages' learning. Because of these beliefs, he offered an explanation of how a lowly worker could become a sage or hero. His view—that Confucian learning got off track during the Han but still remained recoverable—also exhibits his concern about philosophical discontinuity and social disorder.

Quoting a statement by Wang Gen's disciple Wang Dong, Li wrote that everyone—literatus, farmer, artisan, and merchant—could still share in learning even though there were differences in occupation. Although Confucius had 3,000 disciples, only 72 were from the upper class and so understood the six arts. The remainder were from the simple and illiterate masses. When the Qin destroyed learning and the Han revived it, only those who had memorized and recited the classics of the ancients became prominent as teachers. As they compiled the classics again, they became more elitist than before, teaching and learning only from each other. They designated Confucian learning as the occupation of classical scholars and literary men alone, and so the learning that a thousand ancient sages had originally comprehended and taught to everyone was destroyed and no longer transmitted. But, Li continued, Wang Dong suddenly realized that he should think of Confucius and Mencius and point directly to the heart-mind. Then the illiterate and simple people would all know that even their moral natures were complete and sufficient by themselves and that morality did not come from intellectual or textual knowledge. And then the teachings that had not been transmitted for two millennia would be restored (EQQJ, 22.6b–7a).

Referring to Qin and Han events, Li thus suggested how the sages' learning had lost its focus on action in society and became linked with the occupation of textual scholars. Confucius had intended his teachings for everyone, but in recovering what the Qin had destroyed, Han scholars wrongly narrowed his teachings to the concerns of classical scholars and literary men. Confucian learning became a matter of texts, not social practice. Even though its transmission to the common people had been cut off for twenty centuries, this learning could still be recovered by a direct personal realization, for everyone had the same moral capacities. An aspect of being human, the Way was not dependent on texts for its survival. Even laborers could contribute to the harmonious ordering of society through their teaching, if they had comprehended the Way. A government post was not needed and was not even the source of genuine moral authority.

Although Li and other Confucian philosophers did not dwell on questions concerning the relationship between human capacities and particular characteristics of society, they did realize that cultural knowledge is "stored" in many ways, some of which we are more aware of than others.[92] Exemplars were one of the more important non-textual sites in the Confucian philosophical system for preserving and transmitting knowledge. The use of exemplars was effective for transmitting knowledge because much Confucian knowledge was a matter of behavior rather than words. By not presenting values as abstract concepts, exemplars conveyed practical information, for their actions demonstrated values. An exemplar also allowed a range of interpretation and so could teach different lessons to different people. Since reading was not a requirement for learning from exemplars, the use of them enabled teachings to be directed to everyone, low as well as high. Finally, the hero was significant for Li because of his fundamental assumption that a ruler should lead by governing and by teaching. In Li's view, this aspect of rulership had been neglected for too long, and his call for a hero was a plea to shoulder again the responsibilities of a genuine Confucian.

3   *To Teach*

Having examined certain theoretical features of Confucian learning as a body of knowledge, with its characteristic values, issues, and implicit rules, I turn now to a second aspect, or "corner," of Confucian learning—the activity of teaching. The following discussion is divided into three sections in order to help structure understanding of this complex topic. The first concerns different levels of social reality, each of which requires its own kind of teaching. The second addresses those aspects of the personal self that help make the self an important focal point in teaching. And the third discusses critical elements and issues in the Confucian responsibility of teaching. My approach in this chapter is to consider both Confucian philosophy as a system and Li's appropriation of particular aspects.

LEVELS OF SOCIAL REALITY

Like many previous thinkers, Li Yong ranked the Confucian responsibility of teaching and educating as equal in importance to that of governing (EQQJ, 12.3b–5b, 14.7a).[1] Focusing especially on the sociopolitical role and the content of teaching, Li Yong's ideas were organized around several pairs of concepts, each of which had important cultural associations. The complementary concepts of *jiaohua* (teaching and transforming) – *zhenghua* (governing and transforming) and of *shidao* (the way of the teacher) – *wangdao* (the way of the king) brought together Li's ideas on the social and political functions of teaching. The contrasting concepts of *yanjiao* ("word" teaching, or teaching with words) and *shenjiao* ("self" teaching, or teaching with behavior), along with the antagonistic concepts of *jiangxue–jiangshu* (discussing learning – discussing books) and *renshi–jingshi* (teacher of humaneness – teacher of the classics), summarized his ideas on the content of teaching.

When Confucian philosophers spoke about teaching and learning from a theoretical perspective, they employed such paradigmatic examples as root and branches, inner and outer, and higher and lower. Here, however, I apply another theoretical frame, one based on the notion of levels of integration, to analyze the nature of the Confucian teaching responsibilities. This frame recognizes the multiple levels of organization that characterize reality. Although social reality is the concern here, other kinds of realities are of course not denied.

Modern scientists use the idea of levels of integration as a theoretical frame for understanding relationships among various kinds of events.[2] Biologists, for example, speak of molecules, cells, organs, and organisms. Each of these entities exists on a different level, so that on the level of molecules there are no cells, organs, or organisms, and on the level of organs there are no cells or molecules. To offer another example, electrochemical activities in the mouth are not the same as tastes, for these two "events" occur on different levels of reality. The former concern neural impulses, whereas the latter are something adjudicated by the culture.

Since the duration of any event (or entity) is an aspect of that event, events occupy different kinds of time. The time of higher-level entities has a longer duration than that of lower-level entities. An organ thus continues to exist despite the fact that its particular cells change over time, with newer ones replacing those that have died. And a cultural tradition continues to live, even though its apologists come and go, live and die.

Similarly, social reality may be seen as structured by a hierarchy of levels, with different entities on each level. Applying this "map" to Confucian thought, I find three significant levels, each having a separate field of teaching. (This is not to say, however, that there are only three levels.) These levels consist of the personal self, social relationships, and the multi-generational social and cultural tradition. Different (social) entities constitute each level.

The first level consists of persons, whose apparent physiological and psychological individuality tends to obscure the fact that each person is a matrix of numerous relations and activities. That is, the personal self extends beyond the perceivable boundaries of the physical body. The second level consists of relationships, such as the family, community, and government. There are no individual persons on this level, just as there are no electrochemical reactions on the level of tastes or sound waves on the level of sound. The third level consists of the Confucian-dominated cultural tradition itself, measured in a time frame of generations and characterized by various events, values, and ideas.

Although I am suggesting this map primarily as a tool for purposes of analysis, Confucian thinkers also recognized it in some way, but they referred to it quite differently. Early sociopolitical thought took the position, for instance, that families, not individual persons, constituted the state.[3] On the assumption of the reality of the tradition, the term "later generations" (*houshi*) referred to an aspect of the multi-generational level of educative responsibility. Philosophers were referring to this level when they talked about "interrupted learning" (*juexue*) and the idea that Confucius and Mencius had established their teachings to "hang (or, hand down) through the ages" (variously, *chuishi lijiao, chuijiao wanshi*, and *liyan chuixun*).[4] Although Li Yong recognized that Zhu Xi's teaching focused in different ways on all three levels, his statement that Zhu was a teacher of ten thousand generations was premised on the reality of tradition (EQQJ, 7.4a). Such ideas as "later generations," "interrupted learning," and "hanging through the ages" assumed the existence of a social reality logically different from the family (a set of relationships) or from individual persons.

In contrast to the lowest level of the person, the two higher levels of the tradition and certain social relationships tended to involve fewer participants in the teaching concerned with it, and the teachers at the higher levels tended to have higher social status. The issue of survival was important for all levels, but Confucians generally placed greater value on the survival of higher-level entities. That is, the survival of the tradition as the only genuine Way of humanity was more critical than the survival of particular communities, families, or persons. This ordering of value is, we should note, contrary to that of some Western sociopolitical thought, particularly the systems associated with Hobbes, Locke, and Rousseau, and to modern Western ideas of intrinsic human rights and moral worth.

Different kinds of teaching applied to each field, or level, of so-cial reality. A large portion of teaching relevant to the person in-volved the learner's acquisition of skills, ranging from the early learning of tonal patterns to learning to speak and write the language to "dusting and sweeping and answering questions."[5] Teaching at this level, which I shall call "instruction," utilized methods of repeti-tion and memorization, encouraged rote learning, and was a subject on which philosophers rarely wrote. The rudimentary artisanal skills that apprentices were taught, as well as the skills of laborers, includ-ing farmers, also were included in instruction.

Teaching on the personal level involved a further kind of activ-ity, which addressed matters variously described as spiritual, emo-tional, moral, and psychological. Directed more toward the "supe-rior" than the "petty" person, this type of teaching was commonly seen as concerned with the private and hence "inner" aspects of a person. Under the Confucian view that a person's outer behavior reflected the person's inner moral state, however, attention was given to both private thoughts and visible actions in this kind of teaching.

Instead of distinguishing private thoughts from visible actions, the inner-outer contrast here is better seen as referring to the distinc-tion between human moral-social capacities and those sensory ca-pacities that do not differentiate civilized people from the so-called barbarians or humans from animals. Since human behavior could be understood from either perspective, teaching that focused on the personal self always presented the possibility of the "wrong" kind of focus — that is, on sensory-related and selfish actions rather than on moral, socially good actions. Confucian philosophers paid no serious attention to instruction, and they disagreed about what to teach the superior type of person. Emphasizing the necessity of social useful-ness and denigrating literature and art, Li Yong (like Cheng Yi) rep-resented an extreme, but not unique, position.

Teaching for the next level, that of social relations, focused on tasks concerning the family, the community, and the government, and taught values and behavior ranging from the *li* (appropriate be-havior, ritual action) to some aspects of most occupations. These oc-cupations included the "lesser ways" of the common people, rou-tinely categorized as farming, animal husbandry, medicine, and divination, as well as the "great way" of the elite, service in the gov-ernmental bureaucracy (SSFSL, *Lunyu*, pt. 2, 42–43). Implicitly assuming the reality of certain moral-social relationships, Li Yong claimed that it was the *li* that distinguished the superior person from the petty person, humans from animals, and Confucian culture from other ways (SSFSL, *Lunyu*, pt. 2, 48).

Those Confucians interested in social and economic affairs, as Li Yong was, recognized a responsibility toward the "lesser ways," as well as toward the "great way," and some compiled works for these lower occupations. For instance, Li's disciple Wang Xinjing wrote a detailed essay on farming and the construction of different kinds of fields according to the local conditions. A later follower, Yang Shen, compiled an illustrated manual on sericulture, in which the "practical" discussion began with planting the mulberry trees and concluded with selling the silk cloth.[6] Focusing on the second level of social reality, these works were written out of a sense of responsibility to society, and this kind of writing was itself an activity on the level of social relations.

Teaching at the third level pertained to the multi-generational stream of the cultural tradition. This social reality extended hundreds of generations back into the past, at least to the time of Yao and Shun, and thousands of generations forward into the future. Since few thinkers expected a future utopia (in fact it was seldom even conceived until the nineteenth century), the sages' teachings made sense as a guide from the past for the future. The Confucians' attention to this third level, expressed by the classics, philosophical writings, histories, and belles lettres, was in effect a way of taking responsibility for the entire world.

Teaching relevant to this field was discussed in different ways. For instance, in his preface to Li's *Reflections on the Four Books*, Xu Sunquan, the Shaanxi provincial superintendent of education, described the learning of principle (*lixue*) as inner and the events of the world (*shiyun*) as outer. The enduring transmission of the Way and the Six Classics were handed down as an instruction for ten thousand generations from the time when Yao and Shun began the tradition of the Way to when Li completed it. Like the course of the sun and moon across the heavens and the rivers and streams across the earth, the Way always existed. Although it almost ceased after being overcome by Buddhism, thrown into turmoil by Daoism, and dissipated by flowery writing, the sages' learning was recovered in the Song. Guanzhong thinkers then followed the thread of Zhang Zai. In the five centuries since the Song, more than thirty famous (*lixue*) thinkers have appeared, but only Guanxue now teaches the pure and correct learning to the world.

Xu went on to say that after the dynastic change Li Yong appeared in Zhouzhi, discussing the Way and venerating the Confucians. Li's teaching emphasized practical action and reflecting on and investigating the source of morality. Encouraging and kind to students, Li led the way for those gone astray, and he explained the basis of the sages' morality. Xu further noted that Li's *Reflections on the Four Books* illustrated Zhang Zai's teaching about establishing one's aim (SSFSL, preface by Xu Sunquan).[7] By citing Zhang's teaching, with its references to such entities as the past sages and the ten thousand generations, Xu was acknowledging tradition as a responsibility of Confucian teaching.

Others, such as Li Zufa, a contemporary Shaanxi scholar, also pointed out that Li's work was promulgated for the later generations of the world (SSFSL, introduction by Li Zufa). Wang Xinjing noted that Li's *Reflections* was written as a tool to teach people how to read and understand the Four Books. Wang wrote that Li often said that Confucius, Zengzi, Zisi, and Mencius established their words to hang as instruction for the ages and so completed the Four Books. Cheng and Zhu continued this activity during the Song, explaining and clarifying the Four Books. Their instruction, however, was not only for hearing and repeating. They wanted people to embody the ideas in their persons and display them in their actions—to fulfill heavenly virtue in themselves and develop it outwardly as the kingly way, to have essence and application, and to aid the world (SSFSL, preface by Wang Xinjing). Li's work *Reflections* thus was a form of teaching that took the Confucian tradition as its responsibility, and Li's act of writing it belonged to that level of social reality.

Although this hierarchical framework is useful for analyzing the terrain of Confucian teaching, it must be recognized that the boundaries of knowledge were not as distinct as the levels of social reality. Although differing kinds of teaching may be distinguished by the terms "instructing," "teaching," and "educating," my preferred term for general use here is "teaching." The Confucian thinkers themselves regarded educating and teaching, as opposed to instructing, to be on a continuum that began with prenatal teaching (discussed below). The distinction among the three types of teaching has some chronological aspects, for it is true that one must learn characters before one can read, but the distinction is not theoretically a chronological matter. Rather, it concerns different kinds of social entities—individual persons, social relationships, and the sociocultural tradition itself.

Li was interested in many aspects of teaching: the functions and content of teaching, the interdependency of teaching and governing, the conditions of teaching, and the teacher—who and what a teacher was and how a teacher was legitimated. Before examining his views on these subjects, however, we need to look at his understanding of the personal self because of its pivotal role in teaching and learning.

THE SELF

Li's ideas about teaching (and learning) assumed a conception of the personal self that combined characteristics drawn from classical and later philosophical thought. To use modern Western terms, he treated the individual person as a "reflexive self," not an "ego self." This perspective, which has much in common with that of G. H. Mead as opposed to Descartes, focuses on the individual person's appropriate performance of social roles rather than on such problems as memory and personal continuity, identity, personality, and consciousness. More concerned with the self as a social participant and social object, the reflexive self is not concerned with analyzing the "thinking" being, or the "I," or whatever it is that thinks.

There is a fundamental assumption of ongoing activity and that individual people participate in that system of activity. Thus attention is directed to the system that gives meaning to individual acts rather than to the personal or private motivational aspects of people's acts. Li was concerned with the social aspects of the self, regardless of whether such aspects involved "inner" mental and psychological affairs (known possibly only by oneself) or "outer" social and political activities. He did not entertain Western-type questions about the ontological status of consciousness.[8]

The concept of the reflexive self takes society as the context in which human beings are able to become persons. Society (as an ongoing organized system) makes the individual person and, even more, makes the individual person possible. Individuals do not make society. The Confucian conception of the self, from Li's perspective, required (but was not limited to) certain social relations—the family, community, government, and tradition. The genuine person, or the

truly individual person, was an achievement involving these relationships.[9] Such a person was the "human condition" sought, not
that in which human beings began.

Deriving from classical Confucian thought, the notion of a reflexive self belonged to a larger philosophical context that, since the
Song, had been dominated by an interest in ontological questions
pertaining to the patterns of the universe and human beings. Although Li had little interest in investigating the ontological status of
universal patterns and principles, the extrasensory dimension of reality was a given in Confucian thought. Li's attitude was quite similar, however, to that of the late Ming questioner who once asked
Feng Congwu why people talked about "mind and nature" if the
sages' principles were simply to be filial and loyal in the daily practice of human relations.[10]

Still, the Song views were significant because they contributed an
element to Confucian thinking that in turn provided a new justification system for the moral and social thought derived from the classical tradition. By "justification system," I refer to methods for adjudi-
cating and legitimizing ideas. The defining foundation that set the
boundaries of relevancy and the implicit rules of thinking for early
Confucian thought consisted of specific paradigmatic examples (such
as the family or plant) and the particular kinds of relationships that
such examples implied. Song neo-Confucians added a different kind
of defining foundation, namely the universal, extrasensory realities
of principle(s) (*li*) and matter-energy (*qi*).[11] Not concerned with reality in the Western sense of metaphysics or in the Chinese sense of
root and branches, the concepts of *li* and *qi* belonged to another conceptual frame, one that distinguished things as "above (before)
forms" and "below (within) forms."

The older and newer theoretical foundations coexisted in neo-
Confucian (and in Li Yong's) thought. Philosophers never fully
agreed about the meaning of *li* and *qi* and their relationship (whether
one or the other was primary), with the result that both entities
served, for different thinkers, as the fundamental "fact" of being and
becoming. Continuity was a primary claim (or implication) of both *li*
and *qi*, but the continuity of *li* stressed principles and order, whereas
the continuity of *qi* stressed activity and existing.

A primary reason for the difficulty in coming to an agreement
over *li* and *qi* was that instead of establishing new "rules" for thinking when working within the new philosophical discourse, philoso-

phers continued to use the rhetoric and kind of logical thinking associated with thought anchored in the theoretical framework of the paradigmatic example. For example, in talking about *li* and *qi*, thinkers continued to be concerned about what was primary (the "root") and what was secondary (the "branches"), even though the relationship of *li* and *qi* differed from that of roots and branches of the plant metaphor.[12] The logical patterns that applied to the paradigmatic example (i.e., the relation between the primary and the secondary) were carried over into discussions relating to continuity stressing order (*li*) or activity-and-existence (*qi*) and to the hidden and the manifest (or "before forms" and "within forms"). The inappropriateness of applying "root and branches" to the ideas of thinking raised by *li* and *qi* meant that certain conflicts could not be resolved. Moreover, a changed justification system led to changes in the conception of other important entities, including the heart-mind, human nature, and the emotions, and disagreements arose over these concepts for a similar reason, that is, the continued use of old logical patterns in a new theoretical framework.

Song neo-Confucians generally described the nature (*xing*) of human beings as similar to the nature of the universe in that both human beings and the universe were constituted of the same kind of "stuff" (*qi*) and the same kind of principles or patterns (*li*) of activity. These principles were the patterns of life and its processes of birth, growth, maturation, and death, as well as the relational patterns of society and social behavior. As a conception dominated by human perspectives, the universe (heaven-earth-humanity) included phenomena as diverse as celestial bodies, time and the seasons, earth and its physical features, the hierarchical structure of human society, human relationships, and the thinking and feeling processes of human beings. The distinction between animals and humans was more a matter of degree than kind, with the critical difference resting on the social nature and social actions of human beings.

Li Yong accepted the neo-Confucian view of an original, amorphous state giving rise to the experienced world of human beings. This view emphasized the inseparability of *li* and *qi*, although which one took precedence remained in general dispute. Zhang Zai, Lu Jiuyuan, and Wang Yangming have been most identified with a monistic type of view, and Zhu Xi and Cheng Yi, probably with more certainty than is justified, have been associated with a type of dualism.

When Li Yong discussed the personal self, he combined ideas

associated with the two types of theoretical frame, that is, the paradigmatic example and a universal, extrasensory reality of order and continuous change. The two differing perspectives led Li Yong and others to use numerous alternative terms for that original, extrasensory state, the "ground" of existence. For instance, Zhang Shundian, one of Li's predecessors in Guanxue, favored the term "illustrious virtue" from the *Great Learning*, but he also offered familiar alternative terms, such as "knowing benevolence," "centrality and harmony," "utmost wholeness," "utmost goodness," "the one thread," and the "overflowing *qi*."[13]

Li himself used many terms, such as "original essence" (see EQQJ, 1.5a), "origin" (2.1b), "root" (2.2a), "great root" (11.2b), "great origin" (11.2b), "original beginning" (2.6a), "luminous origin" (the term most often used by Li Yong and also used by Feng Congwu; 2.2a–3a and *passim*), "springs of life" (2.4a–b), "original face" (2.6a), and "original truth" (2.7b). Additional terms used by Li and others included "moral knowledge and ability," "the highest good," "the mean," "correct thought or mind," "mind," "the nature," "great vacuousness," and "great harmony."[14]

Since the activities of human beings and the universe were seen as possessing similar fundamental patterns (or nature) and stuff, the characteristics of one applied to the other. Following the disputed formulation of Wang Yangming, Li thus claimed that the original state of human nature (and the universe) was one of absolute goodness with no evil (EQQJ, 1.1a). It was absolutely pure without flaws, and the social concepts of good and evil did not apply to it. This state was easily lost, however, and hence the actual behavior of most people was faulty.

Referring to the source or original state, Li said that the origin of human life was what Heaven (or, the universe) conferred on the individual person (*wo*). When someone or something was born, no new "substance" appeared that was not in the universe previously. And, the death of a thing did not mean that a "substance" was no longer in existence. Birth simply meant that "this" (this thing) had come, and death that "this" had gone (EQQJ, 2.2a). Like others, Li claimed the continuity and unity of existence at the extrasensory level. The birth of something meant that a particular thing had emerged from the ontological whole, and death was its return. "Nothing is begun, and nothing is destroyed" (EQQJ, 2.2b).

Li combined these ideas about extrasensory reality with ideas about social realities. The body as a physiological entity depended on the luminous origin for its functioning, whether it was a matter of the eye or ear, foot or hand. The moral capacities of the self (a social entity), which together were known as human nature or the four sprouts, were identical to this origin. The five relationships, the given social patterns of society, derived from this origin. Moreover, any activity not based in the luminous origin, but only in superficial, phenomenal manifestations of it, lacked a foundation and so would fail (EQQJ, 2.2a).

Li claimed that although the physical aspects of the body changed as one went from youth to adulthood, old age, and death, one's share of the luminous origin was not limited. Like Mencius' flood-like *qi*, it filled up heaven and earth, penetrated past and present, and never rested (EQQJ, 2.2b). The luminous origin was eternal and infinite, whether manifested in a particular person or in its unmanifested state. Echoing Cheng Yi's comment on the inseparability of *li* and *qi*, Li Yong said that "without this luminous origin, there would be nothing by which to perceive heaven and earth, the myriad things, above and below [space], and past and present [time]. Without heaven and earth, the myriad things, above and below, and past and present, there also would be nothing by which to perceive this luminous origin" (EQQJ, 2.2b).

In everyone, the luminous origin was also identified as the (Mencian) moral knowledge and ability (*liangzhi liangneng*) that all humans have at birth (EQQJ, 2.2b). Although human moral knowledge has a specific content, the four sprouts, Li also described the luminous origin in ways that suggested its infinite nature. Echoing the words of the *Book of Poetry*, *Laozi*, and the *Book of Change*, Li said that it is "without sound and odor. It does not look or listen. It is empty and yet it is luminous. It is still and yet it has spirit vitality. Its capacity embraces everything, and its brightness illuminates everything" (EQQJ, 2.3a). Li further described it as the "mind that has no thoughts." "It is a unity and has no duality; it does not form a pair with things" (EQQJ, 2.3b). When applied to the human mind, these terms refer to an absolutely still epistemological state in which emotions and thoughts have not yet emerged. It is only after thoughts and emotions have emerged that the concept of the self becomes a possibility.

Li held that human beings, like the universe, may be viewed from different perspectives, two of which are the phenomenal-social self (*shen*) and a nature (*xing*) identical to the original state or source of being. Li sometimes referred to the self (*shen*) by other terms that more clearly emphasized the self as a particular person, such as *xingfen* (human nature and lot) and the expanded term *rensheng xing-fen* (the nature and lot of a human life; EQQJ, 14.6b, 3b). The human self (*shen*) was based on an endowment of *qi* and *li*. Li, accepting a widely held view, claimed that humans received the *qi* of heaven and earth to complete their selves, and they obtained the *li* of heaven and earth to make their natures (EQQJ, 1.1a). (This dichotomy is clearly quite different from one modern Western dichotomy relating to the self, which opposes thinker-subject to thought-object.)

Li further promoted the idea (found in various ancient texts, including the *Book of Change*, Great Commentary, A6) that the capacity of human nature was as great as that of heaven and earth (EQQJ, 1.1a). By "capacity," Li was referring to a person's creative power (*de*), which included both the power to act and the moral virtues that shape one's actions (EQQJ, 1.1b, 14.2b).[15] Li and others referred to this inherent, "so-of-itself," self-generating power, characteristic of human nature and the universe, as "luminosity" (*ling*). Li conceived of *ling* as a luminosity comparable to that of the sun and moon (both were thought of as sources of light; EQQJ, 1.1a). Like the brightness that emanated from the sun, the vitality of human beings did not depend on any outside force.

Not outside of the sensory world, the self (*shen*) referred to the phenomenal person located in human society. Li assumed that people may differ in their endowment of *qi*, but the quality of *qi* received did not limit a person's achievements (EQQJ, 3.4a). As in the view of Wang Yangming, everyone had the potential to exert moral effort and reach the level of the sages.

One common perspective used by Li to describe the formation of the self involved the paradigmatic examples of a mirror and a pearl. Assuming that mirrors and pearls possessed luminosity like the sun, Li claimed that a person's particular endowment of *qi* (one's *qizhi*) could cloud over and so obscure the brightness and purity of the original state of the nature. Depending on the extent of the obscuration, a person would then behave in a more, or less, moral way. With effort, it was possible to reduce or even remove the obscuration (immoral or antisocial behavior) and thereby regain one's moral luminosity, just as a mirror could be wiped clean or a pearl polished (EQQJ, 1.1a–b). On the level of *qizhi*, the mirror, the pearl, and the sun were the relevant (and interchangeable) paradigmatic examples.

In another perspective, confining relationships and entanglements with others become the dominating image applied to the level of human behavior. Li held that the human self was formed from the influences of the social environment, in a person's interactions with the surrounding world. In Li's view, the most important factors contributing to the social self were emotions and desires, customs and habits, and the circumstances of the times. Emotions and desires led a person to exhibit various kinds of undesirable behavior, customs and habits constrained a person in his or her activities, and the circumstances of the times set the general conditions of life (EQQJ, 1.1a).

The primary factors contributing to the formation of the self thus included a psychological-physical level of emotions and feelings, a social and personal level of customs and habits, and a social and political level of contemporary conditions. The personal self was the result of the interplay between external or social factors and internal factors, whether inherited, psychological, or intellectual. Li was particularly concerned, moreover, with the negative effects of society on the self (EQQJ, 10.4b and 2.4a). He held that, in the case of most people, the formation of the self meant a deterioration from a state of original purity to one hardly different from that of the animals. Sensory knowledge misled people into becoming vulgar and coarse. The movement was so gradual, however, that people were unaware of their decline. They did not realize they were becoming petty persons, but the further they diverged from the original state, the further away they were from becoming superior persons.

Li gave final responsibility for the formation of the self to a person's conscious efforts, to "the turn of a thought" (EQQJ, 1.2a). Immoral behavior was due to the lack of appropriate intention and effort, not to human nature or *qi*. No matter how one behaved, one's nature, that is, one's capacities, remained congruent with the original state of being. A person could take responsibility in various ways, for example, by "calming the self" (*an shen*) or by "establishing one's destiny" (*li ming*, realizing the moral standards derived from Heaven; EQQJ, 2.2a). The heart-mind was responsible for a person's intentions and efforts. Used in different senses, "heart-mind" could refer to the source or luminous origin. Important here, however, was its sense (noted in Chapter 2) of the human mind functioning in the world of everyday experience. Li sometimes called this latter mind the *shenxin*, the body-mind or the self-mind. This mind referred to the thinking that a person did in relation to his or her self-cultivation, learning, and behavior in general.[16] Since this thinking (this mind) was an aspect of the self, the *shenxin* could become "obscured" like the self. However, it was also responsible for getting rid of those obscurations, so that the original, pure heart-mind could be recovered. (Although Li's view reflected the common neo-Confucian opposition between the human mind and the mind of the Way and shows similarities with the Buddhist distinction between the ordinary mind and the Buddha-mind, Li did not use those terms.)

After thoughts began to appear, the distinction between desires and principles emerged and so also the opposition between good and evil, right and wrong, and correct and depraved (EQQJ, 2.3b). These distinctions belonged to the (social) realm of the self and the self-mind, and they did not exist in the extrasensory realm. Li's ideas were similar here to those of Feng Congwu, who composed a chart that distinguished between the paths of goodness and selfishness, a fundamental distinction in Confucian thought.[17] The former path led to the way of the sages, and the latter to the common person and the way of evil. Like most Confucians, Li and Feng believed that a person had to make a deliberate decision to follow the path of goodness.

Interested in the self and self-mind in social terms, Li simply did not address how from a psychological viewpoint a person made this decision. Instead, he emphasized that the mind "shifts and turns according to conditions" (EQQJ, 2.1b). That is, humans act in response to, and in the context of, social phenomena. Li was not suggesting a mechanistic type of response, but was saying that thinking happened in the midst of the social world.

Although Li held that ideas should be prior to moral actions, he did not claim that social conditions are fully prior to ideas. Rather, both of these "events" (conditions and ideas) continually occur in some fashion and in an inseparable relationship. Even if one is not aware of conditions, the mind still acts in relation to them. In a Buddhist-like fashion, Li said, "When the mind arises, then conditions arise. When conditions exist, then the mind exists. The mind and conditions are blended together; only then is it phenomenal reality [*shiji*]" (EQQJ, 2.4a). "Mind" here refers to thinking, the functioning of the self-mind. Li was suggesting that we contribute to making the reality we experience and that thinking depends on conditions. Like seeing or hearing, thinking implies a relationship with conditions.

The conditions to which Li referred were not only the more obvious phenomenal and psychological ones, those of "sounds and forms, goods and profits," or those things that clearly tempted people. Conditions were all those things that one's emotions led one into anticipating and pursuing. Using stereotypic rhetoric, Li said that these things included failure and success, gain and loss, slander and fame, longevity and untimely death (EQQJ, 2.4a). Conditions were all the things that led a person away from the state of perfect unity.

In sum, Li combined ideas relating to the extrasensory reality of *li* and *qi* with classical, and other, ideas about the heart-mind to form a multi-dimensional conception of the self. The idea of a universal unity was a critical assumption, implying that all spheres of human experience possessed the same patterns and principles of activity. Although the personal self constituted only one level of social reality, the principles that applied to it extended to other levels as well.[18] Thus, efforts to teach and educate a person always had ramifications beyond the immediate focus of attention and extended to the levels of society and tradition.

THE RESPONSIBILITY

Teaching and Educating (jiaohua) *and Governing* (zhenghua)

The widespread twentieth-century view that the goal of teaching is to convey content knowledge or help develop skills has not always been paramount, in either China or the West. The Chinese and Western philosophical traditions were, instead, concerned with teaching the whole person. Both traditions suggested that a person can be looked at from the perspective of various contexts, including social, cultural, spiritual, and extrasensory. The Platonic view, for example, held that teaching enabled a person to strive for moral and spiritual perfection. Another pervasive Western view saw teaching primarily as a matter of guiding the development of inherent human capacities. A third position, the pragmatic stance, envisaged the teacher as one who provides an environment that helps direct the course of learning of the student. Although the teacher offers standards, the teacher tries especially to adapt methods to the capacities and responses of the student. The pragmatists especially emphasized the interplay between organism and environment.[19]

Westerners and Chinese shared an assumption that teaching

ideally extended beyond elementary skills and content, but they also had important differences. This is not the place for extensive comparisons, but one area of difference needs to be recognized because of its relevance to understanding the Chinese position. This area concerns the nature of society and the individual person and, consequently, the entities involved in teaching—particularly, the teacher, the student, the conditions, and the material. For Li, as for many others, the reference of teaching was often the tradition rather than the student. That is, the teacher taught not for the student's own benefit, but for the sake of the tradition. In such a case, the focus of time for the teacher was what I call "scholar time," in contrast to "teacher-student time." Shorter in duration, the latter kind of time referred specifically to the student as an individual person.

Li's comments indicate that he saw teaching as the core activity sustaining the Confucian tradition. He knew that many philosophical concepts dealt with topics relating to teaching and that philosophical thought often developed in the conversational encounter between teachers and students. He reaffirmed the position of Mencius that teaching was an aspect of governance, the most fundamental of all Confucian concerns.

Following a long tradition of thought, Li did not conceive of teaching as separate from the sociopolitical context. Since governing in its best sense was thought of as putting the world in order, the ruler's task was to act so that the multiple dimensions of the social and natural worlds functioned together in harmony. The Confucian ideal of governing was not that the ruler would impose a rigid order on formless and passive masses, but that the ruler would work to create conditions permitting the successful performance of activities pertaining to all levels of social reality, from the individual person, to society, to tradition, and even to nature (EQQJ, 12.5b). From a theoretical perspective, good government functioned in such a way that the people properly ordered their own behavior. Li used the terms *zhenghua* and *zhihua*, governing and transforming, to convey the two components of governing. The masses would become civilized as their behavior became morally and socially good under the guidance of a benevolent ruler.

From a practical standpoint, the government had to fulfill certain responsibilities in order to maintain a society that upheld the cultural values of the ancient sages. These responsibilities involved long-range tasks of preserving and transmitting values as well as more immediate tasks of regulation (EQQJ, 12.3b).[20] Li thus emphasized the kind of teaching that would lead to desired changes in people's behavior in society. He even claimed that such teaching, termed *jiaohua*, "teaching and transforming," was "the first duty of government" (SSFSL, *Lunyu*, pt. 2, 83).

Li saw governing (*zhenghua*) and teaching (*jiaohua*) as confluent, with each occupying different sociopolitical niches. The activity of governing was carried out both in the formal actions of the imperial government itself and in the nonofficial activities of the local leadership class, and Li accepted the common distinction between those "above" in the capital and those "below" in the provinces. He applied this distinction to those serving in official posts in the bureaucracy and to those not in office who were teachers in the provinces (EQQJ, 5.2a). With this contrast in mind, Li then claimed that "moral knowledge was the root of one self [*shen*], and [many] selves were the root of the states of the world. Cultivating the self established the great root of the world. Above, governing [*zhenghua*] arises in the self. . . . Below, teaching [*jiaohua*] arises in the self" (SSFSL, *Daxue*, 9). Not viewing governing and teaching only as aspects of the same "event," Li also saw both as developing from the cultivation of human moral capacities.

Li's emphasis on the unity of teaching and governing was based on his assumptions that social behavior is learned and that society indeed has the particular characteristics attributed to it by the Confucians. That is, actions of social consequence were not simply a matter of exhibiting inherited characteristics without thought, effort, and development. Although Li believed that everyone has a similar capacity to know and to do what is morally good, he as well as others accepted that people differ in their actual behavior. It was hence thought important to help moral capacities grow through teaching.

Li Yong claimed that "what one does is based in what one has learned" (SSFSL, *Mengzi*, pt. 1, 4). If a person learned benevolence and rightness when young, then that person's actions as an adult would be benevolent and right. The same was true for immoral and antisocial behavior. If a person learned to behave selfishly when young, then that person's adult behavior would exhibit selfish characteristics. Thus, teaching mattered, and teaching that resulted in a change of behavior toward the good contributed to social order and the overall efforts of governing.

Accepting the necessity of teaching for achieving social order, Li held it was critical to distinguish the genuine activity from others that masqueraded as teaching. This goal entailed keeping one's focus on the three levels of social reality as they pertained to scholar time. That is, teaching (*jiao*) had to refer to teaching and educating, not to instructing. The first two activities helped people develop themselves — in thought and behavior — whereas the last only helped people acquire verbal skills and the information in texts but did not designate their use. The use of knowledge was, moreover, a critical Confucian issue, just as it has been in the West.[21]

To distinguish the genuine from the seemingly genuine, Li contrasted *jiaohua*, "teaching and transforming," with *jiaoshu*, "teaching books" or instructing (EQQJ, 3.9b–10a). The former, not the latter, was a proper concern of a "great Confucian" and formed a class with governing. Teaching (*jiaohua*) referred to civilizing, socializing, and developing moral persons. Just as learning did not mean rote memorization and recitation, teaching did not mean lecturing on factual information or instructing in skills.

Conspicuously absent in Li's views was an appreciation of artistic talents and activities, for neo-Confucian philosophers since the Song had associated art and even particular subjects in nature, such as the pine or bamboo, with specific virtues. Unlike many others, Li did not view contemporary art as having a moral, social, or spiritual content.[22] He simply stated that the modern arts of poetry, prose, calligraphy, and painting had no use in everyday life. They were secondary skills, branches rather than the root. Claiming to follow Zhu Xi (despite Zhu's emphasis on texts), Li further held that poetry and prose were only one danger, with the examinations and books in general being the other two dangers (SSFSL, *Lunyu*, pt. 1, 42–43).

Li thus distinguished "gentlemen of virtue" (*daode zhi shi*) from "people with skills" (*jiyi zhi ren*). Gentlemen of virtue aimed at the Way, whereas the skilled aimed at the arts. People with skills followed the outer and rejected the inner; they had the "appearance" but not the "reality." Li was not wholly opposed to art, however, for he did allow for some pursuit of the arts, but only after adequate social and moral action. He claimed that the six arts of the ancients (rites, music, archery, charioteering, writing, and mathematics) differed from the four contemporary arts (cited above), for all six were necessary and had been useful in daily life. Also, the goals of the ancients were not these arts per se (SSFSL, *Lunyu*, pt. 1, 42; EQQJ, 16.15a). The ancients aimed at the Way.

Although extreme for a Confucian, this view is partly understandable in terms of Li's lifelong poverty. Living conditions were harsh in the northwest, and its culture was stern in contrast to the wealth and extravagance found in the south. Li thus tended to view art as ornamental and as something merely on paper, as opposed to virtuous action (SSFSL, *Lunyu*, pt. 2, 2; see *Lunyu*, 12.8). It was certainly not what the ancient sages relied on in achieving the "great Way" (SSFSL, *Lunyu*, pt. 2, 42).

As suggested above, Chinese thinkers referred to the three fields of teaching in a way that differed from the framework of social realities that I have distinguished here, but what they said can be seen in terms of this framework. Li's contemporary Wu Guang pointed out, for instance, that Li regarded the purpose of his teaching to be "to extend your moral knowledge and practice it vigorously" (EQQJ, 10.23a). In other words, Li's teaching was concerned with a moral (and spiritual) development on the personal level and with the patterned (social-moral) behavior on the level of social relations. Li was referring to this second level in his comments that teaching and educating were concerned with the "human way," that is, with the patterns of proper social behavior. Using totally conventional terms, Li stated that this kind of teaching focused on such things as "being filial when at home and having fraternal respect when in society, being careful to live up to one's word and being fond of the masses, loving those who are close and liking others" (SSFSL, *Lunyu*, pt. 1, 5). All these prescribed kinds of behavior assumed the reality of social relations.

Given the perceived crises of the times, Li was determined not to let instructing, with its focus on a limited self, be disguised as teaching and educating, which took others into account. Li lamented that in his own time teaching had become hardly more than instructing — supervising students as they became skilled in writing compositions in order to pass the examinations. This was merely "paper" learning, not "useful" learning.[23] To correct this problem, he taught that students should first study such works as the *Classic of Filial Piety*, Zhu Xi's *Elementary Learning*, and books on ritual action (*li*). Then, "after the great root is established," they could study poetry, history, and literature, all secondary matters for Li (SSFSL, *Lunyu*, pt. 1, 5).

Genuine teaching involved efforts to develop good behavior, and it affected all aspects of a person, not just the intellectual, psychological, moral, or even aesthetic side. Although these differing perspectives might be used to discuss changes once they became apparent to others, all changes had to be grounded in the heart-mind, or the root. Genuine teaching was directed toward the moral and social self, that is, toward both the "private" self and the self in society. Since a person's visible, public behavior was regarded as manifesting the private moral state, these two aspects of a person were seen as mutually reinforcing each other and providing opportunities for constant self-examination and self-adjustment. Thus, despite some focus on the private aspects of a person, the context of genuine teaching was tradition and society.

In contrast, the context of instruction had a narrower frame of reference, the limited self. Li could not philosophically justify this restricted focus, for his defense of the Confucian cultural world entailed a broad sociopolitical frame of reference. If instructing were allowed to dominate the intellectuals' world, then the importance of the contexts beyond one's immediate self would be reduced, the application of knowledge would be ignored, and the imperative to act would be lost. These were unacceptable consequences.[24]

Li's view of teaching and educating continued previous, well-known philosophical positions. During the Song, for instance, Zhu Xi had talked about Confucian teaching as concerned with behavior in society and with an understanding of the reasons for that behavior. Zhu had said that, as one grew from a youth to an adult, teaching expanded to include not only specific items of behavior but also understanding of that behavior. That is, teaching included things, events, and affairs, as well as their principles (*li*).[25] The social realities that were the reference of Li Yong's ideas existed here too.

Even earlier, in ancient China, Mencius and Xunzi had been instrumental in establishing the government's responsibility to educate as part of the Confucian position. Mencius made teaching part of the kingly way, and Xunzi emphasized that the teaching of appropriate social behavior, or ritual action, was a primary responsibility of the Confucian.[26] Although Li Yong elevated the activity of teaching, in relationship to governing, perhaps more than most previous thinkers had done, the link between these two activities was a fundamental one, based philosophically on a concern with the social realities of tradition, society, and the individual person and on a belief in the interdependency of governing and teaching.

The Way of the Teacher (shidao) *and the Way of the King* (wangdao)

Since classical times, Confucians had promoted the notion of a benevolent government concerned with the welfare of the people and taking responsibility for teaching and the establishment of schools (see, for example, *Mencius*, 3A.3). Called the "way of the king" and developed by Mencius, this ideal was opposed to the way of the hegemon, without benevolence or legitimate authority. To stress the importance of the Confucian role of teaching, Li referred to it as the "way of the teacher." By pairing the way of the teacher with that of the king, Li evoked, for the way of the teacher, the cultural power of the ideas associated with the kingly way.

The relationship of these two ways was seen as complementary, resembling that of inner (sage) and outer (king), or essence (*ti*) and application (*yong*). The teacher's way preserved and transmitted the Confucian cultural values (*ti*), and the king's way implemented (*yong*) them. Two aspects of the larger activity of ordering the world and comparable in importance, education and government together formed what Li alternately called the Way, the sages' learning, or the learning of essence and application (SSFSL, supplement to *Mengzi*, pt. 1, 2–6).

Li Yong acknowledged that both ways were difficult to maintain, even under favorable conditions. Teaching and educating (*jiaohua*) struggled against inappropriate (often non-moral) instruction (*jiaoshu*), and the way of the king could succumb to the way of the hegemon. Even when the sages' learning was in its ostensible heyday during the Song and Ming, teachers who attempted to teach the sages' learning of *mingti shiyong* (clarifying the essential values and putting them into practice; see Chapter 4) had had to contend with the popularity of literature and art, mere skills in Li Yong's view. Li thus praised Hu Yuan (Anding) of the Northern Song, along with several others (Cao Yuechuan, Hai Gangfeng, and Zhang Lüting) for their noteworthy struggles to maintain the way of the teacher (SSFSL, *Mengzi*, pt. 1, 10).

Li maintained that in his own day there was little teaching, although schools were everywhere. The fact that teachers instructed (and taught for the examinations) but did not teach and educate contributed to the current disorder in society, which in turn was a threat to the survival of society. It was important, however, for schools to strive to educate and not simply offer instruction, because good government depended on a good populace and on the hiring of talented people. Such people would emerge from schools that employed genuine Confucian teachers (SSFSL, *Mengzi*, pt. 1, 9–10). Teachers were needed both for those who would some day take office and for those who never would, because good governance entailed a reciprocal relationship between the rulers and the ruled.

Given this exalted theoretical view of teachers, the actual attitude of many people toward teachers raises questions. Various records, particularly fictional accounts, reveal that in Li's time respect for teachers was by no means universal. Many teachers were ridiculed and treated with disdain.[27] In addition, teaching itself did not have the social status of obtaining an examination degree and becoming an official. The disparity between the ideal of the respected teacher and the reality of the ridiculed instructor can be understood, however, by recognizing that the Chinese, like others, did not separate the teacher from the specific kind of teaching. It mattered what one taught and the conditions under which one taught.

Not interested in the teacher as separate from the tasks of teaching, Confucian philosophers did not think of the teacher as an abstract concept. What was taught was inseparable from who taught. The social role, not the individual person, was the focus. As a teacher, a "great Confucian" differed greatly from a village schoolmaster. The Confucian was concerned with teaching and educating; the schoolmaster instructed. Since the teacher and the kind of teaching formed a single activity, the term "teacher" had more than one kind of referent. Those teachers treated with scorn by Li, and others, were engaged in instructing when they should have been teaching. The respected teacher was occupied with teaching and educating.

Teachers were a matter of concern because thinkers in Li's time and earlier commonly accepted the necessity of having a teacher. For instance, during the Tang, Han Yu had helped to revive the ancient emphasis on the teacher. Combining several ideas, he had argued that a teacher was necessary to transmit the Way, to impart learning, and to help resolve doubts. Since even lower-status people like sorcerers, doctors, musicians, and craftsmen had teachers, there was no reason that scholars should not have them. Han Yu acknowledged that one may have more than one teacher in one's life and urged that age and social status not interfere with selecting a teacher. The important criteria were that the teacher already understood the Way and "specialized in the art of instruction."[28] Song thinkers, for example, Cheng Yi, Yin Tun, Zhu Xi, and Lu Jiuyuan, continued to emphasize the teacher's importance.[29]

Distinguishing between the sage and the ordinary person, Li held that most people need a teacher and that only a sage can achieve what Confucius did without a teacher. Although Confucius supposedly learned the Way (of Kings Wen and Wu) from the people of his time and did not have a regular teacher, he was a sage and so his achievements were possible for him (SSFSL, *Lunyu*, pt. 2, 45; reference to *Lunyu*, 19.22). Many customs and teachings are not in accord with the Way, however, and other paths are prevalent. Not knowing which way to follow, people thus need teachers to learn the genuine Way of the ancient sages (SSFSL, *Lunyu*, pt. 1, 14).

Despite the general agreement on the need for a teacher, other Confucian philosophical ideas do not necessarily lead to this conclusion. Emphasizing self-direction in learning, Confucius said that if he were in a group with two others, he would make one of them his teacher (*Lunyu*, 7.21). Mencius' idea of human moral knowledge did not require, at least in theory, a teacher to help a person develop the moral capacities (*Mencius*, 2A.6, 6A.6). And the stages of learning set forth in the opening passage of the *Great Learning* emphasize self-efforts and do not mention a teacher.

Although the explicit statements of philosophers did not uniformly support the necessity of a teacher, this belief had a firm theoretical grounding in implicit assumptions of the culture. The elite, of course, had reason to keep knowledge as restricted as possible, because their hold on certain kinds of knowledge helped them maintain their privileged social position. A further factor is, however, relevant, namely, the coerciveness of the logic of certain paradigmatic examples. That is, thinkers had no way not to think in terms of the implicit patterns and assumptions of the dominant images. Several of these can be identified.

First, the conception of the family and lineage provided assumptions critical to the position of the teacher. Traditions of thought were conceived in terms of the familial framework, which required a first ancestor and descendants. Thus, it was as necessary to have a teacher as it was to have a father. One could not teach oneself, just as one could not father oneself.

Occupational specialization provided another assumption. Characteristic of the highly stratified Chinese society, specialization was seen as a "natural" aspect of society. Mencius had given voice to this assumption by noting that there were those who governed and those who were governed; there were those who were fed and those who feed others (*Mencius*, 3A.4). Seen in these terms, self-teaching was as unacceptable as self-government. (Nonetheless, there were those, Li Yong among them, who claimed to be autodidacts.) Teaching oneself was comparable to a ruler's growing his own food. Thus Li said, "To build a house one must find large trees. To polish jade one must hire a jeweler. It is foolish indeed to govern and not be concerned with seeking for wise men, and to learn and not be concerned with obtaining a teacher" (SSFSL, supplement to *Mengzi*, pt. 1, 8).

Relevant not only to the question of the "natural" ordering of society, occupational specialization also had a bearing on the issue of achieved versus ascribed status. Some occupations were viewed in terms of personal achievement, whereas others were treated more as matters of ascribed social class. A teacher (achieved status) differed from a farmer or artisan (ascribed status) in respect to how the position was attained. Ideally, one became a teacher, a "genuine" teacher, only through deliberate effort and hard work. In contrast, a person was seen as born into the class of farmers or artisans. Teaching oneself was a difficult, if not impossible, enterprise.

Education was also understood in terms of the cultural pattern of initiation and completion (*shengcheng, shizhong*), a pattern based on the biological cycle and set forth in the opening passage of the *Great Learning*. Accepting the relationship of student and teacher, the *Book of Documents* (4.8.3.5) states, for instance, "To teach is half of learning." Teaching began and learning completed a person's changes and development. In order for something to be completed, it had to have a beginning, and even more, the success of the teacher's teaching depended on the student's learning, and vice versa.[30] Assuming teaching to be inseparable from (subsequent) learning, Li enlarged Mencius' statement that if one lived in idleness without being taught, one would be close to the birds and wild animals, by adding, "If one lives in idleness without learning, then one is close to the birds and wild animals" (SSFSL, *Mengzi*, pt. 1, 11; EQQJ, 10.12b; reference is to *Mencius*, 3A.4).

Whether a person thought in terms of the implicit logic of lineage continuity, occupational specialization, achieved status, or the life pattern of living things, it was so important to have a teacher that one's teacher was invariably identified and the lack of a teacher produced statements of amazement (and admiration) at the person's success. For instance, Gu Yanwu said of Li Yong: "Enduring hardships, he studied diligently. He had no teacher and yet he succeeded. I do not equal Li Zhongfu."[31] Wang Sigen, an older Guanzhong scholar, described Li: "When young he was orphaned, and he had no teacher. He struggled arduously, and he established his aspirations by himself" (EQQJ, 2.3a). And in his account of Li's trip south, Yang Yu, a scholar from Piling who heard Li lecture there, reported how Li was described to him — first, that Li was the magistrate's teacher, and second, that when young, Li was an orphan [that is, he had no fatherly teaching], but still he established the learning of the north (EQQJ, 10.24a).

When Li spoke about others, he often identified that person's teacher or noted that the person had no teacher. All the biographical accounts in Li Yong's *Record of Observations and Impressions* indicate whether these exemplars taught themselves or learned from others. The conditions of learning were treated as a critical aspect of these accounts, as significant as the teachings of these unusual people.

In sum, the necessity of having a teacher was based on assumptions (applied to teaching and learning) that derived from various theoretical frames, including those of genealogy, social order, specialized knowledge, and life in a biological sense. Having a teacher connected a person to the ongoing cultural tradition, and the line of past teachers stretching over numerous generations helped to form the tradition. Just as a ruler theoretically received his authority from heaven, a teacher at least in part received his legitimacy from his teacher. This link was part of a person's participation in the tradition, the Way.

Legitimation involved more, however, than having a teacher. Another question was how a person became, and became recognized as, a "genuine" teacher. This issue was linked to the context of the teaching, not to success in the examinations. Regardless of whether one took the examinations, several conditions were necessary if one were to be acknowledged as an educator or teacher, in contrast to simply an instructor. Although one might become a teacher in government schools through success in the examination system and official appointment, those qualifications did not make one the kind of teacher that interested Li. He considered most teachers in government schools to be mere instructors. He felt that their neglect of education forced it to find support in other settings, including private academies, local Confucian temples, and the homes of the teachers.

The recognition of one's peers was required before one could be acknowledged as a genuine teacher. A teacher's reputation was confirmed first by his peers and later by the tradition. A person could not simply claim special status, for recognition lay in the judgments of others. An instructor, in contrast, was legitimated by students' examination success or by students' behavior, since the examination system itself or the students themselves were the reference of the instruction.

A person gained recognition as a teacher, or "great Confucian," through the right kind of participation in the literati's world. No exam would do it; hence Li's decision not to take the examinations did not disqualify him from becoming a teacher. Li knew, at least in part from his own experience, and Li's mother knew that participation of the wrong kind would probably be an insurmountable obstacle.[32] Since a person's eventual recognition as a teacher depended upon his impact on people (both literati and commoners) and on their acknowledgment of the significance of his teaching, a Confucian did such things as talk, exchange letters, and visit with other scholars; write essays and commentaries; and lecture to groups and work with individual students. Li not only did these things, but he also had close advisory relationships with educational and other kinds of governmental officials.[33] It further helped, but was not absolutely essential, to have some close followers to carry on the teacher's ideas and some admirers to promote his special qualities. Li did have both followers and admirers, in his own time and later.

Third, and perhaps the key to all the conditions, was the ability to teach people appropriately. A teacher had to recognize the nature of his audience, teach at a level that reached that audience, and offer aims appropriate for it. Otherwise there would be no success and, given the Confucian perspective, indeed no teaching. Li apparently knew this. Although he directed much of his teaching to those in the educated, elite class (the would-be teachers or officials), he also addressed people at lower levels of society. His method of teaching was to adjust his teaching to the type and level of student, a method emphasized, incidentally, by Buddhists.

Li Yong lived at a time when Confucians were notably concerned with the question of the audience of teaching. By late Ming and early Qing times, many Confucian philosophers addressed future officials and the masses with their teachings.[34] Li taught all kinds of people and all sizes of audience, and one account reports over a thousand gentry and commoners in the audience (EQQJ, 5.1a). Li apparently took pride in making his teaching appropriate to his listeners, and it is reported that many regarded him as tremendously successful. Unlike some, however, Li rarely, if ever, spoke about the ruler himself as his audience. Although the phenomenon of addressing a large audience was popular during his lifetime, the size of the audience did not fundamentally change the goals of Li's teaching. If the crowd were large, teaching might be seen more as a lecture than a philosophical conversation, but the aim of teaching to change behavior was still present. Teaching was not instructing or lecturing in order to transmit information.

Li and many of his contemporaries openly rejected the view that the audience be potential officials. This issue had been raised as far back as the Song period and had been treated then in different ways. Some philosophers, like Lu Jiuyuan, had addressed large, socially diverse crowds. Others, like Zhu Xi, continued to restrict their talks, but not all their writings, to the elite.[35] Although Zhu Xi may not have lectured personally to the masses, many of his teachings, particularly those concerned with behavior and Confucian rituals, were still directed toward them.[36]

The historical and philosophical reasons for broadening the audience for Confucian teachings were not altogether the same in the twelfth and seventeenth centuries. From a historical perspective, it has been suggested that the growing complexity of Song society presented the masses with alternative models of behavior. In order to keep Confucianism attractive, educators during the Song had to expand Confucian teachings to allow the masses to practice rituals once restricted to the elite.[37] The direct teaching of large crowds thus was related to the effort to broaden the application of Confucian practices in the face of Buddhist and Daoist challenges. From a philosophical viewpoint, teachers provided a supplementary authority, based in the moral heart-mind possessed by everyone. This authority augmented that of the classics.

In Li Yong's time teaching the masses was spurred by a variety of factors, some political, social, and economic, and others intellectual, moral, and spiritual. From a philosophical viewpoint, Li's teaching of large crowds was perhaps most related to his sense of the critical need for practical moral and social action in the face of turbulent social conditions. He thus paired the teaching to apply one's moral knowledge with the ideas that everyone can become a sage and that knowledge and action are one. In wanting to spread his teachings to everyone, Li resembled some of the radical teachers of his age who were followers of Wang Yangming's thought.[38] Unlike them, however, he did not attempt to flout conventional standards of behavior. He went to the other extreme.

A further factor in Li Yong's remarkable reputation as a teacher appears to be his open embodiment of Confucian ideals. In appearance and manner, he was described as serious, moral, determined, and totally committed to teaching. Although many of these descriptions were given by scholars who heard Li when he made his trip south, that is, by people who were particularly struck, even shocked, by the difference between the more luxurious southern cultural style and Li's severe and conservative northern style, other similar accounts were offered by scholars and students in his home province. The reports indicate that they, too, were greatly impressed (EQQJ, 10.20b–28b).

Qiu Hongyu, a scholar from Piling in Jiangsu, for example, described the extraordinary impact that Li Yong made when he went south to teach. He said that as a person Li was quiet and solemn and sought nothing of this world. In his learning, Li emphasized stillness, reverential respect, self-reflection, realization of the Way, and self-renewal through criticism and removal of one's faults. When Qiu asked why Li had come to Piling, he learned that Li had earlier taught Piling County Magistrate Luo when Luo had served in Zhouzhi district. Li had been moved by Luo's virtue and so had responded to his invitation. Li came to teach in Piling to help the magistrate in his educational efforts, and together they helped bring about a great change in the people's hearts and customs. Huge crowds came to hear him, and everyone admired his virtue. Qiu concluded that Li's and Magistrate Luo's accomplishment was not less than that of Mencius (EQQJ, 10.20b–22a).

The account by Wu Guang, another southern scholar, was equally favorable to Li, with comparisons also made to Mencius, and Yang Yu's account was no less effusive (EQQJ, 10.22a–24a). Yang said of Li, "In discussing learning, when he was speaking to those above, his words were lofty, and to those below, his words were lowly. The old, the robust, the young—each according to what was fitting; he established his teaching according to the person" (EQQJ, 10.25a). Yang further reported that people were said to be encouraged and stimulated by what Li said.

Other favorable accounts from the south were written by Zheng Jue and Yang Qiu (EQQJ, 10.26b–27b, 10.27b–28b, respectively). Xu Chao and Zhang Junsheng, both from Piling, took especial note of how Li answered questions without tiring and how exuberant all his auditors were (EQQJ, 5.8a). And at home, the retired Shaanxi scholar Wang Sigen wrote that everyone came to hear Li, from the gentry and the scholars down to the farmers, craftsmen, merchants, and youth. Those of high class and low class, the wise and foolish, and those from far and near all admired and praised him (EQQJ, 2.3a).

Bai Huancai, Li's student from Tongzhou, Shaanxi, described Li's teaching in glowing terms and referred to Li as a "genuine teacher" (*zhen shi*; EQQJ, 2.5a–b). Wang Xinjing, Li's foremost follower and compiler of the account of Li's southern trip, reported that huge crowds, of several thousand people of all classes, came to hear him (EQQJ, 9.9b). Magistrate Luo Zhonglin agreed; it was not just the commoners—all the worthies and the officials respected Li Yong as a teacher (EQQJ, 12.1a). A student, Zhang Er, contributed further to the accounts of Li by recording how Li's teaching had encouraged him to abandon the dissolute life he had been living and to reform himself (EQQJ, 7.1a–b).

Such accounts indicate the judgments that led to Li Yong's being hailed as a "genuine teacher." There was no formally recognized process comparable to the examination system by which Li (or anyone else) became acknowledged as a genuine teacher. It can be seen, however, that as a teacher Li behaved similarly to some of the great Confucian teachers of the past, such as Lu Jiuyuan and Wang Yangming, who had taught all classes of people. The genuine quality that people perceived in Li's actions helped gain him the respect of those whom he taught. The "genuine" teacher served as a clear, moral alternative to the self-serving degreeholder.

The recruitment of students was an additional aspect of the issue of the genuine teacher. Since there was no formal recruitment process, Li attracted students to him by his teaching and personal behavior. Some became students or followers after having heard him speak, and some, as in the case of Magistrate Luo Zhonglin, after having been impressed by his filial actions. Some were older than Li, and some were younger. Recruitment depended upon the interest of those wanting to learn.

Although one might wonder whether Li's focus on the way of the teacher was linked in some way to the Confucian imperative to establish a name for oneself and so acquire lasting fame, an answer to this question is outside the scope of this study — if the question is asked strictly in terms of personal motivation.[39] This imperative in its best sense concerned the goal to be seen as an embodiment of the ideals of the Confucian tradition, not as a particular historical person with unique characteristics. That is, the focus was not on the private self and individual personality but on the social self as a carrier of cultural values. If we assume that Li wanted to be recognized as a "great Confucian" or "genuine teacher," we must also recognize that, when Li Yong discussed himself at all, he discussed himself in reference to others and the cultural tradition, not in personal terms. Indeed, the most personal characteristic recorded about him was that his behavior throughout his life was greatly motivated by his sense of filial duty.

Li Yong was adamant that a genuine Confucian did not aim at such things as fame, wealth, or rank. A Confucian's goal should be achievements for others, and if he were successful, like Yao, Shun, Yu, or Confucius, fame would naturally follow. The motivations for a person's acts were seen as critical and distinguished a superior person from a petty person (SSFSL, *Lunyu*, pt. 1, 53–56). In Li's view, the aim of becoming a "great Confucian" was a quite different matter from that of merely "establishing one's name." He saw the former as setting one's sights on the primary task of achievement for society, whereas the latter sought secondary, and ultimately selfish, matters.

In sum, the way of the teacher completed the way of the virtuous king. The way of the teacher was to teach for society and for the ages, and it had its own implicit rules of legitimation. Becoming recognized as an educator or genuine teacher occurred apart from the official structures of the examination system. The teacher's way was seen as having been begun by the ancient sages and Confucius and followed by such later teachers as Zhu Xi and Wang Yangming. Li saw his own behavior in reference to this tradition. Invoking the great teachers and sages of the past, his formal appearance and restrained behavior gained cultural significance from the facts that he was participating in the multi-generational way of the teacher and that he was recognized by others as doing so.

Verbal Teaching (yanjiao) and Behavioral Teaching (shenjiao)

Li's interest in the aim of knowledge led him to address the issue of the proper content of teaching, an issue that had occupied philosophers since the time of Confucius. The paired concepts of verbal or "word" teaching (*yanjiao*) and behavioral or "self" teaching (*shenjiao*) pointed to the central conflict, which was also suggested by another pair, the teacher of the classics (*jingshi*) and the teacher of humaneness (*renshi*; SSFSL, *Lunyu*, pt. 1, 46). Possessing an ambiguity exploited by philosophers, the terms "verbal teaching" and "behavioral teaching" could refer to teaching texts (words) and teaching appropriate behavior, they could refer to teaching with words and teaching with behavior, and they could (and did) mean both.

Not accepting the primary importance of textual knowledge, or knowledge contained in words, Li claimed that behavior, not words, was to be taught (see, for example, SSFSL, *Mengzi*, pt. 2, 16, and *Lunyu*, pt. 2, 116). The behavior in question consisted of knowing how to act appropriately in any situation. The teacher tried to teach the learner how to know a situation, to recognize critical junctures, and to shape his or her actions accordingly. What was appropriate varied with the person and situation (SSFSL, *Lunyu*, pt. 1, 43).

Although not always the case, words were usually necessary in this kind of teaching. For Li, the danger was that the learner's interest would stop with a mastery of the texts and would not go on to a realization of the ideas (SSFSL, *Lunyu*, pt. 1, 41–42). Li considered both teaching with words and teaching with behavior important, and he recognized the difficulties of the latter (SSFSL, *Lunyu*, pt. 1, 45–46). On the learner's side, learning the words was important, but certainly it was not identical to their practice (EQQJ, preface by Wang Xinjing; SSFSL, *Lunyu*, pt. 1, 41–42, pt. 2, 21). The appropriate practice was also not sufficient, for the learner should understand the broader cultural significance of the behavior.

Li implicitly supported the assumptions that much behavior is a form of knowledge and so can be taught and that knowledge is a form of behavior and so does not necessarily require words. These ideas were related to the philosophical question of whether knowledge becomes knowledge only when expressed in words. This issue was argued early in Chinese thought, and a well-known reference to it occurs, for example, in a passage in the *Mencius*, in which Gaozi was charged with relying too heavily on words. Gaozi supposedly believed that if something were to be known, it had to be known in words (*Mencius*, 2A.2).[40] Other kinds of knowledge, such as "knowing how" or "acquaintance," were not at issue here.

Li held that genuine knowledge is not something gained from outside oneself, as is the case with the content of texts, nor is it something just from within. It is a person's "natural" and appropriate responses to the ever-changing circumstances of life, and it further involves reviewing and correcting one's thoughts and actions. Borrowing a Daoist phrase, Li said it is "actionless action" (SSFSL, *Lunyu*, pt. 1, 47). This kind of knowledge is closely related to the adaptive concept of *quan*, to weigh a situation and act accordingly. Given that principles were seen as unchanging whereas events constantly changed, Li maintained that genuine knowledge consists of knowing how to adapt and act while still following the Way (SSFSL, *Lunyu*, pt. 1, 54).

Like others before him, Confucians as well as Daoists, Li recognized in some way that not all knowledge is stored in words and that the human capacities to be developed from teaching have both behavioral and verbal aspects. The capacity that Li emphasized, that is, to judge a situation and act appropriately (in a moral sense), has some similarities to what Lisa Raphals has termed "metic intelligence." Not culturally recognized as a distinct type of knowledge, and including wisdom as well as cunning, this kind of knowledge is a practical (as opposed to theoretical) kind of knowledge and is based on the assumption that "reality and language cannot be understood (or manipulated) in straightforward 'rational' terms but must be approached by subtlety, indirection, and even cunning."[41] Li's conception is not quite the same, however, in that, for him, genuine knowledge has definite moral dimensions and refers to social realities more extensive than a person's immediate personal circumstances.

Whether this kind of knowledge can be taught was a real question, for Li Yong, and others, suggested that some things can be learned but cannot be taught. In matters of genuine knowledge, a teacher can only point the way. Although the Chinese were not especially interested in analyzing this problem, for in a sense they already "knew" the answer, a modern explanation for this could be that such knowledge was (and is) not fully understood. Although it can be learned, not enough is known about it in an analytic sense to teach it in a deliberate and explicit way.

Ancient Chinese thinkers of all philosophical schools recognized behavioral knowledge, or aspects of it, but they were interested in it in different contexts. Confucians usually (but not always) thought of it in terms of social and moral situations, Daoists emphasized a sagely and a skillful type of "knowing how," and military thinkers related it to strategy. Zhuangzi, for instance, referred to this kind of knowledge when he spoke of wheelwright Pian, who said of his knowledge, "I can't teach it to my son, and he can't learn it from me."[42] Sounding like a Daoist, Mencius also acknowledged that "a carpenter or a carriage-maker may give a man the circle and square, but cannot make him skillful in the use of them."[43]

Li recalled that even Confucius had confronted the problem of students' paying more attention to the words than to what they were concerned with. Li said that Confucius demonstrated his teachings with his actions, and yet his followers only sought his teachings in his words. Confucius therefore explained his "not-concealed" qualities (the behavior that he was teaching) to admonish them. Li further noted that the idea here was similar to Confucius' point that Heaven did not speak and yet the four seasons and all things were produced (SSFSL, *Lunyu*, pt. 1, 45; references to *Lunyu*, 7.23, 17.19).

Recognizing the difficulty of teaching this kind of knowledge, Li said that the teacher had to use both verbal teaching and behavioral teaching. Even verbal teaching, however, still had the purpose of teaching "this behavior." In Li's view, moreover, verbal teaching did not equal the lessons a student learned by observing and responding (SSFSL, *Lunyu*, pt. 1, 45). Li used the paired terms *guan gan*, "observe and respond," to indicate what the learner must do. The learner must observe situations in which the teacher was demonstrating something and then try to apply to other situations what he or she had learned. What was learned, however, was not something that the learner had grasped to the point of being able to say it in words. That is, neither the learner nor the teacher knew in a fully conceptual or analytic way all aspects of what was taught and learned.

Providing some examples, Li claimed that the way Zengzi taught

Gongming Xuan ranked second to the way Confucius taught his followers (SSFSL, *Lunyu*, pt. 1, 45–46). For instance, when Gongming Xuan went to Zengzi's gate, he saw Zengzi sitting in the courtyard making threatening noises, but they were not as extreme as those of a dog or horse. At another time Gongming Xuan saw Zengzi responding to guests in a respectful and restrained way, and yet he was not remiss. A third time Gongming Xuan saw Zengzi sitting in audience with the king. Zengzi was stern to his subordinates, and yet he did not injure them. Gongming Xuan learned from all three situations by observing and responding. Li concluded (reminiscent of Zhuangzi) by noting that wordless teaching did not enter through the ear but was received by the mind. After it was rooted in one's mind, it was seen in one's actions (SSFSL, *Lunyu*, pt. 1, 46).

In addition to teaching behavior with behavior, Li tried to teach with behavior that epistemological state of stillness seen as comparable to the extrasensory state of the whole. Only a few examples of this kind of behavioral teaching are found in the accounts of Li. There was, for instance, the occasion when the classics scholar Ma Yushi asked Li about the main teaching of the Six Classics. It is recorded that Li became silent, thus demonstrating it with his stillness. Uncertain at first, Ma Yushi suddenly realized what Li was doing. When asked to explain, Ma replied, "The soundless and odorless are what the Six Classics emerge from and also are what the Six Classics return to" (EQQJ, 9.8a–b).

Another time, in the evening when the moon was low and everyone had finished his tea, those gathered around asked Li for instruction. Li sat silently for a long time. When the crowd saw that he did not speak, they again asked. Li then laughed and said, "I already have spoken" (EQQJ, 10.6b). In these cases the root or the Way, conceived as an original state of silence and stillness, was the goal of learning, and Li was attempting to demonstrate its ontological and epistemological dimensions.

Even the sophisticated teachings of the philosophers were recognized as based on earlier stages of behavioral teaching. Prenatal teaching by the mother was the first step in the teaching process, which was seen as a continuum from the earliest molding to instruction and schooling and eventually to education in sagely learning. The way the mother behaved in all matters, including sitting, walking, eating, and standing, was thought to influence the baby's development. The *Biographies of Virtuous Women* says, for instance,

> In ancient times, when a woman was pregnant, she slept without lying on her side; she sat without leaning to one side; she stood squarely on both feet; she did not eat things with bad flavors; she did not eat meat cut incorrectly; she did not sit on mats not straightened; her eyes did not look at wicked sights; her ears did not listen to depraved sounds; at night then she commanded the musicians to chant poetry; and with correct reasoning, she adjusted affairs. If she behaved like this, then her child's appearance would be correct and his talent would surpass that of others. [44]

Other texts (cited by Li) reflected the importance of teaching by behavioral example, including the *Book of Rites* and Zhu Xi's *Elementary Learning*.[45]

From the time a small child could eat or talk, even as early as one year, it was taught behavior appropriate to its age and ability. The teaching of moral and social behavior was supplemented by instruction in school. Once the student learned to read, the distinction between moral knowledge as behavior and moral knowledge as things known abstractly or intellectually became increasingly pronounced. To indicate his disapproval of the separation between the text and the moral behavior it taught, Li referred to those who focused on the texts as "sections-and-phrases pedants" (*zhangju shusheng*), not students (*xuesheng*; EQQJ, 16.34b).

Recognizing, however, that verbal teaching (in both senses) was necessary, Li addressed two key topics disputed by Confucian thinkers. One was whether teaching texts and reading books were necessary parts of learning; the other concerned the activity called "discussing learning" (see, for example, SSFSL, *Lunyu*, pt. 1, 45–46, and pt. 2, 83; also EQQJ, 3.9b–10a, 16.35b). Although Li's contemporaries held a variety of attitudes toward texts and reading, Li was most critical of those whose interests were literary and seemed to focus on the texts themselves.

> The Confucian school [originally] regarded virtuous action as its root and literature as its branches. Later generations, however, have solely regarded literature as their concern, and so one can see the changes in the times. After later generations began to emphasize only literature, the superiors regulated the inferiors with it, and the inferiors responded to the superiors with it. Fathers and teachers taught it, and sons and younger brothers learned it. . . . But what benefit to the heart-mind and what aid to the Way of the world do the marks on paper have? (SSFSL, *Lunyu*, pt. 2, 70)

Li did not condone the rejection of texts and reading, whether for reasons of contemplative thought or "practical" social and political action. Like Zhu Xi, Li believed that reading was essential to becoming a Confucian, and he advocated an extensive program of reading that included the major classical, philosophical, and historical texts, and a few literary works as well. Li emphasized that the object of reading was still the kind of behavior presented in the texts.

> The Six Classics are the words of the ancient sages and worthies for saving the world. Every word and every phrase was established for the [moral] mind and nature of later generations of people. Today people only pay attention to the written words when reading and do not embody the teachings of the ancients. . . . Therefore, they investigate the classics until their hair is white, and in the end there is no benefit to their own mind and nature. The teaching of the *Book of Poetry*, for instance, originally aimed to teach people to copy what is fitting for them to copy and to avoid what is fitting for them to avoid, to do good and to expel evil. (SSFSL, *Lunyu*, pt. 1, 9)

Li Yong remained skeptical about literature. When he was asked whether it was permissible not to study literature, he responded that it depended on the kind of literature. Many things, such as knowledge for the future and from the past, imperial plans, and the transmission of the Way, would not be spread without literature. One had to study this kind of literature. However, there was a natural order to follow in learning. A person first had to "establish the root"; only then could he engage in literary activities. Otherwise, even if one produced writings as great as the histories of Ban Gu and Sima Qian and the poetry of Li Bai and Du Fu, such writings would still be nothing more than the work of a mere essayist or poet (SSFSL, *Lunyu*, pt. 2, 2).

Li approved of reading because texts were necessary for preserving and transmitting cultural experience beyond the boundaries of one's own life. The implementation of certain values was always the goal, however. Reading was a tool—valued, useful, and indispensable—but not an end in itself. Probably no Confucian truly regarded texts as an end in themselves, but many valued them far more than Li did. Li's argument was not with texts, but with what he regarded as misplaced aims and a wrong conception of knowledge.

A second issue connected to verbal teaching was the activity called "discussing learning" (*jiangxue*).[46] By the seventeenth century this controversial practice was associated especially with Wang Yangming and was severely criticized for lacking the "factual" and "concrete" nature of evidential research and historical learning. It (and Wang's thought) had become so discredited that Yang Yu commented in amazement that Li regarded discussing learning as the first thing to do and that Li's ideas expanded on those of Wang Yangming (EQQJ, 10.24b).

For Li, the *xue* (learning) in *jiangxue* (discussing learning) referred not to ideas but to a person's efforts to act morally (EQQJ, 10.7a–b, 10.13a). This was Li's point when he said, "The ways of teaching [*jiaofa*] are that by which one nourishes human talent."[47] And, "That by which learning is learning is this cultivation of virtue. If virtue is not cultivated, then learning is not genuine learning. Discussing learning is precisely the method of clarifying the cultivation of virtue. If one does not discuss, then one will not have a path by which to enter virtue" (SSFSL, *Lunyu*, pt. 1, 41). Li went on to mention the importance of having a plan and then actually taking action.

Li's advocacy of this practice was tied to his view of genuine knowledge. If knowledge consisted of verbal skills and the content of texts, discussing learning indeed made little sense as a way to teach and learn. For Li, however, a purely textual and abstract conception of knowledge was erroneous. And the task of determining the correct wording of ancient, possibly corrupted, texts had no relevance to Li's view that philosophical knowledge involved forming and acting on appropriate ideas in particular situations. For Li Yong, knowledge was developed in part in the context of the philosophical conversation, an activity that emphasized the relationship of the social context to philosophical thought. Having reference to social matters, philosophical ideas emerged in relation to issues and situations. The very manner of the presentation of ideas was an aspect of what was being taught. That is, while recognizing that particular responses could not be taught ahead of time, teachers taught the behavior of responding to content and adapting it to specific situations.

Evidential research scholars claimed to oppose the practice of discussing learning because of its association with neo-Confucian speculative thought, which they rejected. In Li's view, however, this link was based on faulty analysis. Although Li was not an evidential research scholar, he, too, attacked speculative thought for its lack of practical usefulness, but unlike the evidential research scholars, he supported the practice of discussing learning. Li held that this practice was a teaching activity appropriate to a particular conception of knowledge, one that differed from that assumed by evidential and historical research scholars and by those interested in ontological speculation.

Li claimed that the practice of discussing learning was not about clarifying and explaining ontological concepts and their relationships but was concerned with helping people examine their thought and conduct so that they could improve themselves. Since learning was not the memorization and recitation of words and phrases, discussing learning was not the discussion of these same words and phrases. Learning consisted of efforts to "preserve the mind and restore the nature in order to fulfill the oughtness of the human way," and so discussing learning meant that one discussed both ideas and action (*ti* and *yong*), not only ideas (EQQJ, 11.3a).

Li further pointed out that rightness, the Heaven-decreed standard of right and wrong (*ming*), modesty, and shame were the basic virtues a person cultivated in establishing the self. If any of these were defective, then the foundation lacked stability. One therefore did not need to talk about the mysterious or discuss the marvelous. As long as one exerted effort on the foundation, one was a follower of Confucius and Mencius. Otherwise, learning was just a case of "ten thousand words and one thousand terms." A person may know all the characters to complete the classics but would be able to do nothing in regard to transmitting them to future generations (EQQJ, 10.7b–8a).

Li suggested that textual scholars did not engage in discussing learning because they missed the point of what learning truly was. On one occasion, for instance, Li approached a group of scholars disputing alternative explanations of the classical texts. Questioning what they were doing, Li insisted that there was nothing in what the classics transmitted that was not the Way of cultivating the self and ruling others. Previous thinkers had led the way by clearing up doubts and pointing out delusions. When they had discussed and had clearly understood a path, then they took that path. Once a path was completed, there was no harm in discussing another path. If, however, one just closed the door, discussed things repeatedly, and explained faults over and over as these scholars were doing, in a little while one would be speaking of having gone ten thousand miles, when in actuality one had not taken one step. This, Li claimed, was the trouble with evidential research scholars (EQQJ, 10.11b). They disputed the words without reference to the contexts of action.

Li also pointed out that discussing learning had to be done regularly. A person's spirit and feelings became active from discussing, and so became more refined and advanced every day. When one did not discuss, one's efforts declined, one lost one's aim, and morality became obscured. One became just like those people who shut their doors and sat quietly. They discussed all day long but never went out to investigate the road (EQQJ, 3.11b–12a). A person who did not discuss was like the traveler who started out without carefully determining the way beforehand, while saying, "I value action, not talk." Such a person, Li claimed, ended up simply going around in circles (EQQJ, 3.12a). Actions were important, but they were useless unless focused, and that focus was attained through the practice of discussing learning.

Emphasizing the importance and daily necessity of this practice to the learner, Li claimed (echoing Mencius) that benevolence was more important to the people than were water and fire. People could perhaps go without water and fire for a day, but certainly they could not do without learning for a day. Hence they could not dispense with discussing for a day. Li said that when they discussed, people knew their affinities. If they daily and monthly washed out their impurities and faults, moral principles would be constantly preserved, and the human mind would not be destroyed. Those who did not engage in discussing learning would become reckless. Because they would not know the aims they should pursue, they would act blindly and without restraint and would only follow their passions (EQQJ, 12.5a–b; reference to *Lunyu*, 15.34, and *Mencius*, 3A.4).

Li assumed that human passions were natural and emerged without effort. They were not learned, and they did not have a pattern or direction in themselves. Behavior based only on passions, however, without any deliberate direction given them, could not help but be disorderly and unfocused. This kind of uncontrolled behavior was thought to be characteristic of wild animals and barbarians in contrast to the civilized Chinese, and of the lower classes in contrast to the elite.[48]

Li held that the practice of discussing learning was essential for all spheres of activity and all classes of people. To use Li's terms, "to establish oneself as a person and succeed at being a person, to change customs and alter behavior, to attack disorder and restore order, to revolve *qian* and turn over *kun* [live in harmony with the movements of the natural world]" — all these things lay completely in discussing learning. Whether one were "superior and [so] virtuous, or inferior and [so] vulgar," there was nothing not due to discussing learning. If the practice were stopped, the original *qi* of the universe would be lost and the springs of life destroyed (EQQJ, 12.5b).

Although discussing learning was an activity that applied to everyone, most people required help. A great man was needed to provide the leadership to extend the practice from one person to all persons and from one place to all places, so that everyone's moral capacities would be realized. The great man restored social order by helping people develop their own moral capacities, not by forcing them to adhere to fixed standards. Although the actions of individual people were important, history (as understood by Li) convinced him that social order would never just emerge if all people behaved morally on their own, without strong guidance.

Li further held that the duty of the great man was to act like Confucius, who acted on behalf of Heaven, to reveal and transmit the human (moral) mind, and to awaken the world from its sleep. Confucius, Li claimed, preserved the subtle and the rare on behalf of the world and the myriad past generations. Although other sages had relied on political power to accomplish their achievements, Confucius was different, for he had no political position. That is why he was a sage, and a sage that others could not equal. Li went on to say that Confucius was like the wooden clapper of a bell in spreading the teachings for all to hear. "Establishing his words and hanging up his instructions, he was the wooden clapper for ten thousand generations" (SSFSL, *Lunyu*, pt. 1, 25).

Li's style of engaging in the practice of discussing learning reflected the contemporary interest in verifiable evidence. His answers are thus filled with historical data and citations from the classics, although admittedly in a highly selective way. Often selecting great men, or exemplars, from the recent past, he especially favored Wang Yangming and Feng Congwu. Li claimed that Wang's efforts enabled learning to become as brilliant as the midday sun (EQQJ, 12.6a–b; see *Mencius*, 6A.8 and 6A.11).

Li also recounted how, when Feng was once lecturing in the early 1620's, he was asked how he could discuss learning at a time of such political turmoil. Feng's reply was to ask how could one not discuss learning at such a time, for this practice made clear the duties between father and son and between ruler and minister and aroused feelings of loyalty and love to ruler and country. It was precisely the first-order task in urgent times (EQQJ, 12.6b). When Feng was pressed further about the need to discuss such duties, since these moral principles were (believed) inherent in everyone, Feng replied that they should not be discussed if everyone did not have them. That would be as futile as polishing a brick to make it shine. But, he asked, if these principles were possessed by everyone and only obscured by obsessions with achievement and fame, position and wealth, then how could they not be discussed? Discussing learning was like polishing a mirror to make it bright (EQQJ, 12.6b–8a).

Although evidential scholars and those, like Yan Yuan, who emphasized practical action criticized this practice as a cause of current problems, Li could not agree. Discussing learning was an activity of teaching appropriate to the kind of practical moral knowledge that teachers and leaders aimed to develop. It was compatible with a conception of knowledge (or learning) that did not separate knowledge and action. The criticisms of it were based, however, on a different conception of knowledge, one conceived primarily in terms of textual content.

In addition to reading and discussing learning, academy regulations and guidelines constituted a third kind of verbal (and behavioral) teaching by Li. Regulations for learning were seen as necessary for schools and academies, and Zhu Xi's "Articles for Learning" served as the primary model for numerous Song and Ming academies.[49] In addition to Zhu Xi's articles, several Ming versions were important to Li, including the school regulations of Hu Juren (1434–84) and the assembly compact of the Donglin Academy. Li's regulations for learning highlight his conception of learning and can be seen in his assembly compact, written for the Guanzhong Academy (EQQJ, 13). Whereas Zhu Xi's articles were general in nature, offering fundamental moral principles, Li Yong's regulations, and those of other academies, provided detailed guidelines for daily conduct.

In his preface to Li's assembly compact, Hong Zong, the provincial superintendent of education, discussed the relationship between Li's view of teaching and his regulations. Hong pointed out that there have always been warnings, prohibitions, and regulations to help guide people in their moral conduct. Zhang Zai's *Western Inscription* and Cheng Yi's "four prohibitions" were two examples from the Song. Confucians assumed that if one understood moral principles clearly and practiced them fully, then external self-regulation allowed one to nourish what was inside. Carefulness at the beginning led to success at the end. Hong said that Li was responding to the provincial governor's plan to "transform the people and perfect their customs," and learning was the first step. Relying on the comprehensiveness of the classics, Li had recorded the essentials of the ancient sages and worthies and had used other writings, from the Song and earlier. Hong observed that Li's comments were divided into three sections—Confucian behavior, the assembly compact, and the learning schedule—and thus his learning truly was the practical learning of "manifesting the inner." Although people now were interested only in written words, not in discussing learning, Wang Yangming and others had benefited from that practice. Hong also noted that Zhu Xi's regulations for the White Deer Hollow Academy had had a great influence on Li (EQQJ, 13.1a–2b).

Acknowledging that he based his articles for the Guanzhong Academy on the *Book of Rites*, Li emphasized that a true Confucian was so by his behavior, not by the "surface" characteristics of his Confucian clothes or Confucian words. Li's schedule for learning stipulated explicitly what to do from the time of arising in the morning to the time of retiring at night. Recommended activities included reading, working, and meditating (EQQJ, 13.3a–15a). Giving instruction on how to be a genuine Confucian, Li's regulations were thus compatible with those written earlier by others.

Li thus viewed teaching as the primary responsibility of the Confucian philosophical tradition. As the actions of the ancient sages and sage rulers demonstrated, this task was inseparable from governing. The size and shape of the responsibility of teaching varied widely, for teaching existed in reference to different time frames, ranging from the time of particular tasks to the time of social relations to the time of governmental concerns to the time of history. Despite the teacher's importance, the teacher did not bear all the responsibility. The learner was ultimately responsible for learning.[50] For Li Yong, teachers were the great heroes who periodically appeared and saved the age (EQQJ, 12.6a). Without them, civilized society had no chance of enduring.

4 Li Yong's Teachings

THE NATURE OF PHILOSOPHICAL TEACHINGS

This chapter examines four specific teachings of Li Yong in view of two different contexts. One is epistemological; the other sociopolitical. The epistemological perspective involves consideration of Li's teachings in terms of fundamental assumptions and issues. The sociopolitical perspective treats certain historical conditions, which Li regarded as a critical aspect of the theoretical structure of teachings.

For Li, the task of philosophy was to diagnose the ills of society and then offer teachings that provided the most appropriate treatment. Although the teachings of the ancient sages were highly valued, they could not be duplicated literally in later times. The fundamental values remained, but the manner of their implementation had to change with historical and social conditions. Not intended for all time, the successive teachings of the philosophers were applications of the sages' standards to specific conditions.

As early as the pre-Qin period, philosophers of different persuasions had used the concept of timeliness (*shi*) to indicate the idea of an interdependent relationship among the ideas, practices, and conditions of an age.[1] Li's position that philosophers' teachings, like ritual action, are context-bound reflected this view. The notion of timeliness is seen, for instance, in Li's teaching that method properly begins with one's illnesses (*bing*), or in his defense of Wang Yangming's views on the basis of their appropriateness to the times, not on the basis of some abstract rightness (EQQJ, 6.4a, 16.2a). Nonetheless, Li Yong and others were aware of how the value of timeliness could be subverted, for as Feng Congwu pointed out, the sages had established certain practices (*quan*) in order to preserve the constant values (*jing*), but later people had used the practices to cast aside the values.[2]

Philosophical teachings consisted of more than a thinker's explicit statements. They were set within the framework of the sages' unchanging values, and they implicitly included ideas about the relevant context of their application. Teachings appropriate for one time were likely not to be appropriate for another. This did not mean that novelty was prized—it was not, if it meant challenging the sages' values. Li did hold, however, that a certain originality in responding to the conditions was needed (EQQJ, 16.17a). On one level, Li Yong's teachings addressed the particular social and political problems of the age, but on another they can be seen as responses to certain perennial philosophical issues. Li's ideas had reference to both a philosophical and a political context, and the philosophical context provided the implicit theoretical concerns that shaped explicit philosophical positions in the political world.[3] Existing in a reciprocal relationship, the two contexts legitimated each other.

Philosophical teachings were often encapsulated in slogans, called "prescriptions" (*fang*) by Li and his Guanxue predecessors Feng Congwu and Zhang Shundian. Overlapping and mutually reinforcing, the four that best represent Li's position during the period of his political engagement consist of: "clarify learning" (*ming xueshu*), "comprehend the essence and put it into practice" (*mingti shiyong*), "[learn] for the sake of the self" (*wei ji*), and "criticize and eliminate your faults and renew yourself" (*huiguo zixin*). As Li became increasingly reclusive with the realization that the Manchus would be successful in establishing a new dynasty, he turned to advocating the teachings of "silently know through reflective contemplation" (*fanguan moshi*) and "deeply examine human nature" (*qianxin xingming*).[4] Only the first four are discussed here, however, because they are the ones particularly relevant to teaching and learning.

THE TEACHINGS

Clarify Learning

Directed toward Confucian teachers and bureaucratic officials as the leaders in society, Li's prescription to make learning clear focused on

Confucian learning itself as critical to solving social and political problems. Li used this teaching to attack contemporary intellectual trends and to raise (and answer) the question of the proper conception of learning. Stressing both analysis and action, Li addressed, among other aspects, the reasons that learning should be clear, what will happen if it is or is not clear, how to characterize unclear learning, and what to do to make it clear or understood.

Li organized his ideas around two originally separate, but mutually reinforcing, cultural themes: the necessity of a powerful leader to lead the (formless) masses, and the utility of correlation and resonance to understanding behavior. Both of these themes are found in ancient thinkers and persisted through time in some form; the belief in the need for a leader especially recalls the thought of Mencius and Confucius, and the explanation of behavior in terms of correlation and resonance is found in the *Book of Change*.[5] Closer in time to his own age, Li continued the efforts of Feng Congwu and Zhang Shundian with this teaching.

Li began by stating that learning should be made clear in order to attain the Confucian aim of peace and harmony in the world. He claimed that all the sages, or "the first apprehenders" (*xianjue*), had advocated ways to aid the world and attain order according to the conditions of the times. Just as a sick person takes medicine fitting the illness, so their teachings (*dao*) were designed to fit specific conditions. To Li, society, like the human body, had different kinds of illnesses, which needed different medicines. In his own time, the sages' teachings were obscured, social problems were widespread, and people did not know what to do (EQQJ, 10.7a–b).

To show how the teachings of past philosophers had functioned in a therapeutic way, Li briefly reviewed selected historical illnesses and the teachings that had cured them. Although Li's selection of events was similar to that in Zhu Xi's account of the *daotong* (transmission of the Way), his interpretation of history differed. Zhu was interested in establishing the correct line of the transmission of the *dao*, whereas Li emphasized the healing function of philosophical teachings. According to Li, learning (*xueshu*) had been characterized by a broad pattern of recurring decline and revival from the Warring States period to the present age of decline (EQQJ, 10.7a–b).

Following Mencius, who represented a revival of learning, there was a decline until the Song Confucians. After Zhu Xi, learning again declined, but the world was saved by Wang Yangming. The decline after Wang was reversed by Gu Xiancheng and Gao Panlong of the Donglin Academy and Feng Congwu of the Guanzhong Academy. However, contemporary learning was once again exhibiting illnesses (EQQJ, 10.7a–b; for a translation of this passage, see p. 52). In further comments on the current decadent state of learning, Li mentioned that the Ming thinker Luo Qinshun (Zheng'an) had truly followed Zhu Xi's teachings, but now those teachings were no longer clear and people did not know the meaning of genuine learning. Those Confucians interested in morality pursued pedantic concerns about chapters and sections, whereas those who were refined and elegant cared only for frivolous writings. It was impossible to overstate the harm done to the Way and the human mind. Li noted that Feng Congwu had appeared after Luo and attempted to counteract the trends of corruption and pedantry (EQQJ, 15.9b–10a).

Although the Chinese tradition offered a variety of terms to refer to the sage rulers, Li chose a term (*xianjue*) associated with (and used by) Mencius and Confucius that particularly emphasized the idea of understanding a situation before others. For Li, such intellectual capacities as perception, understanding, and analysis were critical features of sagely rule. If the ruler's analysis were correct, good rule would follow, just as health was thought to follow a good diagnosis and appropriate treatment.[6] A great leader had to be perceptive; nothing could be done if great officials do not care about this world. Those who do care must begin by grounding their efforts in "the great root of the world," that is, the human (moral) mind, and by arousing people to action. "And yet if one would arouse human minds, [one must] make learning clear. Today this is the most important thing to do to save the world" (EQQJ, 12.3a).

Placing the responsibility on leaders, Li claimed that if learning is clear, the world will have order. If it is not, there will be disorder. Order and disorder are due to the uprightness and depravity of people's motivations, and motivations reflect the clarity and obscurity of learning. Clarity and obscurity of learning arise, moreover, from what officials love. Genuine learning will be clear if they love genuine learning, and if it is clear, then people's motivations will be correct. If their motivations are correct, then the transforming power of good rule will prevail. Genuine learning will be obscured, however, if officials are fond of "words and phrases," and if it is obscured, people's motivations will not be correct. If their motivations are not correct, the transforming power of good rule will not flourish.

"What the superiors love the inferiors complete. The mechanism of movement and response works like a shadow or an echo" (EQQJ, 12.4b).

Li further emphasized the moral responsibility of those in higher political positions. Using political terms that applied to the Warring States period, Li claimed that if the emperor truly carried out his teaching of criticizing and eliminating one's faults and renewing oneself (*huiguo zixin*, discussed below), the perfection of the ruler would be established and the world would consequently become pacified. If the feudal lords carried out this teaching, the standard of the lords would be true and their states would consequently be well ordered. If the great officials did this, then the way of the minister would be established and families would consequently be in harmony. If the officers and commoners followed this teaching, then virtuous activity would daily prosper and the self would consequently be cultivated (EQQJ, 1.3b).

Alluding to Mencius, Li said that the harm of physical danger, like flooding water and wild animals, is limited to the body, but the harm of unclear learning is far more serious, for that affects the heart-mind. People can escape physical harm, however severe. But not so mental harm, for that makes one unaware of oneself. It is like being drunk or deep asleep in a dream. Li feared, moreover, that the government's activities would result in mental harm (EQQJ, 12.4a). Without a superior person, a hero, Confucian learning would not become clear, and people would not know what to do. Li compared the appearance and the power of a hero to the luminosity of the sun — its brightness comes from within itself. And yet, like the brightness of the sun, the effectiveness of the hero's actions depends on external conditions.

The hero had to be a teacher, for various, unwanted kinds of knowledge could flourish when moral learning was not known. Li claimed that some kinds were deficient forms of Confucian knowledge, but others represented separate systems of thought altogether. Not only could broad (Confucian) learning be erroneously confused with mixed learning, but there also existed the dangerous other paths of Daoism and Buddhism (EQQJ, 14.6b). Great teachers were the Confucian philosophers, whose teachings fit the urgencies of the times. People needed teachers to show them the sages' way, just as they needed political leaders to bring about order. Despite being a notable exception himself, Li Yong held that it was the rare person who could successfully teach himself (EQQJ, preface by Wang Sifu, 3a, to *juan* 2). Not having a constant teacher usually resulted in confusion. Even Zhu Xi, who in Li Yong's view became "the master teacher of ten thousand generations," had no teacher and therefore no direction in his youth and so become entangled with Buddhism and Daoism (EQQJ, 7.4a, 1.9b). Very few could overcome a handicap as Zhu Xi had.

Li Yong's admonition to make learning clear further relied on the ideas of correlation and resonance to understand the pattern of how things happened. Whether phrased in terms of beginning and completion, or movement and response, this pattern suggested that the genuine accomplishment of one aspect (the beginning or movement) led to the other (the completion or response). And the completion or response confirmed the beginning or the movement. A great teacher thus began by making learning clear, and this action, in turn, led to behavior by people that completed the teacher's effort. That is, good behavior and harmonious order confirmed the action of teaching. When learning was not clear, however, scholarship declined, the people suffered, and bad fortune prevailed (EQQJ, 14.3a–b). Wang Suoxi and Liu Kuang, two contemporary followers of Li, claimed that nothing was to be more feared than muddied learning, but the current misguidedness of scholarly trends was not necessarily the fault of all scholars. They pointed out that Li hoped the deluded ones would become enlightened and a great awakening would gradually spread. Such a development would benefit not just scholars but all people in the world (EQQJ, 14.7a). These ideas reflect the Confucian commitment to the continuity of tradition. Li apparently assumed, as did others, that the social power of the Confucian scholars was so great that all of society would suffer if the Confucians undermined the sages' values. The scholars' pursuit of secondary, literary interests was more than an academic issue, for all scholarly activities had broad social and political consequences.

Li held that learning was so obscured in his own time that conditions were truly desperate. Instruction in the classics should serve to support morality, and schools should serve to gather people together to discuss morality, but the task of teaching and transforming had deteriorated so much that people pursued selfish benefits. Therefore, the supervision by fathers and older brothers, the leadership of teachers and friends, the actions of government functionaries, and the practices of sons and younger brothers amounted to self-aggrandizement. Except for the pursuit of examination learning, no one even knew why schools were established or what purpose there was in reading. Genuine learning had become so impoverished that people could not even bear to talk about morality anymore (EQQJ, 12.3b).

Li supported this position with historical evidence. That is, he reminded people of what had happened in the past, especially in regard to the opposing views that Mencius had faced. In looking at the world as one family and the ten thousand things as one body, Mozi supposedly aimed at benevolence. In actuality, however, he rejected compassion and supported personal profit. Yang Zhu, on the other hand, aimed at rightness, but neither he nor his followers would pluck out one hair to save the world. Li acknowledged that the views of Yang and Mo differed from the current practices of "phrases and sections, fame and profit," but all were similarly distant from genuine morality. In Mencius' view, Mozi's position would lead to social disorder. The result would be like not having a father or a ruler, or like flooding water and wild animals (EQQJ, 12.3b–4a). Mencius worried that the learning of Yang and Mo would destroy later generations, since they regarded "trampling on benevolence" and "treading on rightness" as their duty. Li pointed out that even though Yang and Mo ended up deluded, they started out at a point only slightly divergent from genuine morality. The problem was much worse in the present, for the current pursuit of examination learning and fame and profit began at a point further away from morality. Li insisted that contemporary scholars were so far from the source of genuine morality that they could not even become deluded. Thus, their selfish focus certainly was a threat to later generations (EQQJ, 12.4a).

In teaching the necessity of clarifying learning, Li was following a course begun earlier by Feng Congwu and Zhang Shundian. Feng had pointed to two hidden illnesses of Confucian learning in addition to the paths of Buddhism and Daoism. One illness was characterized by an inappropriate and excessive concern with other people and other affairs; the second consisted of attacks on the Confucian tradition itself, particularly the Song thinkers. Feng likened these defects, first, to stepping over the plates in a ritual ceremony and so losing proper form and, second, to entering one's house with a spear in hand. In Feng's view, these illnesses disrupted the unity of Confucian learning, a unity based on the assumption that learning meant "learn the Way" (*xue dao*)—and there was of course only one Way.[7]

Zhang Shundian also urged the restoration of the unity of learning by getting rid of its illnesses. In his preface to Zhang's writings, provincial superintendent of education Xu Sunquan described two illnesses that Zhang had found in contemporary scholars: speculative talk about "nature and destiny" accompanied by an unwillingness to exert practical effort, and excessive admiration for the ancient sages to the point of regarding them as divine. Zhang saw these attitudes as a denial of the possibilities of practical learning, with the result that scholars were passive and did not exert themselves.[8]

Xin Quan, a follower of Zhang, pointed out three illnesses of learning that troubled Zhang. False learning of human nature used the same terms (mind and nature) as Confucian learning but with different meanings, and so threw truth "into turmoil." False learning of statecraft confused wealth and rank with merit and fame and written works with moral behavior. It was a learning that "followed the times." False learning of morality was single-minded and one-sided and hence biased. It was learning that "held onto one thing."[9]

Li's answer to the question of how to make learning clear was to engage in discussion of it (EQQJ, 12.5a–b). Li offered past examples of this practice, from Confucius and Mencius to the Song philosophers to Feng Congwu, and he also practiced it himself (EQQJ, 12.6b–7b). Unlike some of his contemporaries, Li agreed with Feng that it was wrong to attribute social disorder to the practice of discussing learning. Rather, this practice helped distinguish genuine learning from other kinds of learning, so that the Confucian dual emphasis on values and their implementation could be pursued. As in the past, this pursuit would be led by great Confucian teachers and heroic leaders.

Clarify and Practice the Essential Values

A second prescription of Li Yong's was to clarify and comprehend the essential values and to put them into practice.[10] Although the common people were not excluded, this teaching was directed especially toward Confucian teachers, scholars, and governmental officials, particularly those involved in educational activities. It reaffirmed the Confucian commitment to self-cultivation on the personal level and harmonious order on the social and political levels. The interrelationship of these two goals made achievement of one dependent on achievement of the other.

Li Yong promoted this teaching to correct what he perceived as contemporary distortions in Confucian learning. The times called for social and political action, but scholars were too often interested in the secondary matters of textual studies, literary and artistic accomplishments, and wealth and fame from success in the examinations. Although scholars therefore emphasized "practice," it was the wrong kind of practice, based on a mistaken understanding of the essential values.

Li was also aware that his struggle to maintain essence and application was part of a philosophical tension as old as Confucian thought. When applied to the personal level, this tension could be seen in the competing lines represented by Zengzi and Mencius. As noted above, Li claimed that Zhou Dunyi, the Cheng brothers, Zhang Zai, Zhu Xi, Xue Xuan, Hu Juren, Luo Qinshun, Lü Nan, Gu Xiancheng, Gao Panlong, Feng Congwu, and Xin Quan represented the stream from Zengzi, which stressed copying the ancients, praising the former worthies, and sincerely believing in the sages. Lu Jiuyuan, Wu Yubi, Chen Xianzhang, Wang Yangming, Wang Gen, Wang Ji, Luo Rufang, and Zhou Rudeng represented the stream from Mencius, which emphasized self-reflection and self-knowledge. Li noted that the Mencian thinkers did not emphasize textual knowledge, but neither did they deny it (EQQJ, *fu* 15.3b).[11]

Li further held that both streams had legitimate ideas and actions but, to be complete and unbiased, Confucian learning needed both these emphases, along with a focus on the world as well as on the self: "To establish the self, one must have virtuous acts; to be of use to the world, one must have achievements. To have virtuous acts, one must be like Yan [Hui], Zeng[zi], [Zi]si, Mencius, Zhou [Dunyi], [the] Cheng [brothers], Zhang [Zai], and Zhu [Xi]. To have achievements, one must be like Yi [Yin], Fu [Yue], [the Duke of] Zhou, [Duke] Shao, Zhuge [Liang], and [Wang] Yangming." Only then, Li thought, "will one have essence and action and not tilt to one side" (EQQJ, *fu* 15.3b–4a). Li thus viewed his teaching of *mingti shiyong* as belonging to philosophical and historical contexts. He saw it as a version of Confucius' teaching of broad learning and restraint by ritual action, a teaching that (he said) Zhu Xi later obtained and restated, in terms more appropriate to his times, as thoroughly investigating principle and abiding in reverential seriousness (EQQJ, 15.4a–b).[12] Modifying Zhu's teaching, Li also proposed thoroughly investigating principle and extending knowledge as an alternative expression for his own *mingti shiyong*. The important point was, however, that only a correct understanding of essence could lead to the right kind of practice.

The *ming* in *mingti* suggests both comprehending for oneself and clarifying for oneself and others, and its object is *ti*. Li understood the concept of *ti*, essence or the essential values, as the ways in which humans ideally ought to act toward each other. In fact, these ideal relationships define a person as a human being, that is, a social being. These relationships, as well as the ability to know them and act in accordance with them, are part of one's human "gifts." Seen as both normative and descriptive, the essence does not require or make a distinction between the "ought" and the "is" (EQQJ, 14.3b). If it is not developed, a person loses his or her distinctively human characteristics.

In viewing the essence as the origin of properly human behavior, Li described it as the root of benevolence and rightness, the pivot axis of the Way and of creative power, and the source of social regulation and individual participation. The essence applied to all kinds of activities. From discussing theories to examining one's thoughts, Li held that there was nothing not concerned with this essence. He compared the person who rejected this root and sought fundamental values elsewhere to someone careless with his own family's valuables and yet always looking for his neighbors' common utensils (EQQJ, 15.3a).

The essential values were located not only in the person but also in relationships. Suggesting the relational character of values, Li claimed that the superior person valued the broad but not the mixed in learning. Such a person comprehended the mechanism of cultivating the self and ruling others. He understood the pattern of beginning things and completing affairs. Like Yi Yin, Fu Yue, the Duke of Zhou, and Duke Shao in antiquity, and Han Qi, Fan Zhongyan, Fu Bi, and Sima Guang in the Song, he was able to aid the world and benefit the people (EQQJ, 15.3b).[13] Li further noted that scholars did not always distinguish broad learning from mixed learning, but the two were different. Mixed learning would not enable a person to comprehend the Way and preserve the mind, on the one hand, or to regulate the world and manage things, on the other (EQQJ, 15.3b–4a).

In Li's view, how a person applied the essential values indicated his understanding of them. Employing the cultural dichotomy of inner and outer in the sense of self and other, Li claimed that the inner application of his teaching would lead to genuine personal cultivation, and its outer application would enable a leader to aid the masses (EQQJ, 14.3b). When he restricted this dichotomy to the context of the individual person, Li indicated that action (*yong*) applied both to behavior seen by others and to that known only to oneself.

Purposeful thought was, for instance, one kind of action. Following the formulation of the *Doctrine of the Mean* (20.19) and thinking specifically in terms of *mingti shiyong*, Li said that learning consisted of broad study, thorough questioning, careful pondering, making clear distinctions, and personal implementation. If any one of these were lacking, a person was not engaged in learning, for learning had to be extended to action both inside and outside a person (EQQJ, 11.3a). Li Yong drew further from this classic in holding that inner behavior referred to the activities of the heart-mind and was known only to oneself. Hence, before thoughts arose, a person was careful and cautious, and nourished the heart-mind. Just at the moment when thoughts arose, he (or she) reflected on and investigated the budding of thoughts and illuminated the point at which principles and desires appeared. He restrained anger and controlled desires, repressed evil and encouraged good. Not allowing any of the selfish human desires to remain, he retained only goodness. Through these actions, a person nourished the center, the heart-mind.[14] When learning was manifested on the outside, a person's actions were visible to others. Everything that a person did had (according to the *Book of Rites*) to be appropriate and respectful, from the movement of one's feet, hands, head, eyes, and mouth to the way one stood, walked, sat, and talked. All the external actions of self-control were done to nourish the inside (EQQJ, 11.3a–b). The mutual nourishing of the inner and outer aspects of the self enabled one to develop one's moral capacities. Much effort was required at first, but eventually a person could act appropriately, seemingly without effort. Li did not regard such efforts as actual learning, however, until a person successfully exhibited his full moral capacities (EQQJ, 11.3b).

Li's ideas about essence and application gained authority, from a theoretical perspective, from their grounding in the generative (theoretical) frame. That is, it made sense to understand and experience the world in terms of the relationship of root and branches and other analogous polarities. Li's view was also supported by Wang Yangming's stress on the inseparability of essence and application. Substituting his own concept of loving the people for Zhu Xi's concept of renovating the people, Wang had said, for instance:

> The main thing is that root and branches should not be distinguished as two different things. . . . It is precisely because the tree is one that its parts can be called root and branches. . . . If it is realized that manifesting the clear character is to love the people and loving the people is to manifest the clear character, how can they be split in two? What the former scholar [Zhu Xi] said is due to his failure to realize that manifesting the character and loving the people are basically one thing.[15]

In Li's view, achieving a balance between the two aspects of essence and application was critical for genuine learning, and a bias favoring either aspect distorted true Confucian learning, making it become a deviant or other path (EQQJ, 14.3b). The sought-after balance involved more than attention to these two aspects, however, for the surrounding circumstances conditioned what needed to be done.

Although, Li suggested, Wang's and Zhu's teachings were not appropriate at all times, one could in the present circumstances use the teachings of Wang to understand the essence, and the teachings of Zhu to implement it. To respect one and attack the other led to a sickness of both inner and outer (EQQJ, *fu* 15.2b). "Respecting one's virtuous nature" does not forestall "constant inquiry and study" — the latter is how one engages in the former. These teachings are not two separate things, and emphasis on one aspect should not imply neglect of the other (EQQJ, *fu* 15.3a). Rather, the emphasis chosen should reflect the surrounding circumstances, which might demand more attention to one aspect than to the other in order to achieve an effective balance.

Li claimed, however, that many of his contemporaries simply did not know what was involved in Confucian learning. His typical lament ran, "Today learning is not understood. Other than the memorization and recitation of phrases and chapters, the educated are completely ignorant about what kind of affair learning is" (EQQJ, 16.22a; see also 15.9b). People paid attention only to secondary activities and gave minimal thought to the underlying and justifying values. But by not fully understanding what the essence was, they did not know what genuine action was. Confucian learning involved practical action, not knowledge transmitted in books; human accomplishments, not mere talent; aiding the world, not withholding such aid or ignoring one's responsibility (EQQJ, *fu* 15.4a–b).

Learning that emphasized textual studies, art, and literature was biased and so not the genuine learning of the sages. In support of this view, Li cited several examples of past philosophers, one of whom was the Ming philosopher Xue Xuan, who wrote poetry when young. Li recorded, with approval bordering on glee, that upon realizing his error, Xue had burned his literary writings (EQQJ, 1.11b). As noted earlier, Li would not prohibit artistic endeavors, but felt they should follow the completion of virtue and benevolence (EQQJ, 16.15a). He thus criticized those who engaged too quickly in the secondary types of activities. He questioned whether prose writings, like those of the historians Ban Gu and Sima Qian, and poetry, like that of Li Bai and Du Fu, are of any use to the human (moral) mind or help resolve the problems of the times (EQQJ, 16.15a). Poetry, he suspected, is both useless and harmful, and chatting about poetry and discussing literature do not constitute Confucian learning. He urged action, because those who do not act or speak out give no aid to the world. "Literary courage" (*wenzhang qijie*), as he called it, is not sufficient (EQQJ, 16.7a, 14b–15a, 26a); nor is "literary morality" (*wenyi*) (EQQJ, 15.4b).

To emphasize the complementarity of *ti* and *yong*, Li used various popular terms and phrases. For instance, sometimes he spoke of the learning of principle(s) and ordering (the world) and aiding (the people; EQQJ, 17.15b–16b). Other times he contrasted moral teachings, like those of Zhou Dunyi, Cheng Hao and Cheng Yi, Zhang Zai, and Zhu Xi, with practical accomplishments, like those of Han Qi, Fan Zhongyan, Fu Bi, and Ouyang Xiu; or, alternatively, moral actions, exemplified by Yan Hui, Zengzi, Zisi, Mencius, Zhou Dunyi, the Cheng brothers, Zhang Zai, and Zhu Xi, with practical actions, like those of Yi Yin, Fu Yue, the Duke of Zhou, Duke Shao, Zhuge Liang, and Wang Yangming (EQQJ, 17.38b, *fu* 15.4a).

Li maintained that unless one's learning values both essence and application, it is just vulgar learning. "If one makes clear the essence but does not extend it to practice, one is a pedant. If one has practical application but does not base it on a clearly understood essence, then one is an opportunist, like the ancient hegemons" (EQQJ, 14.3b). Li thus acknowledged two kinds of vulgar learning, that which lacked social action and that which was not grounded in fundamental values. The pedants were those whose textual and literary studies had no practical application, and the opportunists were those who acted, but without virtue.

Vulgar learning is a deficient form of Confucian learning. It falls short of the Confucian ideals not only because it does not adequately incorporate both essence and application (knowledge and action) in a balanced relationship, but also because it is not an appropriate response to the needs of the time, and responding appropriately is critical to achieving effectiveness. Li claimed that in his own time vulgar learning consisted of a preoccupation with texts, since the circumstances called for action. The focus of his contemporaries on textual commentaries, evidential research, and literary writings indicated insufficient understanding (of the times and of learning) as well as inadequate action.

Li urged people not to be fooled by terminology. In attempting to clarify genuine Confucian learning, Li said that *daoxue* (the learning of the Way) was simply Confucian learning (*ruxue*) in a particular historical context, and like *ruxue* it contrasted to vulgar learning. As noted above, the term *daoxue* applied to the thought of the Song philosophers who had "recovered" the Way of Confucius and Mencius. Li saw the distinction between the learning of the Way and the learning of the Confucians as a matter of history, not of philosophy. "Actually, *daoxue* is *ruxue*. It is not the case that in addition to *ruxue* there is something else called *daoxue*" (EQQJ, 14.3a). That is to say, both consist of *ti* and *yong*, and the application (*yong*) is appropriate action. Although the values remained constant, the actual ways they were applied differed from one period to another. "Application" does not refer to all types of practical action (even if appropriate to the context), but only action that is an outgrowth of the fundamental values. In this we can again see the logic of the generative metaphor and the example of a plant with its root and branches.

Li approved of action that belonged to the great Way of the superior person, in contrast to the lesser ways of the commoners (SSFSL, *Lunyu*, pt. 2, 41–42). Li's view of the decline among Confucians is apparent in his comment that the lesser Ways were now poetry, literature, calligraphy, and painting, although they had once been farming, gardening, medicine, and divination. They might be pleasing, but they did not aid the (moral) heart-mind or the times, and so they did not belong to the great Way. These lesser Ways were comparable to technical skills. Li further said that pursuing secondary activities, like textual studies, and regarding them as learning revealed a love of antiquity, not learning (SSFSL, *Lunyu*, pt. 2, 41–42).[16] Li's objection was comparable to Confucius' objection to those who confused the jades and silks used in ceremonies with ritual (*Lunyu*, 17.11).

Li rejected some activities because they were clearly based on faulty values, but he found the status of other activities sometimes ambiguous. For instance, in spite of the civil orientation of Confucianism, Li did not flatly reject knowledge of military affairs and techniques as a legitimate aspect of *ti* and *yong*. He accepted that officials needed practical knowledge to bring order to society, even military knowledge if it were appropriate to the conditions. When discussing Zhang Zai's intellectual development, for instance, Li claimed that military affairs were not a proper concern of the Confucian. Li supported this claim by quoting from a letter that Fan Zhongyan had sent to Zhang Zai when Fan had learned of Zhang's interest in the military (EQQJ, 1.8b). On the other hand, Li included in his reading list a multivolume work on military topics, the *Record of Military Preparations*. Citing the military and official achievements of Wang Yangming, Li emphasized the importance of such knowledge for Confucian officials (EQQJ, 7.8a–b). Military knowledge was desirable if its need and practice stayed within Confucian ethical bounds. As for Zhang Zai, however, he was still a young student and had much to learn before studying military affairs.

Learning for the examinations was another activity whose status was ambiguous. Even though examination learning and Confucian learning shared the same classical texts, their uses of textual knowledge often differed. To defend his view that examination learning was a vulgar (opportunistic) form of the sages' learning, Li cited the positions of, among others, the Ming philosopher Luo Rufang (Jinxi). Luo and others accepted the distinction between Confucian learning and examination learning. Luo's view was that he followed Xue Xuan in pursuing self-cultivation rather than examination learning (EQQJ, 1.12a).

For Li, the problem lay in people's aims and understanding. Contemporary scholars paid attention only to thoughts of merit and fame, and this was "truly a blemish on the glory of the Confucians." If one took the examinations and obtained a degree, it was acceptable to call that merit for oneself, but one could not say that it was merit for others. It was also acceptable to say that one had the fame brought by wealth and rank, but one could not say that one had the fame brought by achievements (EQQJ, 14.4b–5a). Li further said, with obvious approval, that in the past people regarded achievements as the way to merit and fame. Those who aimed at learning regarded the kingly way and their own vital luminosity (*shengling*), or the root, as their aim. Therefore, they constantly tried to clarify the essence of ruling and understand the affairs of the times. When they had completed their learning, their merit and fame were established naturally and effortlessly (EQQJ, 14.5a). But now, people regard only wealth and rank as merit and fame. Having set their aim on learning, they regard taking advantage of opportunity and pleasing others as their goal. Therefore they constantly engage in frivolous literary writing. When they complete their studies, they have no merit that can lead to fame. It is a great shame, Li concluded, that because the meanings of the words "merit" and "fame" are not comprehended, scholars do not know the supporting pillars of Confucian learning (EQQJ, 14.5a).

Li recognized that it could be difficult to keep one's mind appropriately on the root (the essence) while pursuing the branches (application) for the sake of the root. Both are necessary, but one cannot pursue the branches for the wrong reasons. The foundation is so important that if one discards the root, one's actions and skill will be deficient even if they are as great as the actions of Sima Guang and as skillful as those of Zhuge Liang.

Although Li was critical of the preoccupation with textual studies in his own time, he admitted that the examination system was not bad in itself. It simply was not a proper aim because it was action, not essence. What was wrong was people's understanding, their comprehension of the essence. People may use the examinations and degrees to establish merit and fame, but they must not reject the root and follow only these branches (EQQJ, 14.5b). Li abhorred not the system, but how Confucians used the system. He noted that apologists for the system claimed that it had its good aspects since it cultivated the work of essence and application. Specifically, examinees were questioned on the Five Classics and Four Books to encourage them to attempt to comprehend the essence. They were examined on the treatises to promote reserved manners. They were questioned on policy so that they would study current affairs, and so forth. Li con-

cluded that if the examinees truly comprehended the root and followed it in practice, then the examination system would be in reality
a matter of virtue (EQQJ, 11.5a).

Li's position contrasted to that of some who felt, like Feng
Congwu, that the examination system (during the Han, Tang, and
Song) had no relationship to moral thought and action, and so was
not at all an affair of the sages and worthies. Although people read
the sages' books and admired the sages' words, some believed that
the examination system did not express the sages' thoughts and ideals. Therefore it could not help a person engage in sagely work or
establish sagely qualities (EQQJ, 11.4b).

Although Li would have been the first to acknowledge that
learning the moral knowledge contained in books was not the same
as personally realizing that knowledge, he was not opposed to
books. They were "the tile for knocking on the gate" (EQQJ, 11.4b).
He was adamant that, in order to engage in Confucian learning, one
had to read its books. Li accordingly offered an annotated list of
books in both the *mingti* (clarify the essence) and *shiyong* (put into
practice) categories (see Chapter 5). The first category addressed the
moral cultivation of the self and was subdivided into two parts:
comprehending the fundamental moral and social values (*mingti*)
and their application (*gongfu*). Books in the *mingti* category were primarily those of philosophers identified with Wang Yangming and Lu
Jiuyuan, whereas those in the *gongfu* category stressed the writings of
people identified with Cheng Yi and Zhu Xi (EQQJ, 7.2a–6b). The
second category (*shiyong*) referred to statecraft, the governing of state
and society. The subjects of books in this category ranged from music
and ritual to grain transportation, the salt administration, and the
military. Many of the books in this category on Li's list were compilations intended for officials (EQQJ, 7.7a–10a).

In Li Yong's view, reading helped a person begin the effort of
comprehending the essence, but one could not stop there. Values had
to be implemented, and actions had to be guided by moral principles
(EQQJ, 7.10a). Thus, the learning of the Confucians was the learning
of *mingti shiyong*. If one wanted to engage in this learning, one had to
read its books. No one had ever been successful in Confucian learning who had not read its books (EQQJ, 7.1a [preface by Zhang Er],
16.35b). Li identified the Six Classics and Four Books as the basis of
the learning of *mingti shiyong*. But just reading these texts would not

necessarily enable a person to comprehend and implement the essential values. Anyone who read the texts but did not think about this teaching, however profound his research and lofty his discussions, desired nothing more than to "boast of the subtle and strive for the obscure." In such a case, it would probably be better not to read the classics (EQQJ, 15.2b).

Li lamented that the sages had worked so hard to "establish their words and awaken the world," but their efforts had degenerated into the elaborate theories and commentaries of scholars. Although acknowledging that vulgar learning did not arise in one day, he claimed that it was now so prevalent that it imperiled the classics as much as the Qin book burning (EQQJ, 15.2b). It was not that Li opposed the accumulation of knowledge, for he thought it was good. But he emphasized that one should first understand the moral root. And, generally, a person who "knew everything" was tremendously ignorant and consequently confounded his root (EQQJ, 15.3a).

Li taught that moral knowledge and action were necessary for realizing the ideal society and for developing the ideal person from a Confucian viewpoint. These activities were interrelated and interdependent. He criticized current Confucian learning for its action without virtue and its virtue without action, and he held that legitimate activities pursued for the wrong reasons could not lead to Confucian goals. Appropriate action only followed genuine understanding, and thus it was critical first to make learning clear.

Learn for the Self

A third prescription of Li was "learn for the sake of the self," that is, one's moral self. It was directed toward people in all social niches, both those in leadership positions and those not, and it addressed disagreements over Confucian learning and problems of social disorder (EQQJ, 3.3b). Pointing to the way for a person to act responsibly in reference to others and to the tradition, this teaching did not focus on the unique personality of each person.

Li summarized this teaching with the popular neo-Confucian phrase "for the self," which derived from the *Lunyu* (14.25), and like his predecessors, he contrasted learning for the sake of the self to learning for the sake of others.[17] The first focused on self-cultivation, whereas the second involved efforts to impress others and to gain fame and profit (EQQJ, 3.3b). Although Li regarded a person's aims as the initial distinction between these two types of learning, their pursuit also led to considerable differences in practice.

Among the many thinkers who had addressed the issue of the relationship between a person's aims and actions was Confucius, who held that the superior person was distinguished from the petty person by his aims (*Lunyu*, 4.16). In illustrating the tension between social responsibility and selfish interest, Confucius said the superior person aimed at rightness and the petty person at personal profit. Mencius also regarded rightness and profit as antagonistic, and Song and Ming thinkers reaffirmed the opposition (*Mencius*, 1A.1).[18] Indeed, in a famous neo-Confucian lecture, Lu Jiuyuan spoke on this topic at the White Deer Hollow Academy in 1181 at the invitation of Zhu Xi. In his own teaching, Li Yong applied the opposition between rightness and personal profit to the specific context of learning.

A person's aims were considered important because (moral) behavior was seen as beginning with a person's aims and decisions about what to do. The comparison of aims to the root and actions to the branches linked the question of aims and actions to one of the most powerful cultural images, one that emphasized that all things have beginnings and ends and that a thing's development depends on how the source is nourished.[19] That is, the branches of a plant will wither and die if the root is not nourished, and streams will dry up if the spring becomes blocked. Rightness and profit were understood in this framework. Li's teaching of learning for the self was associated with nourishing the root, whereas its counterpart, learning for others, was understood as looking after the branches. Li also thought in terms of a medical framework. Concerned with treating the "complaint" of social disorder, he first had to diagnose the illness before he could offer any prescriptions. In his view, misplaced aims and a faulty conception of knowledge were leading causes of social disorder, and his teaching of learning for the self could provide the basis for a solution.

The concept of teaching and transformation (*jiaohua*) provided the framework of this teaching. Transformation involved the "recovery" and the development of a person's moral capacities or moral knowledge, which Li called "this heart-mind." Li taught that people must "comprehend this heart-mind, embody these principles, and cultivate this self" (EQQJ, 3.3a–4a). (Li also referred to "this heart-mind" as the place where thoughts first arise and as being clear and luminous; EQQJ, 11.8a.) Moral knowledge differed from other kinds of knowledge in that it referred to a person's capacities to develop certain kinds of behavior deemed good by society. Li was not concerned with other kinds of knowledge — whether in the form of statements, as awareness of, or familiarity with. Although moral knowledge included the ability to distinguish between good and evil, and right and wrong, it was easily obscured by ordinary or conventional knowledge (EQQJ, 11.8a).

Li classified ordinary knowledge (*zhishi*) into four kinds but offered no extensive explanation. He simply said that one kind is produced from opinions; another is obtained by depending on special talents and understanding; a third enables one to engage courageously in affairs; and a fourth kind is based on everyday circumstances. Combining experience and particular abilities, "all of them are sufficient to be considered as obstacles to emptiness and luminosity" (EQQJ, 11.8a). Drawing on the past both to illustrate and to give authority to his position, Li claimed that most of the brave heroes of ancient times had succumbed to the errors of these four kinds of knowledge. Even the great hero Liu Bei, the founder of the Shu-Han dynasty, encountered failure because he allowed a surge of *qi*, the third kind of ordinary knowledge, to overrule the necessity to be patient in warfare (EQQJ, 11.8a).[20]

To learn for the self, the learner must conquer and expel these ordinary kinds of knowledge so that "this heart-mind" may be empty and luminous, thereby becoming the "constant ruler." That is, one cannot let oneself be guided by, or merely respond to, the petty thoughts and feelings arising from everyday circumstances. Such things only obscure a person's moral knowledge and prevent its development. From a modern perspective, we can perhaps compare this clearing of the mind to the idea of "unlearning" outdated concepts, particularly in the sciences, because some premodern views seem to obstruct and even prevent the acceptance of newer concepts.

Li used a number of philosophical concepts, or prescriptions, to suggest the idea of development. He particularly favored Wang Yangming's concept of extending moral knowledge, but he also employed classical concepts such as investigating things and making manifest the illustrious virtue from the opening passage of the *Great Learning* (EQQJ, 11.8a, 10.13b–14a). One of his own special prescriptions was that one must first know the head (EQQJ, 3.6b). The head referred of course to the root.

In addition to the four kinds of ordinary knowledge, excessive desires (which were seen as immoral) hinder a person's moral development. Li recognized the difficulty of removing some desires, particularly when the distinction between them and moral principles was barely apparent. Li acknowledged that lusts, or excessive desires, emerge naturally and without effort, just as moral principles do (EQQJ, 15.11b). Lusts, however, are ultimately a part of human knowledge (*renzhi*) in Li's view, and human knowledge derives from experience, not from one's human moral capacities. Any similarity between lusts and moral principles is, therefore, only apparent and not actual. Still, the difference between the beginnings of moral principles and those of human desires is so slight that unless their boundary is extremely clear, a person cannot discriminate between them. This difficulty is the reason that the superior person values the thorough investigation of principles (EQQJ, 15.12a).

Since moral cultivation consists of both knowledge and action, moral knowledge has to be realized in some concrete way. Li thus augmented the concept of "comprehending this heart-mind" with the concepts of "embodying these principles" and "cultivating this self." Deliberate effort is required, and moral principles have to be translated into action. It is not enough just to eliminate those actions and thoughts that are in some way obstructive. Basing himself especially on ideas from the *Doctrine of the Mean* and *Mencius*, Li regarded moral behavior, that is, the functioning of the heart-mind, as analogous to the optimal functioning of the sense organs and other parts of the body.

Li assumed that when thoughts begin to emerge, the four sprouts of the heart-mind are stimulated and appear in behavior. Li claimed, echoing Mencius, that one knows what to do without having to learn and one is capable of acting without having to ponder (EQQJ, 4.5b–6a). Since he conceived of moral behavior as the development of the four sprouts, two aspects of a person came into play in his conception—actual behavior and human nature, alternatively referred to as principles, moral capacities, or "this heart-mind."

As noted earlier, Li's view was that human nature (*xing*) and phenomenal endowment (*qizhi*) are inseparable, for the nature adheres to one's phenomenal endowment and the so-called goodness of human nature becomes manifest only because of (or through) phenomenal endowment or *qi* (EQQJ, 4.6b). To use Li's example, the eye's activity of seeing is a matter of phenomenal activity (*qi*), but clearness of vision is the goodness of the (eye's) nature. That is, the capability to see constitutes that aspect of one's nature which pertains to the eye, but seeing itself is a phenomenal activity and so is a matter of *qi*. Clearness in seeing is the highest achievement of the capability to see, and so clearness of vision is the goodness of the nature (as it relates to the eye).

Li gave comparable examples for other parts of the body. Thus, the ear's hearing is a phenomenal activity, and acuteness in hearing is the goodness of the nature (as it relates to the ear). The hand's grasping is a phenomenal activity, and respectfulness in grasping is the goodness of the nature (relating to the hand). Movement of the feet is a phenomenal activity, and solemnity in moving is the goodness of the nature (pertaining to the feet). All the movements of the body are phenomenal activities, and each part of the body fulfills its *dao* as it moves. Without the original goodness of the nature, none would be able to do so. And, if there were not this phenomenal activity, even though the nature is good, there would be no way to see its goodness (EQQJ, 4.6b). In other words, Li conceived of the goodness—or goodnesses—of human nature as the highest degree of the functioning of some aspect of the phenomenal or physiological self. To support this position, Li quoted Cheng Yi on the nature: "If one discusses the nature and does not discuss phenomenal activity [*qi*], then it [the nature] is not complete. If one discusses phenomenal activity and does not discuss the nature, then it [phenomenal activity] is not complete" (EQQJ, 4.6b).

Li did not want ideas about self-cultivation to become divorced from action, for self-cultivation was not something outside daily effort and the realization of the unchanging moral principles of human relations (EQQJ, 3.4a, 10.13b–14a). Borrowing a phrase from the Ming thinker Zhan Ruoshui, Li stressed that principles can be comprehended "at any time and in any place" (EQQJ, 3.4a). There is no need to talk of the "mysterious" and the "wonderful." The foundation for establishing the self is found in such principles as rightness, the moral standards of heaven, compassion, and a sense of shame— all principles for practical action (EQQJ, 10.7b). Li held that one starts with the self, the root, and all principles are complete in the self (EQQJ, 10.14a–b).

Li used examples from ancient authorities to provide specific details about learning for the self. For instance, according to Confucius (*Lunyu*, 16.8, 16.10), a superior person is in awe of three things and has nine wishes. The three things are the mandate of heaven, great men, and the words of the sages. As for the nine wishes: "In seeing, he wishes to see clearly. In hearing, he wishes to hear distinctly. In his expression, he wishes to be warm. In his appearance, he wishes to be respectful. In his speech, he wishes to be sincere. In handling affairs, he wishes to be serious. When in doubt, he wishes to ask. When he is angry, he wishes to think of the resultant difficulties. And when he sees an opportunity for a gain, he wishes to think of rightness" (EQQJ, 3.4a).[21]

In a further historical example, Li stated that when Confucius taught Zixia, his teaching contained a distinction between scholars who are superior men and scholars who are small-minded men. This distinction was a matter of establishing one's aim and valuing distinctions (EQQJ, 3.3b). One had to decide to take the moral course and to value it. Also relevant were the teachings of being cautious and watchful over oneself when alone, from the *Doctrine of the Mean* (chap. 1), and the teaching of Mencius (*Mencius*, 6A.11) to seek the lost mind (EQQJ, 4.7a). Li said that these teachings were intended to encourage people to take care of their human heart-mind so that they did not lose (that is, not develop) their moral principles. Therefore, the ideas of Confucius, Mencius, and the *Mean* formed the basis of the sages' — and Li's — teaching of learning for the sake of the self (EQQJ, 3.4a).

In addition to the aim and content of learning for the self was the question of who could pursue this goal. The answer changed over time. Although early philosophers, including Mencius and Xunzi, repeated the commonplace that everyone can become a sage, much of early philosophy was directed to the ruler and those in the scholar-official class. During the Song, many thinkers broadened their focus to include the masses; some, like Lu Jiuyuan, did so more explicitly than others. By Li Yong's time, audience was no longer an issue; everyone, high or low, was considered worthy of being taught.

Universality was an important characteristic of human moral capacities. Li stressed that "this heart-mind" and "these principles" are the same in everyone, from the sage to the "ignorant husband and wife," just as is the ability to distinguish black and white (EQQJ, 3.3a–b). Like seeing, the functioning of the heart-mind does not change over time. As Li said, everyone has the root, the luminous brightness of the one mind of knowing right and wrong. It is the "great root of heaven and earth," and it is what everyone has to establish (EQQJ, 4.5a). Practice differs from capability, however. Taking a position as old as Confucius, Li held that the learning of the ancients was for the most part learning for the sake of the self, whereas that of his contemporaries was learning for the sake of others (EQQJ, 3.3b). (Not only was the contrast between past and present behavior relevant to current political concerns, but from a theoretical perspective, it enabled the past to continue as a viable aspect of the present. It affirmed the relevance of the past as a standard of authority.)

The question of universality was important because of the concern whether the sage differs from the common people. A frequent answer was that the sage and the commoner differ insofar as the sage is born knowing, whereas commoners know only by studying. This difference results from a different natural endowment (EQQJ, 9.5a). Li, however, did not want to make sagehood inaccessible, and reversed this common view. According to him, all the common people were born knowing, and the sage knew only by studying (or learning). Moreover, everyone received the same endowment. Li clarified his position by noting that as a child one knew to love, and as an adult one knew to respect. Anyone seeing a child fall into a well would feel empathy. The abilities of knowing to approve of right and to disapprove of wrong and knowing to love and to hate are in the human heart-mind all the time. And this knowledge is the same in the common people and in the sage (EQQJ). This (moral) knowledge is innate and does not depend on learning. The sage differs from the commoners only in being willing to learn. Taking responsibility, he is able to complete these capacities, and he is called a sage because of his actions. The masses are not willing to study, and therefore they are constantly being destroyed. They turn their back on this knowledge, and so they are called commoners (EQQJ, 9.5b). For Li, the distinction between sage and commoner lies in the distinction between learning and not learning. There is no difference in their human moral potential or their inheritance (in the sense of *xing*, nature; EQQJ, 9.5b). No matter what one's phenomenal endowment is, everyone can work to attain the status of a sage by exerting effort for the self, not for others (EQQJ, 3.4a).

In a comparable manner, evil must be "achieved" in one's behavior. Li claimed that the nature cannot be discussed in terms of close or far, even though Confucius said that we are by nature close together (*Lunyu*, 17.2). "Close" and "far" apply to the phenomenal aspects of the self, one's inherited endowment. Evil occurs when people are controlled by their emotions and by the circumstances of their environment. Although many people behave in evil ways, it is not true that some people are born evil. Good and evil are characteristics of phenomena, *qi* (not human nature, *xing*), and so can appear only after thoughts and actions emerge (EQQJ, 4.6a).

Although many of these ideas about cultivating the self display the logic of the generative metaphor, Li's thinking also depended at times on the reflective metaphor, with its images of the mirror and water. Utilizing this other perspective, Li stated that the common person is a sage at birth, and the sage is a common person, because the common person's "not-learned" and "not-pondered" goodness is complete at birth and not in the least deficient. A common person disrupts his own goodness and willingly destroys it, however. A sage is called a sage not because he adds anything to the "not-learned" and "not-pondered" goodness but simply because he does not allow the original goodness to become dirty (EQQJ, 10.11a–b). In this framework, sagehood is conceived as a potential, equivalent to the perfectly bright luminous source, and it is maintained only by protecting it from the dirt of everyday life. The generative metaphor emphasizes capacities (goodness) to be developed, whereas the reflective emphasizes luminosity (goodness) to be kept bright. Although the two frameworks conceptualize a person's actions in different ways, both claim that the root or the source is the same in everyone.

Nonetheless, many people did not behave in moral ways. Li believed that a major reason was incorrect teaching. Young people were being taught the wrong things, and these teachings were apparent in their behavior.

> Today, when people teach their sons and younger brothers, from the time when they begin to read at six and seven *sui*, it is only wealth that is valued and profit that is pursued. As soon as sons and younger brothers begin to be taught, people plant the seeds of devoting attention to externals. Therefore, what they pursue from morning to evening is only fame and profit. When they meet with others and their conversation reaches the subject of fame and profit, they are pleased. When their conversation reaches the subject of cultivating the self and ruling the people, they either regard it as irrelevant or strange. This is how people of the past and present are not the same. People now do not understand the meaning of the two words "meritorious fame." (EQQJ, 3.4b)

Claiming that learning for others involves mistaken goals, Li asked why people pursue the wrong goals. He held that meritorious fame follows naturally from the pursuit of learning for the self, but that setting one's aim directly on attaining those results leads only to petty and secondary types of knowledge. Setting one's sights low is characteristic of the small person, not the superior person. Li felt that if he could correctly diagnose the roots of such behavior, he could find a solution and get people to change (EQQJ, 3.4b, 14.5a). Addressing the question of why people aimed at fame and profit, that is, learning for others, Li emphasized their lack of understanding. Li stated that persons with meritorious fame, like Yi Yin, the Duke of Zhou, Confucius, and Mencius, had accomplishments for all directions, for the entire world, and for ten thousand generations.

> They did not seek fame and yet fame naturally followed, just as a form must have a shadow. To have accomplishments is to have fame. Now, however, as youth advance in learning and the second-degree holders take the exams, they only know to enrich themselves and their family and to preserve their wives and sons. One can say that they have wealth and rank but not meritorious fame. (EQQJ, 3.4b–5a)

Misunderstanding the nature of genuine fame, people set their sights on the wrong goal. As a result, they cannot achieve genuine fame, for that comes only from accomplishments. "One does not plan for meritorious fame, and yet when the opportunity arrives, one follows in response. Meritorious fame will be established naturally by itself" (EQQJ, 3.5a).

Li's argument was not with attaining fame, but with aiming at fame. He approved of the examinations and degrees. "If one uses these things [exams and degrees] to establish meritorious fame, what is there to disapprove of? It is only that one should not follow the branches and reject the root" (EQQJ, 14.5b). In Li's view, learning for the self is genuine learning and is defined by one's aims, rather than by what one does. The only worthy aim concerns the root, that is, developing one's self and aiding society. The branches of wealth, rank, profit, achievements, momentary fame, and literary writings would flourish naturally if the root were nourished (EQQJ, 4.4a).

Elaborating further on the necessity of aiming at the proper thing, Li said that "if I know the root and truly implement it in my efforts, then that is the Way and its creative power, and yet I do not know the so-called Way and creative power. If I advocate things in words, then those things may turn into writing, but in the beginning I do not aim at writing." Li applied the same idea to a person's accomplishments and courage. No one aims at either, and yet both are obtained. Li Yong made a further comparison with the emergence of streams—the water obtains a name according to where it flows. These secondary results are not aimed at, and yet they are so (EQQJ, 14.4b).

Li's analysis of why people mistakenly aim at the branches evinces a strongly social, as opposed to a psychological, orientation. The failure of people to focus on the right kind of aim is not simply the fault of the individual person, even if educated. Larger than the motivations of individual persons, such failures are due to general social conditions that obscure genuine learning (EQQJ, 3.5a–b). Confusion over the very conception of knowledge lies at the heart of the problem. Because the confusion affects all of society, it has to be addressed on a social, not just personal, level.

In sum, although Li's teaching of learning for the self considered long-standing philosophical conflicts, it focused on developments in his own time. Li argued against a conception of knowledge that emphasizes factual content, skills, and social rewards, and against any desire for fame not based on the right kinds of achievement. He advocated development of one's moral capacities just as one would develop one's physical capacities, and he acknowledged that the use of knowledge was critical. Moreover, he did not accept the possibility that the aims of genuine learning could be expanded, and he could not do so, as long as his thinking was theoretically based in the generative and reflective paradigmatic examples, with their one legitimate root and source. Within this type of framework, other aims of genuine learning are logically impossible.

Criticize and Eliminate Your Faults
and Renew Yourself

The most elaborate of Li's prescriptions, the teaching of *huiguo zixin*—to examine, criticize, and eliminate your faults and to reestablish your original goodness—applied to the personal behavior of people of all classes. It encouraged people to examine their thoughts and actions, acknowledge their errors, and establish themselves on a new course of action after making appropriate readjustments in their ideas and behavior. It emphasized the Confucian imperative (and Mencian sprout) to have a sense of shame; this entailed having a social sensitivity essential to human motivation.

This social sensitivity consisted of an awareness and an appreciation of others, along with a desire to behave well in society and have the approval of others. A sense of shame was necessary for recognizing one's faults, and this recognition helped motivate a person to behave responsibly. Such behavior contributed to the treatment of social problems since, in Li's view, social turmoil was an illness connected to people's lack of a sufficiently developed sense of shame (SSFSL, supplement to *Mengzi*, pt. 1, 11–12).

The phrase *huiguo zixin* has no easy or faithful equivalent in English. *Hui* has been translated by James Legge and D. C. Lau as "repent," which is not entirely satisfactory in this sociopolitical context.[22] This Christian religious term implies that a person should feel guilty and sorry about his or her wrongful acts. In Christianity it suggests asking for forgiveness from God. Li Yong was not talking about this kind of religious feeling, nor was there in Chinese thought any supreme power from which to ask forgiveness. Wm. Theodore de Bary's translation of *huiguo* as "self-criticism" is closer, but it does not reflect the full range of the concept.[23] As used by Li, *hui* suggests the ideas of critically examining one's activities, recognizing and removing those thoughts and actions that are faulty, and making plans for the continued pursuit of moral action. *Huiguo zixin* is based on ideas connected to a sense of shame and implies a deliberate focus on both past and future activities. It does not involve notions of sin, guilt, a divine power external to oneself, or forgiveness, in the way that "repent" does.

Philosophical interest in the idea of examining and correcting one's faults as a method of self-cultivation had existed since ancient times. For instance, Confucius urged people to act so that they had no regrets about their words or conduct, and he urged them not to be afraid to correct their faults (*Lunyu*, 2.18.2, 1.4, 1.8.4; see also 7.10.3, 4.7, and 5.26).[24] Mencius claimed that people can reform themselves, even though they often make errors, and that the superior men of old, unlike those of the present, corrected their faults (*Mencius*, 6B.15, 2B.9; see also 5A.6 and 2A.8). And the partly Daoist *Spring and Autumn Annals of Mr. Lü* (*Lüshi chunqiu*) contains a section (16.4) entitled "Huiguo."

From the Song through the early Qing, philosophers continued to be concerned about faults. In the Song, Cheng Yi, Zhu Xi, and Lu Jiuyuan, among others, made comments on this subject, using a vocabulary virtually identical to Li Yong's. Ming philosophers spoke frequently of the need to correct one's faults, particularly in regard to self-cultivation. Liu Zongzhou (1578–1645), for instance, categorized faults into six major categories and wrote an essay entitled "On Correcting Faults." Yan Yuan (1635–1704), Li Yong's contemporary, also proposed a teaching (*gaiguo qianshan*) that closely paralleled Li's *huiguo zixin*.[25]

Ideas about faults were also tied more immediately to the popular late Ming, early Qing practice of keeping a journal or a diary, especially for recording one's credits and debits.[26] Not concerned only with moral credits and debits, the contents varied widely, with topics ranging from personal thoughts to classical texts to research results. The accounts were as divergent as Gao Panlong's introspective account of his self-cultivation efforts and Gu Yanwu's record of evidential research, *A Record of Daily Knowledge*.

In such a context Li claimed that his teaching had universal applicability, since all people were subject to faults and all could do something to improve their behavior. He was concerned, however, that ordinary people did not have sufficient faith in their ability to change and so gave up too easily. They did not realize that all efforts began simply with the decision to change, or in his phrase, "in the turn of a thought" (EQQJ, 1.2a). Li pointed out that no matter how bad one's previous actions were, one began the journey the moment one decided to change. It was not a lonely journey, for one would receive support from "family and friends, heaven and earth, and the ghosts and spirits." People should begin by taking responsibility for themselves and stop making excuses.

Li claimed that the reason his teaching applied to everyone, not just those aiming at the sagehood, was that everyone has the same moral capacities, an original luminosity, that becomes obscured by human faults. The luminosity of one's original virtue is restored when faults are destroyed. Thus, to renew oneself, or one's original nature, one needs to examine oneself critically and then eliminate one's failings. A common person accumulates more faults than a sage, but self-renewal is still possible (EQQJ, 1.2b–3a).

Li stressed that self-renewal requires constant effort and is not separate from daily life.

One does not need to pursue what is lofty and far-off, or speak of what is subtle and hidden, or talk about the learning of the Way, or discuss nature and destiny. One's efforts should begin in the daily and ordinary relationships, in the constant moral principles, and in the most shallow and nearby places. One must be constantly alert, and every word and every action must be examined so that one does not utter any perverse words and one does not engage in any perverse acts. Even when alone in a dark room, one should act as if one were in a room crowded with people, so that there will be no difference between outer and inner, coarse and fine. And then, one can face humans and heaven in the daytime, and the ghosts and spirits at night. (EQQJ, 6.4b)

This teaching's focus on the individual person led to some concerns, however, for it appeared to some to be a selfish teaching (not too different from the Confucian criticism of certain Buddhist teachings). A questioner thus asked how he could *huiguo zixin* only for himself, since the classics and commentaries embody the principles of regulating (the state) and pacifying (the world). Li's response served as a reminder that the self was not separate from a network of social relations. Li claimed that, given the hierarchical structuring of society, those below would follow if those in high positions pursued his teaching (EQQJ, 1.3b). The success of this and of all teachings still depended, however, on the motivation of the learner. As Li insisted, if a person did not aim at becoming a genuine person, then there was nothing more to say. But if one truly had this aim, one would succeed (EQQJ, 1.4a).

Li Yong's understanding of "fault" was based on his view (noted above) that the human self had two aspects—a perfectly good nature and a phenomenal endowment, with which faults are associated. Faults are evil, but evil is not something with an independent existence. It consists of the extent to which one's behavior departs from one's perfectly good nature. Thus, human beings are closer than wild animals, and superior men are closer than petty men, to their perfectly good nature (EQQJ, 1.1a–b). Li referred to this original goodness as original truth (*benzhen*), and claimed that it was actually the subject of numerous other, apparently unrelated, teachings.

The former sages in teaching later sages taught this [original truth]. The Six Classics in regulating later generations regulated this. The *Great Learning*'s concept of extending knowledge extends this. The *Doctrine of the Mean*'s concept of being watchful over oneself when alone is being watchful over this. The *Analects*' teaching of studying and practicing appropriately in due time is studying and practicing this. Mencius' teaching of requiring the constant practice of this rightness practices this. Zhou Dunyi's establishing the ultimate, the Cheng brothers' recognizing benevolence, Zhu Xi's residing in reverential seriousness and thoroughly investigating principle, Lu Jiuyuan's first establishing its greatness, Wang Yangming's goodness, Zhan Ruoshui's recognizing that there is nothing not returning to this—all these ideas are concerned with this original truth. (EQQJ, 2.7b–8a)

A fault, in other words, was (analogous to) the obscuration of this original truth.

Everyone and everything had faults. To substantiate this claim, Li cited anecdotes about the sages and rulers Yao and Shun, Yu, Tang, Kings Wen and Wu, the Duke of Zhou, and Confucius (EQQJ, 1.7b). Li said that Yao and Shun mistook others as sages, and so they did not regard themselves as without faults. Yu wept when he saw a prisoner get down from a cart and so did not regard himself as faultless. Tang corrected his faults without regret, but he regarded banishing Jie as shameful and so did not think of himself as faultless. King Wen looked at the Way as if he had never seen it, and King Wu gave a warning at the table and engraved it around the window. For the Duke of Zhou axes were broken and hatchets were splintered, and Confucius did not study the *Book of Change* until he was fifty. For all these reasons, Wen, Wu, the Duke of Zhou, and Confucius did not regard themselves as without faults.[27] The natural world also had faults; *yin* and *yang*. for example, brought unseasonable weather, with droughts and floods. Li excluded heaven and earth from his discussion, however, since they had no heart-mind and thus could not think, act intentionally, or take responsibility (EQQJ, 1.8a).

In pursuing the question of how to carry out this teaching, Li said that the superior person begins to act as soon as he recognizes the subtle and incipient stirrings of the heart-mind. Moreover, a person should follow the example of Yan Hui, Confucius' favorite disciple, who acted to get rid of his faults as soon as he became aware of them.[28] He must establish his aim and engage in the practice of quiet sitting, advocated by the Cheng brothers.[29] Li held that this practice would help a person become harmonious with the principles of heaven and earth (EQQJ, 1.6b).

Those pursuing this teaching must examine deeply into the essence and carefully verify things when thoughts first begin to stir and emerge. A thought not in accord with principle is a fault (*guo*), and one has to acknowledge it and eliminate it. Li further said that those not advanced in learning should first examine the faults of the self and then the faults of the heart-mind. Those advanced in learning, however, should eliminate the faults as they begin to arise in thought, and in that way their later appearance in conduct can be prevented. The aim is, of course, to have one's thought and actions coincide with moral principles.

Li emphasized that since people's faults differ, their actions to eradicate them will vary (EQQJ, 1.5b). Some faults are seen by others, and some only by oneself. The latter most obstruct the Way and are easiest to ignore. Although some people think that hidden faults are completely hidden, Li pointed out that there is nothing more obvious than what is hidden. Thus, as stated in the *Doctrine of the Mean* (1.3), it is essential to be "cautious when alone" (EQQJ, 1.5b–6a). Consistent and daily effort is necessary, as opposed to occasional and incidental acts of goodness. Each person must exert effort according to his or her own illnesses. The basic essence is complete on its own when all illnesses are removed, and nothing is ever added to it. If a person does not get rid of his illnesses, however, then all efforts will ultimately be deficient. Therefore, Li claimed that the first principle for entering the gate of learning is to examine and eliminate one's faults and reestablish one's original goodness (EQQJ, 6.4a–b).

Li distinguished between the efforts of middle-level and upper-level people. The upper-level person understands that all faults arise in the heart-mind and that if he immediately cuts out the source of his faults, his efforts will be easier. After exerting effort for a long time, the middle-level person comes to understand the growth of faults, and, although not without success, he encounters more difficulty in his efforts to eliminate them. The upper-level person is more likely to experience sudden enlightenment and sudden cultivation, whereas the middle-level person will pursue gradual cultivation and gradual enlightenment. Li admonished people, however, to hope only for enlightenment, not for its suddenness (EQQJ, 1.6b–7a).[30]

Elaborating on what to do and using familiar phrases from the classics and previous thinkers, Li said that the learning of the sages is both "lower learning and upward reaching," and its beginning is not outside movement and stillness and words and actions and the affairs of daily life. Its aim is to fulfill the (Heavenly) principles, complete human nature, and arrive at the moral standards decreed by

Heaven (EQQJ, 1.7a).[31] If someone has a tiny fault and it remains in the heart-mind, then that person's nature and decreed standards will not be fulfilled and he will be far from the sages. Therefore a person must examine over and over, and renew over and over, until there is nothing left to do. Referring to the different relationships that constitute a genuine person, Li further said that if he were successful, he would not be ashamed before Heaven above and men below, nor during the day or at night. He would be a filial son in the world and a complete person in the universe (EQQJ, 1.7a–b).[32] Today such a person would be a worthy or a sage according to Confucian teachings, and in the future in the obscure vastness, a marvelous luminosity (EQQJ, 1.7b).

Assuming the logic of the luminous paradigmatic example, Li stated that "human nature is nothing other than my own nature, and virtuous power is what I myself have acquired from Heaven. I naturally have them. To renew means to restore this origin." Li compared this origin to the sun's luminosity. "When the sun in the sky sinks in the evening and rises in the morning, its light is not added to or decreased, and today is not different from yesterday. Therefore the sun's luminosity can constantly be renewed." Li warned, moreover, that "if one wishes to add something to the basic substance in order to regard it as renewed, then that is a case of liking the new and loving the different. This is not what is called the 'renewal of the sages'" (EQQJ, 1.5a).

Li was clearly attempting both to explain and persuade as he offered this teaching to a non-elite audience. He sometimes used language close to the vernacular to help make his ideas understandable, and apparently assuming a certain lack of familiarity with the classical texts, he often identified the textual sources of ideas. Although Li wanted people to understand and accept this teaching, there was also something else at stake.

Li wanted his teaching to have a legitimate place in Confucian thinking, and thus he needed to justify it according to the standards of the scholars and teachers. Employing an approach used earlier by Zhu Xi and others, Li claimed that all the teachings of previous Confucian philosophers amounted to virtually the same idea as *huiguo zixin*.[33] People had therefore wasted a lot of words by not using this teaching (EQQJ, 1.2a–b). According to Li, many famous Confucians in the past and present had advocated ways to save the world. Their teachings are represented by such slogans as "reside in reverential seriousness and thoroughly investigate principle," "first establish the mind's greatness," "the spirit of the heart-mind is the sage," "naturalness," "restore one's nature," "extend one's moral knowledge," "embody the Way in any place," "cultivation of resting" (in the highest good), "knowing where to rest," and "the illustrious virtue" (EQQJ, 1.2a–b).[34]

Defending his claim against charges of exaggeration, Li singled out ideas from the Six Classics and Four Books that in some way concerned the notion of faults. He said that the *Book of Change* made manifest the images of wind and thunder, the *Book of Documents* handed down the message of not regretting, the *Book of Poetry* presented songs of reform, the *Annals* concealed the manifest and made known the hidden, the *Book of Rites* refined behavior, and the *Book of Music* made people virtuous. Li further noted that Confucius had said not to fear correcting your faults, and Zengzi had said to regard your moral mind with reverence. The *Doctrine of the Mean* advocated having few faults, and Mencius spoke of the accumulation of right deeds. Li concluded that these teachings had the same aim as his—to encourage people to restore their faultless essence and return to the way of daily renewal (EQQJ, 1.3a–b).[35]

Li's insistence on the functional equivalence of these teachings led some people to question why yet another teaching was needed. Accepting the necessity to justify a new teaching (his own) and realizing that the contextual nature of teachings was not always recognized (or even accepted), Li offered instruction on how to evaluate his teaching. Previous sages and worthies did not see all the principles of the Way in the world, and so some principles just happened to be picked out by later sages, worthies, ordinary persons, and even those advocating other paths (EQQJ, 1.4a, 16.16b). If one wanted to test later teachings—that is, those not originally taught by the sages and worthies—one could select from among them those that seemed to benefit the human (moral) heart-mind. The results of applying those teachings to one's own cultivation would then provide evidence of their worthiness. Li's point here was an important one—that later teachings (those not from the sages) may be just as valuable as earlier ones, and their efficacy is the standard of validation.

To illustrate further that the efficacy of a teaching was more important than its source as a standard of evaluation, Li explained how his teaching of *huiguo zixin* originated. He was a common person, ignorant, fatherless, wretched, and anxious, and in the midst of extreme self-searching, he suddenly realized this truth. Consequently, he was able to decide on and pursue this course of action, with no self-serving aim. He charged that anyone who summarily dismisses this teaching because it emerged from a common person is no better than a man willing to suffer from the cold because he refuses to wear the clothing of a poor woman (EQQJ, 1.4a).

Holding that one cannot judge the truth of a teaching merely by its source, even if the source is the sages, Li did not try to claim that the sages had taught his particular teaching. He justified his teaching, instead, on the fact that it could be validated through application, and that, like others, he had had an enlightenment experience that gave rise to it. A teaching may or may not have a source in the sages' teachings, but its followers' achievements in self-cultivation demonstrated its truth. By Li's time, moreover, an enlightenment experience was accepted as a legitimate basis for knowledge in neo-Confucianism as well as in Buddhism. Li thus used several standards for evaluating evidence that would verify a belief.

Li further argued for his teaching by denigrating the opposing view. Stressing the superficiality of honors and rewards given by society, Li pointed out that an official career can last no more than thirty to fifty years, but a self that is established and a Way that is implemented will not perish in a thousand years. "If one discards the teaching of *huiguo zixin*, however, one cannot establish the self or implement the Way. Each person, however, has to decide for himself" (EQQJ, 1.4b).

Li's claim that his teaching could be verified by its results, rather than by an appeal to classical texts, left him open to the criticism of subjectivity — that there is no sure way to verify the results since success is a personal "inner" matter. Li Yong answered this objection by pointing out that one knows whether one has done it, just as one knows water is cold or hot when one drinks it. Inner virtue is necessarily manifested in observable behavior (EQQJ, 1.5a).

Li provided brief biographical accounts (presented below) of selected historical figures as a way to demonstrate that the actions of historical people confirmed the validity of his teaching (EQQJ, 1.8b–18a). His purpose in citing these accounts was to show that this teaching would result in appropriate action and had already done so under the stimulus of different, but functionally equivalent, teachings. This type of validation worked in Chinese philosophical thinking in those situations, like the present one, in which a secondary premise about the application of the ideas was attached to the primary premise, even if not stated explicitly.

Li began with accounts of neo-Confucian philosophers who had achieved some success in their efforts to eliminate their faults and to reestablish their moral goodness. He wrote about Zhang Zai, Xie Liangzuo, and Zhu Xi of the Song; Wu Cheng of the Yuan; and Xue Xuan, Luo Rufang, Wang Yangming, Nan Daji, and Dong Yun of the Ming. Li then gave accounts, some very brief, of Yang Tingxian, the father of the prominent Song philosopher Yang Jian; Qiu Lan, Xu Shu, and Zhou Chu, three men from the third century C.E.; and six people from the pre-Han period, Zizhang, Yan Zhuoju, Duan Ganmu, Gao He, Xian Zishi, and Suo Lucan. As we shall see, Li's accounts mention different kinds of faults committed by people with widely varying positions in society—officials and commoners, good and bad persons.

Zhang Zai (1020–77) was interested in military matters as a youth, and so he sent Fan Zhongyan (989–1052) a letter describing the regional military situation when he learned that Fan had become the commander in Shaanxi. Fan's response was not encouraging, for he wrote that the concern of Confucians was moral behavior, not the military. Fan gave Zhang a copy of the *Doctrine of the Mean*, and after reading it, Zhang reset his aim on the Way. Zhang still floundered around, however, studying Buddhism and Daoism. Finally he realized their errors and his own in pursuing these traditions, and he began to study the Six Classics. At the beginning of the Jiayou period (1056–63), Zhang went to the capital to visit his nephews, the two Cheng brothers. Although they were younger, their learning was considered vast and profound, and Zhang discussed the essentials of the learning of the Way with them. Subsequently reaching great understanding, he exclaimed that "our" Way was sufficient by itself. Zhang then completely cast aside the other paths (EQQJ, 1.8b).[36]

When Xie Liangzuo (1050–1103) was young, he went to study with Master Cheng. Xie quoted so much from texts that Cheng Hao finally became critical and said that Xie memorized too much, that he had "lost his aim by trifling with things." Ashamed of himself, Xie asked Cheng about the essentials of learning and was told to practice quiet sitting. Xie did so, and he also kept a diary, in which he recorded the ritual correctness of his daily words and behavior as a way to measure himself. He wrote in his diary about the difficulty of "restraining the self." When Xie spoke with Cheng Hao a year or so later about his progress in learning, Xie said that he had rid himself of only one word—boasting. When pressed to explain, Xie said his heart-mind still cherished obstinate obstructions and self-deception, and his temperament still produced baseless arrogance and self-aggrandizement. Cheng, however, was pleased with Xie and praised him as a learner who asked urgent questions and who thought about what was nearby (EQQJ, 1.9a–b).[37]

When Zhu Xi was young, he did not have a permanent teacher, and so he studied a little of the Confucian classics, as well as Buddhism and Daoism. At the age of fifteen or sixteen, his admiration for Buddhism led him to follow the Buddhists. At the age of 24, he met Li Tong (Yanping) for the first time, and when their conversation reached the subject of studying Chan Buddhism, Li just said Chan was wrong. At first Zhu doubted Li, but Li would not say much more and simply instructed Zhu to look at the words of the sages and worthies. After studying the classics for a long time, Zhu eventually realized their worth as well as the inconsistencies in Buddhism. Zhu then felt regret and remorse and realized his errors (*hui-wu*), he earnestly corrected his previous illnesses, and he rid himself of errors permanently (EQQJ, 1.9b–10a).[38]

At the age of five, Wu Cheng (1249–1333) was already memorizing several thousand words a day and was reading all night until dawn. Although his mother worried that he was working excessively, he continued his studies until he understood all of the Confucian classical tradition. Wu's classical learning was so impressive that even an official praised him for his vast understanding. Wu wrote insightful commentaries on the *Book of Change* and the *Annals*, and his work on ritual was especially critical for those studying this subject. When older, however, he felt regret and remorse and realized his errors. He came to regard only "honoring the virtuous nature" as important, and he wrote two pieces, the *Foundation of Learning* and the *Transmission of Learning*, to enable people to realize the root of learning (EQQJ, 1.10a).[39]

Li Yong then summarized the general ideas of juan 22 of Wu's collected writings on following the virtuous nature and pursuing the path of inquiry and study. That whereby heaven produces humans and humans become human is the virtuous nature. When the sages' tradition and the scholars' learning were discontinued, during the thousand years from the Han through the Tang, the source was obscured, even though Dong Zhongshu and Han Yü came close to it.

When Zhou Dunyi, the Cheng brothers, Zhang Zai, and Shao Yong flourished in the Sung, people began to be able to comprehend Mencius. From the Chengs to their four disciples to the subtleties of Zhu Xi — ever since Mencius there had never been such a person as Zhu Xi. But the learning of Zhu's followers eventually degenerated into the vulgar learning of scholars who memorized and recited words and phrases. This was the defect of the later followers of Zhu Xi after the Jiading reign period (1208–25), when there was no one able to save the Zhu school.

But, continued Wu, what one values in the learning of the sages is being able to complete this virtuous nature, conferred by Heaven on the self. It is both the root of virtuous conduct and the ruler of one's bodily self. One cannot cast it aside even if one's actions are as great as Sima Qian's and one's talent as great as Zhuge Liang's. How much more so for lesser people, those who stop with the minute details of commentaries and theories, such as Chen Chun (Beixi, 1159–1223) and Rao Lu (Shuangfeng, ca. 1210), who were not able to depart at all from the learning of memorization and recitation. The learning of the sages was brilliant in the Song, but how awful that their later followers became like this. Li Yong further quoted Wu Cheng's comments on how he had deeply studied prose writings and morality and had analyzed in detail the most minute parts, and yet still had regarded Chen and Rao as not very subtle. Wu was trapped in the examination life for forty years before he began to realize its falseness. Afterward, however, he spent all his time attending to his virtuous nature (EQQJ, 1.10b–11b).[40]

Xue Xuan (1392–1464) at first spoke to the world through poetry and prose, but then he began to study philosophy. After he heard the writings of Zhou, the Chengs, Zhang, and Zhu discussed, Xue sighed and exclaimed that this was the genuine branch of the learning of the Way. Xue then burned his poetical writings and focused his mind on this learning, even to the point of forgetting to sleep and eat. He often said that although he fervently desired to reach the ultimate of this learning, he was unable to and would ask himself where his illnesses lay. Had he not yet fully eliminated old habits? Old habits were extremely harmful, for one's development was stopped as long as one wished simply to continue old habits. If one wished only to reform them, then one stymied one's efforts at renewal. Old habits were despicable and had to be completely eliminated. Xue also said that if one's self-examination did not reach to the smallest things, one would not act appropriately. And so one should criticize and reject that behavior. One cannot not be watchful (EQQJ, 1.11b).[41]

Luo Rufang (1515–88) began serious studying when he was fifteen years old. His teacher often said that people should vigorously pursue the ancients and not throw the self away by burying themselves in the examination system. Consequently Luo focused on genuine learning with single-mindedness. One day he was reading the passage in Xue Xuan's *Recorded Sayings* in which Xue said that the coming and going of numerous selfish thoughts had jumbled his mind for a long time and therefore he had concluded he ought to get rid of all thoughts in order to complete his pure and clear essence. After finishing reading, Luo burned incense and bowed respectfully, focused his mind, and vigorously exerted effort. Several months later, however, he had not yet restored his essence, and so he went to the Lintian Temple. He set a mirror on the altar and a bowl of water in front of it, and he tried to make his mind achieve a unity with the water and mirror. After a long time he fell ill. Becoming distressed, his father gave him a copy of Wang Yangming's *Instructions for Practical Living*. Luo gradually began to recover after following Wang's teachings.

At the provincial capital, Nanchang, in 1540, he joined a large crowd listening to Yan Jun (Shannong). Having a chance to speak to Yan, Luo mentioned that when he faced a dangerous sickness, or life and death, or gaining and losing, he was able not to become disturbed. Yan did not approve and said that control of one's desires is not how to embody and practice benevolence. Luo then asked how one can embody benevolence if one does not control desires. Yan asked in return whether Luo had read Mencius' discussion that the four sprouts fulfill themselves by expanding. Since benevolence also was realized in this way, how could this realization be equivalent to cutting off the sprout? Yan noted that Luo was anxious about immediate daily needs and yet did not know it, and so he told him not to doubt the breaths of his heavenly nature. Luo felt as if he were waking up from a long dream, and in the midst of the crowd of people he bowed respectfully and acknowledged Yan as his teacher.

Some time later, Luo suddenly met with a serious illness. He lay in bed and had a dream in which an old man came and said that he was now healthy and recovered from his illness of the body but not yet from his illness of the mind. When Luo did not respond, the old man said that all Luo's life his energy (*qi*) had never been truly aroused when he was stimulated. When Luo faced fatigue, he did not try to sleep. When his passions were disturbed, he did not become ambivalent. He slept soundly and dreamed, and yet it was not night. These, the old man said, were Luo's diseases of the mind. Luo became alarmed, and the old man told him to understand things according to the thing and not to have any preconceptions. Luo's possessiveness in a past life (his karma, perhaps) had resulted in these habits, but now he was slowly becoming content and recovering from his illness. Luo had not comprehended that one's heavenly essence is lost gradually. Such habits do not remain only an illness of the mind, moreover, for the body follows along. Sufficiently warned, Luo prostrated himself on the ground, and lay drenched in perspiration. From then on, Luo's obstinate thoughts gradually dispersed (EQQJ, 1.12a–13a).[42]

The learning of Wang Yangming went through three transformations, and his teachings also changed three times. When young, Wang pursued examination learning, and afterward he tried, and abandoned, Buddhism and Daoism. Finally, while living in a "barbarian" region and suffering hardships, he obtained the teachings of the sages. With this third change he attained the Way. When he lived in Guiyang, he first proposed his theory of the unity of knowledge and action. After living in Chuyang, he mostly taught quiet sitting. And after he moved to Jiangyou, he began to advocate his teaching to extend moral knowledge, a teaching that directly pointed to the basic essence and so enabled learners to become enlightened through this teaching. These were the three changes in his teachings (EQQJ, 1.13a).[43]

When Nan Daji (1487–1541) was the prefect of Shaoxing, he studied with Wang Yangming and requested Wang's help in addressing his faults. At Wang's request, Nan listed his numerous faults. Wang then said, "I have said it." Nan asked Wang what his words were. Wang replied by asking, "How would you know it if I didn't speak?" Nan answered that his own moral knowledge itself would know it. Wang agreed that Nan's words were indeed moral knowledge. Nan smiled, thanked him, and left.

After several days Nan again enumerated for himself his faults, going from those less private to those more so. He then returned to Wang and announced that to criticize and correct after committing faults was not as good as saying beforehand that he would have good actions without any faults. Wang said that a person's words were not as good as the purity of self-criticism. Nan smiled and left. After several days Nan again enumerated for himself his faults, this time those even more private. He returned and said that faults of the body could be avoided, but he didn't know about faults of the mind. Wang said that when the mirror case was not open, one could successfully hide one's stains, but now the mirror was bright and reflecting. When one is starting to fall, it naturally is hard to stop one's feet. This precisely is the incipient moment of entering sagehood, and one should exert oneself there. Nan thanked him and left. From then on, to obtain learning he exerted effort at the points of movement (EQQJ, 1.13b–14a).[44]

At 68 years old, Dong Yun (1457–1533), an accomplished poet known throughout the world, formed a poetry society with literary men of his region. Day and night they chanted and recited, to the point of not sleeping, eating, or working. Dong thought that this was the greatest happiness in the world. One day he heard that Wang Yangming was teaching in the mountains and went to visit him. Wang was struck by Dong's strange appearance and his age. He respectfully received him, and after learning who Dong was, they talked for several days and nights. Dong then left and said that hearing Wang's theory of moral knowledge was like suddenly awakening from a deep sleep. He understood that he had previously covered up his essence and followed after fame and profit in the world. If he had not come to Wang's gate to become a follower, his life would have been empty. When Dong expressed concern about what he could accomplish at his age, he was assured that although he was old, his aspirations were youthful and strong. Wang accepted him as a follower, saying that although Dong was older, they were the same as teacher and friend. Somewhat later, because of Dong's great courage in giving up all he had done earlier in life, Wang claimed that Dong was his teacher, and he could not be Dong's teacher. Dong, however, refused to accept this view, saying that his own life had been changed from one of bitterness to one of happiness because of Wang (EQQJ, 1.14a–15b).

When Yang Tingxian (twelfth century C.E.) was young, he was very fierce and believed that there was nothing in the world he could not do. He found no faults in himself, but he did see other people's faults. One day he asked himself why he alone had no faults. After pondering this, he realized what his faults were, and being in great fear of a painful punishment, he vigorously corrected them. He read books and listened to others. He was determined to examine himself, and he reproached himself every time he saw a fault. Even in sleep and in dreams he was extremely watchful, and he corrected the slightest defects in his thoughts, words, and actions. When people praised him, he told them that he had worked to correct his faults (EQQJ, 1.15b–16a).[45]

Qiu Lan (Later Han) was the head of Yangsui department, and he was good at teaching morality. The young man Chen Yuan was not filial, and so his mother visited Qiu Lan to talk about her son. Lan summoned Yuan and charged him to assume his filial responsibility. He gave him a copy of the *Classic of Filial Piety* and told him to read it. Deeply moved and enlightened, Chen Yuan went to his mother's bed and confessed his faults. He said that when he was young, he was fatherless and was his mother's pride. But, as the proverb says, "The orphaned calf butts the udders; the favorite son scolds his mother." From that day on, he would correct himself. Mother and son wept together, and afterward Chen Yuan cultivated and carried out the filial way, eventually becoming a good man (EQQJ, 1.16a–b).[46]

When Xu Shu (third century C.E.) was young, he loved being a knight-errant, attacking others with his knife. He even killed people in anger. Once, when walking along with the white scar showing on his face and his hair disheveled, he was seized by an official who asked his name. When Xu would not tell him, the official tied him in his cart to hold him, and he beat the drum to announce it to the village. When no one dared recognize and identify him, his gang together petitioned to obtain his release. Afterward, he was greatly moved and threw away his knife and sword. He changed into simple, rough clothes and dedicated himself to learning. When first he went to the school, the students were not willing to live with him after hearing about his past as a thief. But he rose early and swept out the place by himself, and eventually his moral behavior became thoroughly refined. He became friends with Zhuge Liang, and together they were famous men of the time (EQQJ, 1.16b–17a).[47]

Zhou Chu (240–99) was fierce by nature, unrestrained and self-indulgent, and his fellow villagers feared him. One day he asked his old father why, with his abundant years, he was now bitter and unhappy. His father sighed and asked what happiness could he have with the three dangers not yet eliminated. Chu asked what they were, and his father answered: the white-foreheaded wild animal of

Nanshan, the dragon under Long Bridge, and his son. Chu replied that if these were his fears, he could get rid of them. Zhou Chu then went to the mountain and killed the wild animal. He then jumped into the water and seized the dragon. Sometimes submerged and sometimes floating, it traveled numerous miles with Zhou Chu hanging on to it. When after a long time it did not emerge, people said that Chu must have died, and they congratulated each other. But Chu killed the dragon, and when he returned, he heard the villagers congratulating each other. He then realized how much people hated him.

He subsequently went to Wu to look for the two Lu brothers, both poets. Lu Ji was not there, but he saw Lu Yun and told him that he wished to cultivate himself. He feared, however, that too many years had already slipped away. Yun replied that the ancients valued hearing about the Way in the morning and correcting themselves in the evening. Although it was still possible to correct his previous faults, he feared that Chu's aim was not firmly established. Why be concerned that one's name is not known? Chu then vigorously set his aim on learning. His aim was fulfilled, his rightness was imposing, and his words were loyal and trustworthy. He died as a pure and virtuous famous official (EQQJ, 1.17a–b).[48]

Concluding his examples with six men from ancient times and quoting from the *Lüshi chunqiu*, Li said that Zizhang came from a lowly family from the state of Lu (yet studied with Confucius). Yan Zhuoju was a great robber from Liangfu and studied with Confucius. Duan Ganmu was a great rascal from the state of Jin and studied with Zixia, the grandson of Confucius. Gao He and Xian Zishi were brigands from the state of Qi who studied with Mozi. Suo Lucan was a great scoundrel from the eastern region and studied with Qin Huali, a follower of Mozi. All six men were executed and died in disgrace. Today, Li commented, not only would such people avoid capital punishment and dying in shame, but they would become famous scholars and distinguished men throughout the world (EQQJ, 1.17b–18a).[49]

Li's teaching of *huiguo zixin* brought together many ideas that went into the development of Confucian thought. Li's quotation of Lü Buwei's work, the *Spring and Autumn Annals of Mr. Lü*, is interesting in that the passage in question is part of a section entitled "Respecting Teachers." Scholars of Li's time would have known the source of the quoted passage, and so there was no need to indicate the source or even to indicate that he was quoting. The lack of documentation here contrasts to Li's presentations to people uneducated in the classics. Lü was an official in the state of Qin (ancient name for the area of Guanzhong), he was a disciple of Xunzi (historically seen as the rival of Mencius), and his work was compiled under Xunzi's sponsorship before the book burning in 213 B.C.E. Lü's work incorporates the views and interests of a number of ancient philosophical schools, including the Confucians, the Mohists, the Daoists, the agriculturalists, and the military strategists. The practical emphases of these ancient schools are clearly still evident in Li Yong's thought and in much of Guanxue (Confucian learning in Guanzhong).

Li's teaching of *huiguo zixin* incorporates ideas derived from, or held in common with, Chinese medicine, including views that assumed correlative thinking and that saw illnesses as caused by demonic possession. Thinkers used both of these approaches in speaking of faults, errors, defects, or those things harmful to the health of the self in all its different aspects. In terms of correlative thought, the way to restore good order, whether in respect to the self or the state and society, required an understanding of the categories to which all things belonged and then action based on that understanding. Li accepted that view, but not that view alone. In his insistence on getting rid of faults, he was also using an idea akin to exorcism. That is, a fault was an illness that destroyed one's original health, and it had to be completely removed before health could be restored.

Li's teaching of *huiguo zixin* required people to examine, acknowledge, and eliminate their faults in order to reestablish their original moral goodness. A person had to plan, perform, and constantly review. In arguing for the acceptance and validity of this teaching, Li did not emphasize a basis in the classics. Rather, he made as his ultimate standard the actual results of self-cultivation (as seen in people from the past) and personal experiences of "enlightenment." Although not fully articulated, the theoretical implication of this teaching was a fundamental shift in authority away from the written tradition to personal experience.

5   *To Learn*

AN ANALYTIC FRAMEWORK

Learning (*xue* and *weixue*) as an activity completes Li's conception of Confucianism as a tradition centered on teaching and learning. Although learning was thought to occur at the level of the individual person, Li (like others) maintained that the benefits extended from the person to society and to the cultural tradition. Li was concerned primarily with two problems: how to characterize the process of learning, including its objectives and the "state" that was sought; and the constituents of the approach, or the actions necessary.

Like earlier Song and Ming thinkers, Li used the term *xuezhe*, "one who learns," to refer to the learner. This term implied that the activity of learning did not necessarily take place with reference to the examination system or the school system. Although a learner (*xuezhe*) could be a student or a scholar in an institutional setting, affiliation with the government's educational system was not mandatory. A learner was anyone, with or without a degree, in any position in society, engaged in the kind of behavior conceived of as great learning. There was also no necessarily close relationship between schools and teaching. No compulsory educational system existed, and government schools were often not the site where teaching occurred. Schools were generally seen as places for taking examinations (a phenomenon lamented by Li), and success in the examinations, not in school, was the route to official appointment. Public and private academies were the exception, for they actually served as places for teaching and learning.

At the highest level of Confucian learning, a person became a great man, a hero, or a genuine person. By embodying the tradition, the genuine person paradoxically became a truly individual entity and the culminating point of Confucian learning. Such a person was regarded as having achieved an ultimate "state" through learning. Taking a position that began with Confucius, Li further held that the viability of society and the tradition depended on periodic appearances of such an extraordinary person. This person was able, in times of great turmoil, to offer a restatement of the Confucian way. The social significance of the great man is, I suggest, particularly illuminated by Durkheim's concept of anomie.[1]

Anomie is a condition that often describes people in societies experiencing tumultuous change. The changes are so great and the patterns so subtle that most people cannot see the patterns of regularity that are present. Because they see only disorder, people label such periods "chaotic." That is, they mistakenly think there are no regularities. Through his ability and his learning, the great man comprehends these situations. Because he can recognize patterns of change that others cannot, he is able to reformulate the Confucian way in a manner relevant to the times and thereby help direct people toward appropriate action.

Confucian culture implicitly attempted to temper the rate of social change by accepting the necessity of the great man's rarity. That is, it recognized the need for the periodic appearance of a "hero," but it accepted that this sagely person appears only rarely, perhaps once every 500 years. Confucians believed that the hero revitalizes the cultural tradition and enables society to remain viable. Confucius was viewed as one such person, Mencius another, and the Song Confucians and Wang Yangming as still others.

Before turning to Li's views on the process of learning, I shall briefly introduce a few modern ideas about learning, to provide a framework for thinking about the Chinese position. The Chinese used different terms, had different aims, and did not do experiments to justify their views, but the implicit theoretical organization of their ideas has significant points in common with some modern ideas. I am not suggesting, of course, that the people mentioned below are the only ones with these (or similar) ideas.

In examining the question of how people learn, cognitive scientists have proposed, first, that learning is a process in which a person goes from being a novice to an expert.[2] This process occurs, moreover, in specific knowledge domains. Different areas of knowledge are called knowledge domains, and each has its own facts, skills, and strategies. To become proficient in an area of knowledge, whether it be physics or chess, one must learn a body of factual knowledge, skills, and the rules of thinking that apply to that domain. These rules, or "strategy," tell a person what information to attend to. Unique to each domain, the strategy concerns the specific kinds of questions asked.

Since facts, skills, and strategy are specific for each knowledge domain, one can be a novice in one domain and an expert in another. Moreover, these three aspects do not transfer in any general way from one domain to another, and therefore they must be learned in reference to different knowledge domains. One can be an intelligent learner, but to become so, one must gain certain metacognitive skills. That is, one must become aware of the different aspects of learning so that one can deliberately change one's behavior to improve one's learning skills. Although easier for some than others, metacognition can be learned and taught. A person can be taught to think critically about what he or she is doing and what he or she should do in order to learn. A person can learn how to learn. Gregory Bateson has proposed three levels of learning: (simple) learning (partly physiological and partly cultural), learning to learn (learning facts, skills, and strategies), learning to learn to learn (metacognition).[3] No matter whether Bateson's terms or those of the cognitive scientists are used, this highest level of learning, or metacognition, was of great concern to Confucian philosophers. A critical awareness of how to learn belonged to their "great learning."

Confucian philosophers typically divided learning into a set of stages, the last of which is of philosophical interest. The activities appropriate to each stage were seen as forming a continuous progression connecting to the highest stage, the knowledge domain called "Confucian learning" (EQQJ, 3.7a–b). Not born a "blank slate," a baby began to learn in the womb. A small child's early learning focused on proper social behavior, first within the family and then in broader social settings. If an examination degree was the goal, the male child eventually acquired the skills of writing and reading, with a stress on memorization and recitation. (Such skills were only selectively encouraged for female children.) Little emphasis was placed at first on understanding the meaning of the words and texts. The early stages of learning, from about the age of eight to about fifteen, were considered elementary learning. After that, adult learning, or great learning, began.[4]

Interpreted as "learning for adults" by Zhu Xi and "learning to be a great person" by Wang Yangming, great learning was, for Li Yong, learning to be a great Confucian (*daru*).[5] Unless one mastered the facts, skills, and strategy of the knowledge domain of Confucian learning (*ruxue*), one could not become an expert in it, or a great Confucian. This great learning was termed "upper reaching" in contrast to "lower learning" or practical studies, but it was not without practical application. Indeed, its imperative for action often subverted its political goals into a crass striving for personal success in the examinations and in bureaucratic life. (Confucians warned against comparable foreshortenings in other areas, such as art, where the concern was that people would focus too much on the objects in the painting, the means, and too little on the end, the moral value of the work.)[6]

Confucian philosophers wanted to become experts not only in the knowledge domain of Confucian learning. They were also interested in metacognition (about learning), or Bateson's third level of learning. Since much of Confucian thought was concerned with teaching people how to learn, Confucian philosophers offered ideas about learning and its objectives, and about the specific kinds of necessary efforts.

CONCEPTIONS OF LEARNING

Like many Confucian philosophers, Li Yong discussed learning in a variety of ways. He used certain paradigmatic examples to describe learning, and he provided a few general definitions whose language and thought assumed one or more of the paradigmatic images. His varied approaches enabled him to conceive of the process and objectives of learning from several perspectives. Overall, Li (like others of his tradition) regarded learning as self-transformation, understood as realizing the Way.

Li most often turned to the paradigmatic examples of the plant, the mirror, and medicine, each of which provided a distinct view of the process of learning. As noted earlier, these and other examples, such as the road and the rite, were thoroughly embedded in the thought and language of philosophers.[7] Although not always compatible or usable together, the ideas suggested by the different para-

digmatic examples were constructively redundant in elaborating on
the learning process. Moreover, it would be a mistake to interpret the
multiple approaches as contradictory in an epistemological sense,
because multiple approaches constituted an important aspect of the
epistemological system itself.[8]

The living plant provided the conceptual frame used by Mencius
in his theory of the goodness of human nature. The potential of humans was compared to that of plants, and the process of learning
was viewed as one of growth, development, and completion. Human
capacities were like a seed, dependent on the right conditions for
germination and development. Among the terms used to refer to
human capacities, "root" clearly brought out the basis of this perspective. The characteristics of the plant were assumed, for instance,
by the questioner who asked what it meant to say that the essentials
of learning lie completely in nourishing and examination. Li's reply
followed appropriately: "One must first understand the head. Otherwise, what is one nourishing and what is one examining?" (EQQJ,
3.6b). Analogous to the root in plants, the head was seen as the
source and the basis of the organism.

Important in two ways, a mirror was thought to have an inner
brightness or luminosity like that of the sun, and it could reflect like
perfectly still water. The process of learning was compared to the
activity of getting rid of those things that obscured or inhibited the
mirror's brilliance. Learning was like recovering or restoring. One of
Li's followers, Lu Shikai, said, "That whereby humans are humans is
that they have this heart-mind. That whereby this heart-mind is this
heart-mind is that its empty luminosity is not clouded over. [This
heart-mind enables a person] to complete the four sprouts and to
unite myriad acts of goodness" (EQQJ, 6.1a). Li said that one must
"first sweep everything clean and not let oneself get entangled in
worldly desires, surges of energy, personal opinions, and clever
knowledge. If one can sweep away all such beclouding things, then
. . . the brilliance of one's nature will be self-illuminating . . . and
one's entire essence will be completely manifested" (EQQJ, 5.3a).

The mirror's ability to reflect provided another conception of the
process of learning, one also important in Buddhism. Li said that
"when one is able to be constantly alert and have no distracting
thoughts, one's mind is then pure and still, and there is nothing
thought or pondered." Someone who has reached this state responds
to affairs and conditions in the same way a bright mirror reflects

things in front of it. "One thinks what one should think without any perverse thoughts, and one ponders what one should ponder without any malicious thoughts" (EQQJ, 4.8b). When someone asked how to achieve this state, described as empty, luminous, boundless, and joyful, Li said:

> One must practice reverential seriousness. If one is reverential and serious, then inner and outer are pure and penetrating, and one is naturally not entangled in excessive desires. This lofty, bright, and vast realm is not hard to reach by oneself. . . . If the learner is able to attain this condition and not let thoughts arise, then there is nothing more to say. If thoughts do arise, all of them are naturally good. When one meets a parent or an older brother, one naturally is able to be filial or fraternally submissive. When one ought to be compassionate, feel shame and dislike, yield, and know right and wrong, then one naturally does all these things. (EQQJ, 4.9a)

The medical example provided Li with a third major way of conceptualizing learning. In this context, the process of learning was compared to diagnosing and treating illnesses. To learn involved a search for health, and becoming expert was comparable to becoming healthy. Thinking in these terms (along with the image of the road), Li said, "If only each person were to shine the light back on himself and search himself for the places of his own illnesses, and to think of curing these illnesses himself after he knows what sicknesses he has, then he is entering the gate [of the sages' learning] and is beginning to learn" (EQQJ, 3.8a–b).

In addition to using analogical thinking focused on particular metaphors, Li also defined the process of learning in more general ways. Still implicitly based on the appropriateness of certain paradigmatic examples, these broader descriptions often addressed specific issues. To use modern terms, one of the most critical issues for Li Yong was the lack of recognition that the knowledge domain of Confucian learning included factual knowledge, skills, and (unwritten) rules of thinking and behaving (a strategy). An expert (a "genuine Confucian") had to master all three aspects, but many Confucians stopped short of the third ingredient.

Li referred to the "rules" or strategy in many ways—for instance, as the marrow and skin of learning. Reminiscent of the distinction between inner and outer, the "marrow of learning" referred to rules on the personal level, such as "calm the self and establish the standards conferred by heaven," whereas the "skin of learning" referred to rules for the social and political levels, including those about engaging in scholarship and government service (EQQJ, 2.3b–4a).

Li was concerned that the strategy or implicit rules were often not recognized (much less followed). This concern is visible, for instance, in his answer to a question why Wang Yangming's teaching was the target of such incessant criticism. Li's answer was that Confucians do not understand great learning. Some people pursue book knowledge and its false morality (rightness seized from outside, not developed from within), but neither enables people to have real achievements. Other people simply advocate personal opinions or strange and lofty theories, particularly successful exam candidates. All these people are deluded, Li claimed, and none engages in practical effort (EQQJ, 3.10b–11a).

Li advised Confucians to follow Confucius, to be "slow in speech and quick in action." He claimed that those who argue and discuss incessantly fail to implement the Way, and so their so-called Way is merely a Way of words (EQQJ, 3.11a; reference to *Lunyu*, 4.24). Despite Shen Buhai's Legalist position, Li compared his view of learning to Shen's view of ruling in terms of their similar emphasis on action. That is, neither learning nor ruling lies in a lot of words. In both cases, one must concentrate on vigorous action (EQQJ, 3.11a–b).

A person does not have to do everything, of course. Li said that it is enough just to implement one or two ideas found in the Four Books. Then, even if for the rest of one's life one does not engage in either moral discussions or writing, there is no harm to one's status as a superior person. On the other hand, no matter how penetrating one's discussions and how rich one's writings, they are nothing more than clever words if one's actions do not embody the Way. Clever words confuse what virtue is, and learners ought to be on guard against them (EQQJ, 3.11b; reference to *Lunyu*, 15.26).

In urging people to recognize the strategy aspect of Confucian learning, Li emphasized the position of Li Tong (Yanping), the Song thinker and Zhu Xi's teacher. Quoting Li Tong, Li Yong said, "Learning does not lie in a lot of words, but in silently sitting, purifying the heart, and embodying natural principles" (EQQJ, 4.9b, 6.5a–b). Facts and skills are not enough. In a similar vein, Li claimed that "one learns in order to fulfill this heart-mind and to recover this nature, not to show off one's brilliance and boast of one's fame" (EQQJ, 6.4a).

Li emphasized that "learning is not the memorization and recitation of phrases and chapters, but is that by which one preserves the heart-mind and recovers the nature in fulfilling what ought to be so of the human way." The "ought to be so" refers to human capacities and their appropriate patterns of realization, or natural principles. After giving examples of the "inner" and "outer" efforts that a person should make, Li observed that "if one's behavior is like this, then one's heart-mind will be preserved, one's nature will be recovered, and one will not be ashamed over how one performs the duties of the human way. Only then can one begin to talk about learning" (EQQJ, 11.3a–b).

Expanding on this idea, Li Yong maintained, "That whereby a human being becomes a person is simply this one heart-mind. That whereby the heart-mind is constantly preserved completely depends on learning" (EQQJ, *fu* 15.2a). Moreover, those one who exclude the heart-mind while talking about learning are merely talking about "vulgar [opportunistic] learning" or "pedantic learning." Neither bears any relationship to the reality of becoming a person, and neither is what Confucians mean by learning (EQQJ, *fu* 15.2a). To learn is to complete the capacities of the heart-mind that are shared by everyone (EQQJ, 6.1a).

Developing one's human capacities involved recognizing the extent of one's responsibilities toward others. The fact that many Confucians reduced learning to the acquisition of facts and skills constantly led Li to reaffirm the importance of social behavior, which entailed a higher level of social reality. Echoing Zhang Zai, Li said, for instance, that he occupied a place between heaven and earth just as a human being, but to be a person, he had to "participate in the activities of heaven and assist in the activities of earth." Only then could he have accomplishments. And only if his accomplishments were done for others — past, present, and future — was he engaged in learning and in becoming a person (EQQJ, *fu* 15.3b–4a). Acting on behalf of others was "establishing the self" (EQQJ, 5.2a). As Li said, "I emphasize practical action and not what has been seen and heard [by others]. I discuss human actions and not talent." Li acknowledged that the superior person is familiar with previous words and actions, but said that he also values extending what is within himself to others and giving aid to the world (EQQJ, *fu* 15.4a–b).

Li was also concerned with the problem of appearing to master the strategy of Confucian learning but not doing so in reality. This distinction is important because it points to another conception of the process of learning and because a genuine realization of the Way was seen as the means by which learning was verified. In addition, then, to the conceptions of learning as processes of developing, completing, restoring, recovering, and diagnosing and treating, learning was understood as perceiving and comprehending. Li (and others) emphasized comprehension by contrasting it with mere imitation: "To learn [*xue*] is to apprehend [*jue*]. One apprehends in order to apprehend what one naturally has, not to apprehend what the ancient sages had. And yet, if one does not imitate what they did, then it is also not easy to talk about apprehending" (EQQJ, 11.3b–4a).

This statement is related to two concerns that grew out of the view that learning involves realizing the Way, that is, that right behavior is a result of learning and is observable by others. One concern was whether the appearance of right behavior indicated that a person had learned, and the other was whether a person could simply copy the actions of the sages—Yao, Shun, Yu, Tang, Wen, Wu, the Duke of Zhou, and Confucius—since the Way was the Way of these sages (EQQJ, 3.13a). In other words, had learning occurred when a person could successfully imitate the behavior of these exemplary persons? Li followed Zhu Xi in maintaining that imitating is not learning, and that even though the root is the same in all people, similar behavior will not result from each person's development of the root.

To answer these two questions, Li addressed the problem of what the Way is. Given that everyone ought to follow the Way, Li argued that the Way is not the sages' particular acts, for each did what was appropriate in his circumstances. The variety of their actions confirmed this view. Yao held fast to the mean, Shun was refined and single-minded, Yu received with reverence, Tang ordered affairs by rightness and the heart-mind by ritual action, Wen did what was right without instruction and entered the path of goodness without admonition, Wu overcame insolence with respect and desire with rightness, the Duke of Zhou thought of combining in himself the sages' virtues, and Confucius sought earnestly. Yan Hui acted as if ignorant, Zengzi behaved vulgarly, Zhou Dunyi resided in stillness, the two Chengs abided in reverential seriousness, Zhu Xi thoroughly investigated principles and extended knowledge, Lu Jiuyuan first established the heart-mind's greatness, Wang Yangming knew the good, and Zhan Ruoshui realized the Way everywhere (EQQJ,

3.13b and 11.4a).[9] Although everyone ought to follow the Way, Li maintained that no one now is able to do so completely. Only the ancient sages were able to. Thus, people have a real need to imitate the sages' acts to help themselves along. "If later Confucians are sincerely able to imitate these early sages and, in following them, able to respect what they hear and carry out what they know, they will be able to perceive the minds of the sages. Doing that will then enable them to perceive their own minds" (EQQJ, 3.13a–b). Imitating others, however, is not great learning.

When beginning to learn, a person thus imitates what the former sages did and may even seem to attain the Way of these sages. When finished, he will clearly have progressed beyond imitation. Such a person will go through a multi-stage process of reflecting on his thoughts and acts, making them clear, completing them, and verifying them; everyone who does this will attain the Way that he himself ought to follow. That Way will not mimic what the sages did (EQQJ, 3.13b–14a). Li stressed this obvious point to argue against contemporary scholarly practices that he judged pedantic. He held that textual scholars were trying to recapture the sages' words and acts literally. Trying to do what the sages did and attain their Way is a case of "rightness seized from the outside" (reference to *Mencius*, 2A.2). It is like neglecting one's own field to weed the field of another. Such actions will not help a person overcome the selfishness involved in imitating others and in chasing excessive pleasure. Even if a person copies the sages' good and humane acts, he or she is not in actuality being humane and right (EQQJ, 3.14a).

Only those acts that are manifestations of a person's cultivated nature and an appropriate response to the circumstances are right. Although the root or the nature is the same in everyone, one cannot duplicate the actions of others, for different situations required different behavior. Copied actions are not right because they do not stem from responses appropriate to the situation. Such actions have no basis in the root but are instead based on its external manifestations, or branches. Right acts that imitate others' right acts possess only an imitation rightness and are not genuinely good. Thus, the appearance of apparently right acts does not guarantee that a person has truly learned, for the rightness of an act does not lie simply in the behavior itself and in its resemblance to a standard.

Li thus affirmed that genuinely right behavior must be rooted in the heart-mind. Beginners may need to base their actions on those of the sages, but they cannot continue to do so. Eventually, beginners need to understand their own mind and do what they as particular persons ought to do. Actions must be appropriate to the particular situation.

> To learn, one must first know the root. When one sincerely knows the root, and the root of the root is obtained, then the branches naturally flourish. It is just like water. This water has a source, and it bubbles up naturally. When it flows out to Sichuan, it becomes the Min River. When it flows toward Yuzhang, it is the Jiu River. When it flows to Jinshan, it is the Zhen River. When it flows to the ocean, it is the Eastern Sea. One names the water according to where it is, even if the source is at first not known. (EQQJ, 4.4b)

That is, rightness and humaneness can appear in many forms, just as the outflow of a spring can become different rivers, but a person does not aim at the particular forms. They appear naturally when the source is nourished.

Li went on to say that "as we learn, if we understand the root and embody it in our actions, then the root becomes the Way and its creative power, even though we may not understand the so-called Way and its creative power." When the Way and its creative power are manifested in words, actions, or "junctures of fate," they become known as literature, meritorious accomplishments, or courage, even though a person does not initially aim to achieve those things. Just as water is named according to where it flows, a particular manifestation of the root happens without deliberate planning (EQQJ, 4.4b). That is, a person's human capacities can be developed in many ways, and the Way when achieved is called by the form of behavior that that development takes.[10] If that behavior is not a result of a person's developing the root, however, it is not the Way.

Li described the root that must be both apprehended and developed as that luminosity (*lingming*) in every person's heart-mind by which a person knows right and wrong. "It is the great root of heaven and earth, and when one establishes the self, this is what one establishes" (EQQJ, 4.5a). Li used other important Confucian concepts to convey the idea of comprehending the root, such as investigating things, thoroughly investigating principles, and extending moral knowledge.

In discussing the idea of investigating things, for instance, Li acknowledged the profusion of theories about the meaning of the term, but his concern was not with the disagreements of others (EQQJ,

5.2b). Citing the *Great Learning*, Li said that investigating things is similar to thoroughly investigating principles. That is, when things are investigated, knowledge is extended and the principles become clear. Things consist of the self, the heart-mind, thoughts, knowledge, the family, the state, and all the things of the world. Li said that all ought to be investigated and in a particular sequence. The root was to be established first. One should examine deeply, eliminate all doubts, and progress carefully from one's own knowledge, thoughts, heart-mind, and self to one's family, the state, and the world. Otherwise it is a case of "putting second what is first and putting first what is second," or "making the root outer and the branches inner" (EQQJ).[11] However, learning ultimately required no separation between inner and outer or between one's mind and external circumstances (EQQJ, 10.13a). Li elaborated by saying that "knowledge" refers to the illustrious virtue (*mingde*) mentioned in the *Great Learning*. "Investigating things" simply means to investigate the illustrious virtue and, further, to make clear the illustrious virtue in each thing, from the self and mind to the state and world (EQQJ, 10.13b). "Illustrious virtue" is thus another term for the root.

When challenged whether examining things is actually a matter of relying on externals, Li claimed that the concepts of investigating things and extending knowledge are equivalent. They do not refer to things only external to the self, but to one's fundamental human capacities. "One extends knowledge to investigate things. One investigates things to extend knowledge. Thus there is nothing that is not the functioning of one's moral knowledge" (EQQJ, 5.3b). The concept of investigating things does not entail a focus only on either the self or the accumulation of external (factual) knowledge. Li insisted that investigating things and thoroughly investigating principles are to help one to cultivate the self, regulate the family, order the state, and pacify the world. These concepts are not concerned with knowing everything there is to be known; such knowledge is mixed and crude and "toying with things." The more one pursues it, the more one loses one's aim and departs from the Way (EQQJ, 5.4a; reference to *Book of Documents*, 5.5.6).

In responding to the criticism that these ideas are Buddhist, Li replied that this is the learning that has been cut off for a thousand years and that people who think that these ideas are close to those of Chan Buddhism are simply ignorant. Li compared the moral knowledge (the root) of human beings to the sun and moon. Without them, the earth would be dark and have no seasons, and without their moral knowledge, human beings would become like corpses, unable to see, hear, speak, and move (EQQJ, 3.10b). This moral knowledge is "the great ruler of the self." Without it there would be nothing to direct one's behavior, and one would have to copy others (EQQJ, 3.10b). By emphasizing the cluster of concepts associated with the investigation of things, Li Yong thus attacked those who, he believed, sought the Way in texts and hence misunderstood what great learning was.

Li described the experience of a person who fully apprehends the root in terms that sound at times like Buddhist enlightenment and Christian rebirth. He said, for instance, that it would be like being aroused from numbness or being awakened from sleep, and one would then begin to understand that whereby the self is the self. Only a person with this kind of experience would wholly understand the Heaven-endowed original face. He would be suddenly awakened one morning, and this awakening would be the birth of a sage (EQQJ, 5.3a).

In sum, Li viewed the process of learning from several perspectives and characterized it as development, completion, restoration, recovery, therapy, reflection, and comprehension. To become an expert in Confucian learning, one had to exert effort in all areas of this knowledge domain—its facts, skills, and rules. Since learning was verified by a person's acts, the issue of imitation was especially important. Moreover, great learning encompassed aims for the social self as well as for the personal self and so included the family, the state and society, and the world.

THE APPROACH TO LEARNING

In their discussions of learning, Confucian philosophers used terms (such as *fa, fang,* and *shu*) that are often translated as "method," a term I prefer not to use, or to use only in a very broad sense, because it suggests implications that are misleading in the Chinese philosophical context. In modern Western educational thought, "method" generally implies techniques associated with supposedly unilinear cause and effect relationships. The modern Western interest in methods tends to be related, moreover, to an interest in the mechanisms of learning, particularly psychological ones.

The Confucian position was different. Chinese thinkers assumed that everyone has the ability to learn, and Confucians even claimed an ethical imperative to learn. The interest in how one should learn focused not on psychological aspects of the problem of motivation but on purposeful efforts. Although the Chinese accepted the notion of cause and effect, they rarely thought of causal relationships in direct unilinear terms. They saw multiple conditions, acts, and events contributing in interdependent ways to situations that then became regarded as effects. Thus their use of the term "method" implied a set of associated conditions that are not implied in the modern Western use of the term.

In discussing his approach to learning, Li was presenting a metacognitive teaching. He emphasized the constant need for an overarching self-awareness as he instructed people on the efforts they needed to make. Drawing on past ideas, he regarded the most important aspects as establishing one's aim, getting a prescription, practicing reverential seriousness and self-cultivation, and reading. Other than the primary activity of establishing one's aim, there was no fixed sequence to the activities, and indeed a learner should regularly engage in all of them. These were also logically different kinds of activities.

Establishing One's Aim

In Li's view, "To learn one must first establish one's aim" (EQQJ, 6.6a). A person needs to have plans before he can act effectively. Since Li was talking about the learning of the "great man," he emphasized that the great man sets his aim on the world, the state and society, and the family. The small man, in contrast, has no concerns outside "planting and herding" (EQQJ, 5.3b).

In putting this task first, Li was claiming that (Confucian) learning requires a person to take responsibility for his actions and to act purposively. A person's commitment and efforts can never cease, and the learner's achievements depend on that person's efforts. Learning does not happen as a result of someone else's efforts or by chance. Although Li's position is typical in neo-Confucian thought, the Song philosopher Xie Liangzuo (1059–1103) expressed the idea especially well by comparing a person's aims to the root of a plant. Growth and development cannot occur if the root is not firmly established.[12] A learner must set his aim on the root (the moral heart-mind), the full development of which leads from a morally cultivated self to peace in the world. Focusing on a secondary type of activity, such as wealth, rank, or fame, would make even a Confucian scholar a petty man. Li often used Zhang Zai's expression "Establish your aim on behalf of heaven and earth" to describe the full scope of a Confucian's aim (EQQJ, 14.6b and *passim*).[13] Regarding Dang Zhan's ideas as a continuation of Zhang Zai's, Li also used the favorite expression of Dang Zhan (Liangyi), a prominent Guanzhong contemporary, to encapsulate what he meant by this phrase: "Establishing one's aim means that one takes responsibility for engaging in first-[i.e., highest-]level affairs in heaven and earth, for being a first-level person in heaven and earth, and for exhibiting effort on behalf of the past and future." One's aim should be to "take responsibility for this great burden" (EQQJ, 6.6a, 21.3b–4a; SSFSL, *Lunyu*, pt. 1, 63). This great burden was, of course, the root.

After establishing one's aim, one should start immediately to work on oneself. Specifically, the first thing to do is to renounce vulgar habits in behavior and speech (EQQJ, 14.2a). Since one's life span cannot be determined in advance, it is best to begin at once to urge this "self that easily dies" to establish the aim and carry out the responsibilities of a great Confucian (EQQJ, 14.6b).

Establishing one's aim required a person to distinguish between the superior person and the masses and to decide to become a superior person by setting standards for one's behavior that differed from those of the masses and rejecting their petty, frivolous, limited, and immoral behavior. One's aspirations had to be vast in scope, encompassing society and the world, in the present as well as in the past and future—and all this because one's self included others. The superior person's self, a higher-level social self, was not bounded by narrow conceptions of time and space. Although Lu Jiuyuan had used different words, this was the issue he had addressed in his talk on rightness versus private profit. In Lu's view, one had to establish one's aim to distinguish between rightness and profit, or to be a superior person in contrast to a petty man.[14] Although a person might aspire to this kind of vastness, Li (like others) emphasized that learning started with what was near and concrete, not with what was lofty and far away (EQQJ, 5.3b, 3.7a). The ultimate goal of world order and harmony could be achieved only by starting with the practical affairs of daily life. As Li said, "To learn, do not devote attention to the lofty and far away, but begin with what is lowly and nearby."

Once a person brings order and harmony to his own self, other selves will also gain order and harmony, until eventually all things are completed. "Therefore the highest moral principles lie simply in the lowest ability to cultivate." Li claimed in many ways that the greatest achievements emerged from the smallest part, the one heart-mind (EQQJ, 3.7a–b).

Although learning started with the bodily self, great learning concerned the social self and one's human capacities for moral and social action. There was always the danger, however, of losing perspective and letting the narrow, "ego" self of the petty man become dominant. Instead of focusing on efforts leading to self-cultivation, familial and social order, and world peace, the petty person became entangled in worldly desires, unruly passions, private opinions, and ordinary knowledge, to use Li's words. One could lose one's aim if that happened; thus, constant effort was required (EQQJ, 5.2b–4a).

Getting a Prescription

After establishing appropriate Confucian aims, a person had to engage in activities that together contributed to the process of learning. One such activity was conceived as getting a prescription. Li's view of learning (from one perspective) as analogous with overcoming illness and regaining health made prescriptions important, but he recognized that no prescription would work for everyone. Indeed, he often made this point. When asked, for instance, how to enter the gate of the sages' learning, Li replied that he had no fixed method for beginning. He wanted each person to plan by himself how to begin (EQQJ, 3.8a).[15]

When asked about those who already knew how to do such things, Li responded that he did not encourage idle discussion or sweeping theories. A person had to discover his own illnesses and decide to treat them. Li maintained that if he set up only one way to begin learning, he could not guarantee the universal appropriateness of that way, for the treatment would not always match the illness. Since learning involved getting rid of one's own illnesses, which varied from person to person, the treatment, as in medicine, must fit the illness in order for it to be effective (EQQJ, 3.8a–b; see also 1.3a–b, 10.7a–b, 11.5b, 13.8b–9a, 15.8b–9a, *fu* 15.2a–3a, 16.18b). Li pointed out that one cannot swallow medicine intended for someone else, and the only person who knows one's inner faults is oneself (EQQJ, 3.9a).

Li's mention of different kinds of illnesses reflected his view that action begins "in the mind." Some illnesses are a matter of licentiousness, some of greed, and others of a hunger for fame. Describing illnesses in terms of people's faulty minds, Li pointed out that people have combative minds, jealous minds, stingy minds, miserly minds, minds that separate others from oneself, and minds that view wrong as right (EQQJ, 3.8b; see 6.3b; see also comments in Chapter 3). He cited the example of King Xuan of Qi, a contemporary of Mencius, whom he diagnosed as having the illnesses of loving bravery, wealth, and licentiousness (EQQJ, 13.8b). The concept of mind in this context is not the heart-mind, but a person's aims, in the sense of purposeful control over one's thought and actions. Despite people's differences, in order to eliminate an illness, one had to restrain and order oneself, and recover by oneself "this origin" (EQQJ, 3.8b). The prescriptions of the philosophers should be used in such efforts (EQQJ, 3.9a).

Although Li spoke of illnesses as defects of the mind, he saw them as more than "mental" states. Illnesses of the mind were manifested in behavior. Since Li believed that the behavior for which one is responsible begins in the mind, with one's intentions and decisions to act, it is necessary to treat the early stages of the illness, not just the visible symptoms. Li was thus talking about mental activity in the sense of "promptings to act," to use Donald Munro's term.[16] Since Li assumed knowledge and action to be a unity, illnesses are disorders of behavior, whether visible or not.

Li's view suggests that illnesses are constantly being acquired and that no one ever reaches a state of unchanging absolute health, with a permanent eradication of all illnesses. Thus learning entails constant effort. This position was unavoidable, given the Chinese understanding of the relationships of things. As discussed above, illnesses were seen not as a matter of a single physiological entity but as involving all the interdependent relationships a person has with the world.

All the varieties of self-cultivation taught by other philosophers were prescriptions to Li. Within the framework of *ti* and *yong*, the prescriptions were *yong* (practical application) or *gongfu* (effort, practice), in contrast to *ti* (essential values). Prescriptions included, but were not limited to, such activities as discussing learning, reading, quiet sitting, being watchful over oneself when alone, reverential seriousness, investigating things, thoroughly investigating principles, extending moral knowledge, nourishing and examining the self, self-renewal through criticism and elimination of one's faults, and the five steps set forth in the *Great Learning*—study broadly, question deeply, ponder carefully, distinguish clearly, and put it into practice oneself.[17]

In Li's view, these and other prescriptions, or teaching slogans of past philosophers, texts, and sage-kings, aim at virtually equivalent results. The apparent differences in the prescriptions are due to the particular characteristics of the context. Deriving from different historical contexts and so responding to different illnesses, the various prescriptions are attempts to capture in words behavior that is not in words or whose primary focus does not lie in words. Thus, different prescriptions reflect different conditions and points of view. Numerous prescriptions had appeared over time in response to the problems of particular situations and had remained in the culture long after the situation had changed. The original differences in meaning these concepts had in their particular historical contexts were unimportant to Li because he was interested in their therapeutic and behavioral results, not in their theoretical relations with other ideas.

Learning thus requires efforts conceived by Li as diagnosing one's illnesses, getting a prescription, and treating one's illness accordingly. The state of health that is the goal in learning consists of an unobstructed development of one's human social-moral capacities. Although the prescriptions of previous philosopher-doctors derived from the classics and Four Books, the ultimate authority was not textual but accomplishments in actual practice.

Practicing Self-cultivation, Reverential Seriousness, and Quiet Sitting

Another effort necessary for learning was the practice of reverential seriousness (*xi jing*), part of the broader category of self-cultivation. The term *jing*, translated here as "reverential seriousness," admits of no easy translation into English. It suggests ideas of reverence, respect, earnestness, and seriousness, but none corresponds exactly. *Jing* is an important religious concept in neo-Confucianism, and it overlaps with other concepts of "mind control" in Confucian, Daoist, and Buddhist thought. In the context of Li Yong and his perspective on learning, "reverential seriousness" refers to both a psychological-mental state and the related behavior that the learner aspires to achieve. Attaining this state and engaging in this behavior go hand in hand with the other efforts advocated by Li. Especially emphasized by the Cheng brothers and Zhu Xi, reverential seriousness was seen as having effects that extended from the person, ideally the ruler, to the entire world.

Li utilized the image of the mirror to locate reverential seriousness in a theoretical framework. "The heart-mind is the nature, and it is like a mirror. A mirror is originally luminous, and yet dust obscures it. Polishing it is how one seeks to make it luminous again, but one does not regard the polishing as the luminosity. If one understands this, then one understands reverential seriousness" (EQQJ, 11.2b). In other words, reverential seriousness, like polishing, was a practice intended to recover an original state. A person aimed at the original state (*ti*), not at the polishing (*yong*).

Reflecting his emphasis on deliberate thought as the first aspect of learning, Li Yong said that no effort to learn should have precedence over reverential seriousness (EQQJ, 6.5a). Li also quoted Zhu Xi with approval: "Practicing stillness is not as good as abiding in reverential seriousness." Li further elaborated: "Learning is not outside reverential seriousness, but the latter is but one activity in the midst of learning. It is permissible for a person to say that he pursues reverential seriousness in order to recover the beginning (the heart-mind). But if one claims that reverential seriousness is the object of learning, then that is a case of merely imitating what the sages did in order to restore reverential seriousness. It is not restoring the beginning" (EQQJ, 11.2a–b).

Li described reverential seriousness as being thoroughly on guard. He claimed that if for a whole day a person could constantly be alert and on guard, to the point that he was not careless in any thought, then the moral heart-mind would be preserved and not lost. And such a person could hope to understand goodness and recover the great origin. Li added that reverential seriousness is effort (*gongfu*), not basic essence (*benti*), and a person recovers the basic essence only after engaging in effort. Effort and basic essence are not the same (EQQJ, 11.2b). On this last idea, Li disagreed with some of his contemporaries, such as Huang Zongxi, who equated the two concepts.[18] For Li, they differ, but both are necessary.

Li claimed that reverential seriousness is relevant to all actions from their beginning to their end. It is critical in all aspects of learning, high and low (EQQJ, 3.7a). The way to practice it is to strive for constant alertness (Xie Liangzuo's term) in one's spirit, to walk in a dignified way, to move and make gestures respectfully, and to pay extreme attention in seeing and hearing. If surrounding circumstances do not change, one must remain patient, continuing to control oneself, so that one is composed in all situations and in all affairs (EQQJ, 3.7a).

Li maintained that if one did these things, the desires and sense experiences of oneself and of all things would be ordered, and the nature and feelings of oneself and of all things would be in harmony. The notions of order (*zhi*) and harmony (*he*) are critical aspects of reverential seriousness as it relates to learning. That is, in learning, one aims to give order to one's feelings by controlling excessive desires and antisocial behavior and to establish harmony between one's human capacities and one's feelings. A superior person is someone who recognizes no separation between the (his) self and others, and the (his) self and circumstances. This idea is no different, Li claimed, from that of cultivating the self and establishing the moral standards of Heaven, completing the self and completing other things. Li thus related the concept of reverential seriousness to the view that a person's actions and even his body are not truly separate from other things. In other words, for Li, a great person's actions are not isolated acts. Rather, there are complementary relations between the subject's acts and surrounding circumstances. A reciprocity exists between the self and the world, and the great person is one who becomes confluent with the world. The behavior of a reverentially serious person is naturally appropriate. In a sense, then, we can say that appropriate behavior "happens," and it is erroneous to conceptualize this behavior according to a narrow subject-and-action sequence.

The results of a ruler's self-cultivation were seen as more far-reaching than those of lesser persons. Citing classical ideas, Li suggested how this worked. The opening chapter of the *Book of Rites* says, "Be grave and austere; if one's thoughts are calm and settled, one's words will calm the people." The *Lunyu*'s phrase "Calm the person, calm the people" and the passage in the *Doctrine of the Mean* "Be sincere and respectful and the world will be pacified" were also based on the reverential seriousness of cultivating the self (EQQJ, 3.7b). Li claimed that if the ruler is composed and serious in his behavior, the people will be in awe. And they will have something that they can copy. If he is calm and peaceful, the people will see that and their stinginess will dissipate on its own. This is, Li said, to treat others with kindness without using words. For Li, reverential seriousness entailed the idea that if the great man orders his self, others will also be ordered (EQQJ, 3.7b).[19] This is possible because he contributes to establishing a situation that in turn elicits ordered behavior from those involved.

A state of reverential seriousness leads to effortless, appropriate behavior by enabling a person to eliminate what is obstructive. In Li's view, extraneous and inappropriate thoughts obstruct one's human capacity for proper behavior. The way to eliminate them is to recognize the "ruler" in the mind, a state that Li described as the whole mind being constantly alert (EQQJ, 4.8b). As noted above, constant alertness is an empty, luminous, boundless, and joyful state.

In other words, in a world in which behavior was in part understood, explained, and justified on the basis of correlations, particular social situations required certain kinds of behavior, just as on the physiological level one's sense capabilities had to match different kinds of sensing. Although they existed on different levels, for example, behaving in a filial way was considered analogous to seeing or hearing. Behavior of all kinds was seen as occurring in accordance with heavenly natural principles, many of which were described as operating according to the pattern of movement and response (resonance). Human desires could obstruct the principles and interfere with their perfect functioning, however. Therefore desires had to be controlled, so that one's human capacities and the conditions of one's life corresponded.

Learning is the process that allows one to achieve this state of unobstructed correspondence. Distinguishing between the inner and outer practices of learning, Li held that internal efforts are known only by oneself, whereas the external acts are visible to others. Li did not make this distinction to rank one form higher than the other. Rather, he regarded this distinction as merely one of convenience. "Inner and outer nourish each other and together complete the whole" (EQQJ, 11.3b). Li further said that one had to struggle in the beginning, but after a long time, one's feelings of love, anger, sadness, and joy would naturally be regulated, and in looking, hearing, speaking, and moving one would be governed by ritual action. The constant moral obligations would be honored, and one would not exhibit carelessness in declining, maintaining, selecting, and conferring. Confusion and danger, and even success and failure or slander and fame, would not stir one's emotions. In situations of life and death, one would not by affected by calamities. Li concluded that a person who could behave like this was learned (EQQJ, 11.3b).

Li Yong's position was, in effect, to advocate the five-step process laid out in the *Great Learning*, which proceeded from broad study to practical action. Taking the conception of inner and outer as the framework, Li made reverential seriousness the first step. This prepared the way for subsequent activities. It also was a continuing state, not ever to be abandoned. In terms of the relation between, and relative value of, inner and outer behavior, Li insisted that they were (at a higher level) aspects of one activity. Thus, a person could not emphasize one aspect to the exclusion of the other. An emphasis on observable behavior led to a disregard of the values that provided the foundation and justification for the behavior, whereas an emphasis on the unobservable aspects led to abstract theorizing without practice.

How can one know if one has accomplished anything; that is, what can be accepted as evidence that reverential seriousness has contributed to the process of learning? Li's answer encompassed what is and what is not visible to others. Efforts are exerted internally to control those passions that hinder the emergence of morally good thought and behavior and to encourage those that are constructive. These efforts are not directly apparent to anyone other than the subject. Since inner efforts emerge in observable behavior, however, the nature of these efforts can be inferred. A person judges his own observable behavior by his feelings of shame, and others judge it by how well it corresponds to ritual action. A person's overt behavior thus is the basis for inferring the nature of his personal efforts. The actual practice of human relational obligations is evidence that the heart-mind has been preserved and the nature has been recovered; that is, it is evidence that one has learned.

Closely related to reverential seriousness was the practice of tranquillity, or quiet sitting. Regarded by Li as too difficult for the beginner, this practice aimed at the control of thoughts and emotions, to the point of eliminating all selfish ones. In advocating quiet sitting, Li Yong drew on a variety of past sources. The Song neo-Confucians, including Zhou Dunyi, the Cheng brothers, and Zhu Xi, had favored it and had done much to develop it in a Confucian context. It was practiced by the Chan Buddhists and the Daoists.

Although the aim of quiet sitting was to achieve a psychological-mental state similar to that of reverential seriousness, the efforts involved were described differently. Reverential seriousness was conceived in positive terms as being constantly alert, whereas quiet sitting was conceived in negative terms as having no conscious intent (EQQJ, 6.3a). The two concepts complemented each other and were often paired. Qiu Hongyu, a contemporary of Li's from the south, expressed the rather typical view, for instance, that Li's "learning took tranquillity as the foundation and reverential seriousness as the essential" (EQQJ, 10.21a).

As with reverential seriousness, Li used the images of a bright mirror and still water as a way to conceptualize the mind in his discussion of quiet sitting. Here "mind" does not refer to the heart-mind, but to thinking and willing and to the whole bodily self. Someone who can achieve a state of mind or self described as perfectly quiet, clear, bright, and reflective has a "still center" in the midst of activity. The idea is to remove all disruptive thoughts and emotions so that the mind, like a mirror, can reflect events without obstruction. Only then can a person respond perfectly to all situations and so practice good behavior. Li Yong referred to this ultimate state of mind and self by various terms, including "no mind," "no thoughts," and "empty luminosity" (EQQJ, 6.3a–4a, 15.10a–b).

The aim of having no mind was a secondary aim; success in this endeavor allows a person to achieve the primary aim of social and moral behavior. Thus, when asked about the mind, Li replied, "Have no mind." When asked further whether this is possible, Li replied that a person has no mind when he has no extraneous thoughts. When thoughts are not yet aroused, the mind is empty and quiet. When an empty and quiet mind is confronted with things, it penetrates them completely. Since the mind is vast and impartial, a person can simply respond to things as they come along. Li claimed that even if one with such a mind is involved in numerous activities, he has a still and luminous center that does not rush along with things (EQQJ, 6.3a). Li was thus striving for a calmness of self that allows a person to act appropriately, without the interference of distracting thoughts and feelings. Quiet sitting was not aimed at eliminating all action.

Some people questioned whether this practice contradicted the teaching to think in a purposive manner. Quiet sitting seemed to suggest passivity and purposelessness. One person observed that in practicing tranquillity it was essential for not even one thought to arise. He then asked how Li could reconcile a former worthy's admonition not to dwell on matters of the future, past, or present with Confucius' statements about having "distant concerns" and "reviewing the old" (EQQJ, 15.10a; reference to *Lunyu,* 15.11, 2.11). Li's answer reflects recognition of different levels of social reality and hence different conceptions of the self — distinctions he felt were lost, however, on all but the superior person. In answering, Li affirmed that the slightest thought should not arise and that this idea meant a beginner should not think about the past, the present, and the future. Li feared that if such thoughts arose, beginners would consider the false to be true and their lives would not be transformed. Their excessive desires and bad behavior would continue to obscure their pure, still, empty, and bright essence. Li noted, however, that he was not opposed to thinking when moral principles confirmed a person's thoughts (EQQJ, 15.10a–b).

Citing a number of passages from ancient texts that urged people to think deliberately, Li emphasized that thinking involves deliberation.[20] A person should think about the future, past, and present, but knowing the basic essence is not a matter of deliberate thinking (EQQJ, 15.10b). The issue of allowing thought was, in effect, a matter of which self was involved. Thoughts that confirmed, and actions that coincided with, moral principles entailed a higher social self, whereas thought that obstructed moral principles was evidence of the self of a petty person.

In a similar vein Li was asked how to reconcile Wang Ji's teaching to "let everything go" with a person's daily moral duties. Li replied that after a long period of "letting everything go" and practicing tranquillity, a person's mind would be empty of selfish thoughts and moral principles would be fully manifest. Such a person would simply respond when things arrived. Like a mirror that reflects everything once the dust is wiped off, his mind's essence would be constantly luminous (EQQJ, 15.10b–11a).[21] Thus, "letting everything go" would not conflict with a person's daily moral duties.

Although he saw quiet sitting as the way to preserve this empty luminosity, Li emphasized that much effort was required. There was no shortcut. If one exerted effort by expelling thoughts and emotions, apprehending things, and preserving what one should, one could make one's mind still. Then, one's mind would remain the same no matter what one did. That is, one would have an inner calm. Li compared the process to making muddy water clear. At first, the water is still muddy. Then it is partly clear and partly muddy. And then, after a long time, it is clear, just as a mirror naturally is when it has no dust (EQQJ, 3.12a). Stillness was thus essential. When the mind was perfectly quiet, it could reflect all day long and yet not be stirred up (EQQJ, 3.12b).

Li thus presented the practice of tranquillity as an aspect of self-cultivation required for learning. A person who successfully rid himself or herself of all disturbing thoughts would be perfectly attuned to the surrounding circumstances. Reflecting things perfectly, he or she would act appropriately. This unity between a person's actions and surroundings was conceptualized in terms of having a perfectly still center.

Reading

Although discussed last here, reading was not last in Li Yong's priorities or his conception of the sequence of learning but was to be done throughout a person's life. Associated with different conceptions of knowledge, the role of reading in learning had been a philosophical issue since classical times. The early Confucians valued texts and knowledge of them, whereas their Daoist opponents generally characterized books and their contents as the dregs of knowledge, best if discarded—even though Daoists also read and wrote. Reading remained a problematic issue among later thinkers, too, particularly Buddhists and the Song and Ming neo-Confucians. Despite the reservations of some thinkers about reading and textual study, Confucian philosophical culture remained a literate and literary culture. Although reading was accepted as necessary at the lower levels of learning, many philosophers interpreted an interest in reading (at the higher levels of learning) as a preoccupation with texts and hence a depreciation of moral and political action. Another aspect of the problem of reading was important as well, although rarely if ever addressed. This was the issue of the two different kinds of information texts contain.

Texts possess both an explicit, openly stated content and an implicit content—the unstated "rules" for organizing and presenting particular kinds of material, that is, the rules governing how the various literary forms are to be written and read. This second kind of instruction concerns the theoretical frames within which ideas are understood, and such frames are rarely in a person's full awareness.

(This instruction is an aspect of the "strategy" portion of the Confucian knowledge domain discussed above.)

Both the explicit and the implicit ideas carried by texts are important in a philosophical tradition, although the explicit ideas receive the most attention. Since reading reinforces the implicit (as well as the explicit) aspect of ideas, or the tacit rules for how ideas should be understood, reading itself is often questioned when ideas are changing. That is, unless new texts with significant differences from those of the past appear, reading simply reinforces older views and interpretations. Challenging the role of reading thus implies a challenge to both the explicit and the implicit ideas in the texts.[22] From Li's comments about reading, it appears that he handled this problem by not recommending certain kinds of texts and by encouraging selective and critical reading of other texts.

Following Zhu Xi, Li Yong regarded reading as essential for the great learning of the Confucians. Although most of Li's comments concerned advanced levels of learning, Li did discuss how a learner should begin and the curriculum that he should follow. (Two chapters in Li's collected works are devoted entirely to his recommendations of texts; these are discussed below.) Many informal suggestions for reading are scattered throughout Li's writings. For instance, when criticizing his contemporaries for not knowing what learning really is and so submersing themselves in dry commentaries and frivolous phrases, he urged people to read Luo Qinshun's *Record of Knowledge Painfully Acquired* (*Kunzhi ji*), Hu Yin's *On Venerating Correctness* (*Chongzheng bian*), and Feng Congwu's *Distinctions in Learning* (*Bianxue lu*), works that would help people realize the true aim and scope of learning (EQQJ, 15.9b–10a). All three works were concerned with establishing genuine Confucian thinking while defending it against "other" ideas.

Even in referring to non-Confucian types of learning, such as geomancy, Li advocated a similar approach, one that involved reading, understanding, and applying fundamental principles. He complained, for instance, that the geomancers understood only earthly patterns and did not understand heavenly patterns. Since they did not know that the former are based in the latter, they should read such books as *On Cleansing the Mind* (*Xuexin fu*), the *Blue Bag Classic* (*Qingnang jing*), and the *Genuine Teachings of Geomancy* (*Dili zhengzong*). He acknowledged that he had thoroughly studied their theories and methods in his youth but had refused to discuss the subject further after discovering that they rejected heavenly patterns and relied only on earthly patterns (EQQJ, 15.13b–14a).

In addition to his comprehensive reading program for all learners and recommendations for particular cases, Li established a daily routine of different readings at different times of day for students at the Guanzhong Academy. Thus, in the morning before breakfast, those who had no chores should read a few passages from the classics with their commentaries and study them until fully understood. After breakfast, one should read several passages from the Four Books, but without looking at the commentaries. If one did not understand the text, then one could look at the commentaries. A single passage should then be selected and studied thoroughly until it became totally incorporated into a person's thoughts and actions. After lunch and meditation, one should read portions of the *Amplified Meaning of the Great Learning* (*Daxue yanyi*), by Zhen Dexiu of the Song, and *Additions to the Amplified Meaning of the Great Learning* (*Yanyi bu*), by Qiu Jun of the Ming. Li said that these works contained critical points about thoroughly investigating principles and extending knowledge. They led to moral cultivation and political action — in other words, the learning of the great man.

Later in the day when relaxing, one may select some poetry and prose to read, such as pieces from the Han and Wei periods. In the evening one should read selections from the *General Outline of the Comprehensive Mirror for Aid in Government* (*Zizhi tongjian gangmu*; a summary by Zhu Xi of Sima Guang's work) or from the recorded conversations of Song and Ming philosophers. Afterward one should sit quietly and examine one's thoughts and actions of the day silently. One should reprove oneself for any depraved thoughts and actions, and every day one should work on becoming virtuous. In addition, when discussing learning with others, one should discuss such (Ming) works as Wu Yubi's *Daily Records* (*Rilu*), Lü Nan's *Recorded Conversations* (*Yulu*), Xue Xuan's *Reading Notes* (*Dushu lu*), and Wang Yangming's *Instructions for Practical Living* (*Chuanxi lu*; EQQJ, 13.12a–15a).

Li's stated rationale for reading was that the sages' minds — that is, their thoughts, ideas, passions, values, and aims — could be understood only by reading their books. Li claimed that if one discarded books, one's words and actions would not support each other. One would be rejecting the sages' words and so also the means for becoming a genuine person (EQQJ, 11.4b–5a). Li's recommendations for reading were clearly not made in isolation from the Confucian context. As one aspect of learning, reading carried with it many assumptions about what a person was doing. Particular texts served specific purposes.

Like much of Confucian thought, Li's position contained an inherent tension in that reading was thought necessary but textual knowledge was not the ultimate aim. A conflict existed between encouraging people to read and discouraging reading used as a substitute for action. Following Confucius, Li phrased this as the "conflict between loving learning and loving antiquity." He refused, however, to make the different approaches to learning exclusive or contradictory — they all contributed.

Li corresponded with provincial educational authorities about schooling, reading, and related matters, and he worked with provincial officials to establish schools. Rejecting the widespread view that schools were primarily places to prepare for the civil service examinations, he believed that the very reason for schools and books was to educate the people concerning their social and moral duties. He held that reading aided in efforts at self-cultivation, and thus the classics and commentaries helped support and nurture the development of human capacities. Schools were also important for bringing people together for discussion and inquiry (EQQJ, 12.3b).

Li's erudition and knowledge of the written cultural tradition are obvious in his recorded discussions, and thus the typically extravagant claims about the broadness of a person's reading may easily have some basis in his case. For instance, Chen Shizhi, a contemporary, reported that there were no books Li had not read and that Li particularly revered the works of Zhu Xi and Wang Yangming. Alluding to an unspoken and mistaken assumption that a person can have only one kind of expertise, Chen lamented that people knew Li only as "Li, the filial son," and not Li, the expert in Confucian learning (EQQJ, *fu* 11.8b).

In his preface to Li Yong's "Reading Sequence," Li Shibin mentioned that the book lists of former worthies were not entirely satisfactory because they did not get to the essentials or because they lacked purity. In contrast, Li Yong's curriculum enabled the learner to proceed gradually from elementary studies to great learning. He noted that, from the classics and their principles to literature and history, Li's list set a target at every step, and contained discussions and judgments for every book. Li Yong's curriculum thus truly helped a learner enter the genuine gate of the sages and to take the "upper road" of learning (EQQJ, 8.1a–b). Li Shibin further claimed that this curriculum contained everything to enable a person to pursue the road of the sages. Scholars who relied on it would be able to overcome their faults of being biased and mixed, and literary men who relied on it would not be licentious and wild. Li Shibin also mentioned that, in addition to this list, Li had given Zhang Er the list of the "complete essence and great application." Together, the two lists made a complete curriculum (EQQJ, 8.1b).

Both lists were recorded in 1669, when Li Yong was 42 and actively promoting practical (Confucian) learning. Because these lists were transmitted orally, it should not be surprising that some outstanding works are omitted, such as Sima Qian's *Records of the Historian* and Zhang Zai's writings, while others are given in variant forms.[23] Elsewhere, however, Li strongly recommended the writings of Zhang Zai (e.g., EQQJ, 17.15b). Li's curriculum displays a distinct bias against literature, but this kind of bias was not uncommon in Li's Ming predecessors, such as Xue Xuan and Hu Juren.

Li's "Reading Sequence" consists of more than 30 items, drawn from three of the four major Chinese bibliographic categories: the classics, the histories, and belles lettres. Philosophical writings, the fourth category, along with some histories and works useful in governmental affairs, are the subject of Li's other book list, the "Complete Learning of Essence and Application." Li's comments on his recommendations reveal a critical attitude, which he encouraged in the learner. Li was surprisingly open in his opinions, even admitting that some of these works were simply too long to read in their entirety. Below, I first discuss Li's "Reading Sequence" and then his "Complete Learning of Essence and Application." Since the second list deals specifically with Confucian philosophy (in Li's sense), I give more attention to each of its items.

"*Reading Sequence*" (EQQJ, 8.1a–9b). The first five books on Li Yong's "Reading Sequence" ("Dushu cidi") were recommended for youths beginning their pursuit of the sages' learning. Li started with Zhu Xi's *Elementary Learning* (*Xiaoxue*), an influential twelfth-century text consisting of material largely drawn from classical sources.[24] After noting that Zhu had collected good words and virtuous acts past and present as the foundation for students aiming at sagehood, Li then quoted from the *Book of Change* to support the importance of

educating youth. Educating was conceived as nourishing uprightness, and educating youth was sagely work. Nothing was more critical for the kingly way than teaching, and youth came first in teaching. Li emphasized that students should become thoroughly familiar
with Zhu's text and should practice its teachings. He also admitted,
however, that this text contained some repetitions from the classics
as well as some unnecessary ancient rituals and difficult characters.
Thus, one had to be selective in reading.

The second item, *Reflections on Things at Hand* (*Jinsi lu*), also a
work compiled by Zhu Xi (along with Lü Zuqian) contained the essence of the learning of Zhou Dunyi and the two Cheng brothers, or
neo-Confucian learning. Li said that it was good for beginners to examine this work, for it established the steps for investigating things
and extending knowledge.

Li's next three recommendations focused on the Four Books—
Cai Xuzhai's *Quotes for Youth from the Four Books* (*Sishu mengyin*),
Feng Congwu's *Record of Doubts About the Four Books* (*Sishu yisi lu*),
and Lü Nan's *Inquiries on the Four Books* (*Sishu yinwen*). Li ranked
Cai's work with Zhu Xi's commentaries (high praise indeed), and he
pointed out that the works by Feng and Lü were written as "virtuous
acts," not as preparations for the examinations. He claimed that they
were very useful for beginners because they helped to elucidate
various passages.

Li turned next to editions of the classics, arranged according to
his view rather than the standard bibliographic order. Listing first
the classics on ritual action, Li included seven compilations. In commenting on the first of these, the *Great Compendium on the Record of
Rites* (*Liji daquan*), Li Yong quoted Confucius as saying that one has
nothing with which to establish oneself if one does not study the
rites. In this way Li reaffirmed the importance of appropriate behavior for learning. Li went on to say that the rites were the gate for the
learner to enter virtue and hence had to come first. He criticized Han
Confucians for adding to the text, but he said that some chapters
(which he named) were pure and should be read every day. Moreover, the compilation by Wu Cheng (Caolu), a Yuan Confucian, was
excellent and should be read.

Li commented only briefly on the next entry, the *Record of Rites
with Commentaries* (*Liji shu*); it was mandatory for a specialist in the
rites, but otherwise it could be read irregularly and in fragments.
However, Li praised the *Zhou Rites with Commentaries* (*Zhouli zhushu*)

as the Duke of Zhou's regulations for ruling the state for ten thousand generations. Li said that later people have avoided it because Wang Mang used it to rebel against the Han and Wang Anshi brought disaster to the Song by clinging to it. Moreover, all the commentaries of Wei Zhuangqu were worth reading.

The next two items concerned the *Ceremonies and Rites*. Li Yong said that the *Ceremonies and Rites with Commentaries* (*Yili zhushu*) was closest to daily life and was *the* classic among the ritual texts. In addition, this text made it clear that it was acceptable to change according to the times. The other work, *Complete Explanation of the Classic and Commentaries of the Ceremonies and Rites* (*Yili jingzhuan tongjie*), developed from a Song conflict concerning the different ritual texts. Li said that people relied on the *Ceremonies and Rites* for knowledge of the rites and ceremonies of the period before the Three Dynasties; the *Record of Rites* was simply a commentary on this text. Later people put the *Record of Rites* in the schools, and the *Ceremonies and Rites* was then not discussed. Moreover, this dispute went back to the Song, when Zhu Xi wanted to designate the *Ceremonies and Rites* as the classic and the *Record of Rites* as the commentary. Zhu wrote memorials to the court with no success, but his follower Huang Gan (Mianzhai) followed Zhu's lead and compiled these historical materials on the rites.

Li's comments on the next two items, the *Ceremonies of the Family Ritual of Zhu Xi* (*Wengong jiali yijie*), compiled by Qiu Jun (Qiongshan), and the *Appendixes to the Four Rituals* (*Sili yi*), by Lü Kun (Xinwu), were very brief. Although Qiu's text was widely read, Li simply said that one should examine it thoroughly. Lü's text, however, was very good for everyday use. Li thus ended his comments on the ritual texts with another reference to the importance of everyday practice.

The next classic that Li Yong recommended was the *Book of Poetry*, for which Li selected two texts: *Great Compendium on the Book of Poetry* (*Shijing daquan*) and *Book of Poetry with Commentaries* (*Shijing zhushu*). Given Li's disparaging attitude toward literature, it is not surprising that he should offer little guidance with this classic. He said that the sounds of poetry being chanted can move a person deeply and that one ought to try to follow the ancient methods even though they were difficult. Because the second work combines the pure and the tainted, however, it is important that the reader be good at selecting what is essential.

Next Li addressed the *Book of Documents* briefly. He simply said that unfortunately he did not have an opinion on the *Great Compendium of the Book of Documents* (*Shujing daquan*) and so, as he had said before, it was important that the reader be good at selecting what is essential.

The next classic recommended by Li was the *Spring and Autumn Annals*, a work particularly associated with Confucius because of the traditional claim (now believed inaccurate) that Confucius had edited it. The fact that Li selected six items related to this classic suggests its importance, at least from Li's perspective, but he still did not have much to say about any of the texts.

Li claimed not to have an opinion on the first one, the *Great Compendium of the Spring and Autumn Annals* (*Chunqiu daquan*). Next on his list were the three classical commentaries, *Mr. Zuo's Commentary on the Spring and Autumn Annals* (*Chunqiu Zuoshi zhuan*), the *Guliang Commentary on the Annals* (*Chunqiu Guliang zhuan*), and the *Gongyang Commentary on the Annals* (*Chunqiu Gongyang zhuan*). Li commended *Zuo's Commentary*, saying that it was a complete record. To study the *Annals* and not read this text first was like deciding a criminal case without using the plaintiff and defendant. It would be impossible to find out the details of the case. Li suggested reading the explanations of the sentences first and then reading the commentary. The other two commentaries, he said, were written to explain this classic and were essential for the study of the classics. The *Gongyang Commentary* was especially penetrating.[25]

For the last two items on this classic, Li Yong chose one from the Song, *Mr. Hu's Commentary on the Spring and Autumn Annals* (*Chunqiu Hushi zhuan*), and one from the Tang, *Mr. Dan's Commentary on the Spring and Autumn Annals* (*Chunqiu Danshi zhuan*). Li described Hu Anguo's commentary as clear and incisive, far surpassing the others, but he warned against its many questionable statements. Li claimed that, in addition to the other commentaries mentioned above, only Dan's among the many available succeeded in getting to the very essentials, but others, such as those by Lu Chun and Zhao Kuang (both of the Tang), could be read.

The next four recommendations focused on the *Book of Change*. Li said that he had no opinion on the *Great Compendium of the Zhou Change* (*Zhouyi daquan*). He described the text of the *Complete Book of Past and Present Literature on the Zhou Change* (*Zhouyi gujinwen quanshu*) as vast, but said it still should be examined to investigate thor-

oughly the changes of past and present. Li had great praise for
Cheng Yi's commentary, here listed as *Mr. Cheng's Commentary on the
Zhou Change* (*Zhouyi Chengshi zhuan*). Li said that its moral principles
were deep, the aim was lofty and ancient, and that Cheng had fulfilled the model of the learning of the *Book of Change*. The fourth recommended text was Zhu Xi's *Original Meanings of the Book of Change*
(*Yijing benyi*). Li Yong pointed out Zhu Xi's view that this classic had
originally been written for purposes of divination. Zhu's work therefore showed respect for Cheng's, but it revolved around the idea of
divination.[26]

Apparently thinking that Li Yong had not given sufficient attention to the *Book of Change*, Li Shibin added his own comments here,
saying that several thousand people had discussed the *Change* since
the Han and Jin periods. He selected nine people as most outstanding from the early period, as well as two from the Song and two from
recent times, and he also mentioned other directions of this learning,
including the tradition of images and numbers. He included Yang
Xiong in relation to the latter tradition, but (surprisingly) not Shao
Yong.

Li Yong ended his list of recommended readings on the classics
with two large compilations, *Explanations of the Five Classics* (*Wujing
yi*) by Deng Qiangu and *Explanations of the Nine Classics* (*Jiujing jie*) by
Hao Jingshan. According to Li , Deng's work exhibited deep thought
and correct understanding, and Hao's explained the garbled views
of past and present and far surpassed other writings.

Claiming that one may read the histories after studying the classics, Li next considered the bibliographic category of history. The
first history he recommended was the outstanding Song dynasty
work by Sima Guang, *Comprehensive Mirror for Aid in Government*,
with Mr. Hu's Commentary (*Zizhi tongjian Hushi zhu*). Li said that one
must first read the annalistic histories, and none was more detailed
than this one. Sima gives a clear account of the traces of order and
turmoil, prosperity and decline, of the past several thousand years,
and Hu Sanxing's commentary contains criticism and argument.

Li also recommended one later annalistic history, the *Complete
Mirror of the Song and Yuan* (*Song Yuan tongjian*), by Xue Fangshan. Li
claimed that this was an extremely detailed work about Song and
Yuan affairs. Indicating again a certain realism, Li admitted that it
was acceptable not to examine other works (EQQJ, 8.7b).

Reflecting his view that recent history was at least as important as ancient history, Li next selected the *Record of the Government Regulations of the Great Ming* (*Huang Ming xianzhang lu*). Li commented that, before Xue Fangshan compiled this work, Chen Jian's *Comprehensive Record of the Great Ming* (*Huang Ming tongji*) had circulated throughout the world. Since Chen's work was marred by inconsistencies and errors, however, Xue had compiled his record. It begins with the founder of the Ming and ends with the Zhengde reign period (1506–22). For histories after this period, there is Mr. Shen's *Account of Things Heard and Seen During the Jia-Long periods* (1522–72; *Shenshi Jia-Long wenjianji*). Claiming that these two works by Xue and Shen grasped the essentials of Ming affairs, Li recommended that people not read other similar books.

Finally, Li selected the *Complete Histories Edited, Parts I and II* (*Hanshi shangbian, xiabian*), by Deng Yuanxi. Li commented that after the annalistic histories, learners should read the dynastic histories to complete their investigations. However, the standard dynastic histories contain far too many documents for a person to read completely. These two compilations are useful because they select the important points. From the highest officials and calendrical methods down to taxes, levies, and grain transport troops, they provide data from the past and so are vital to contemporary statesmen (EQQJ, 8.8a–b).

Stating that one may pursue literature after the histories have been understood, Li next recommended readings from the bibliographic category of belles lettres. Li's limited selections here indicate his ambivalent attitude toward this kind of writing. Only two items are included, *Literary Remains of Eight Great Writers* (*Ba dajia wenchao*) and *Literary Selections of Ten Great Writers of the Great Ming* (*Huang Ming shi dajia wenxuan*). Li stated that, other than the writings from the pre-Qin and Han periods, no writings were more heroic than those of Han Yu, Liu Zongyuan, Ouyang Xiu, the three Su (Su Xun, Su Shi, and Su Che), Wang Anshi, and Zeng Nanfeng. Li admitted that he had not read all the writings of these eight writers, but he did recommend Mao Lumen's compilation as very fine. Consisting of writers (mainly essayists) from the Tang and Song, Li's list was somewhat unusual, for it omitted the great poets and included lesser writers (Wang and Zeng). In listing ten writers from the Ming, Li made brief individual comments about only three, whose writings he described as particularly heroic, clear, and pure.

Li concluded by stating that the classics, histories, and literary works on his list were the most urgent ones for the educated person.

Anyone with the strength, however, to broaden his understanding could take a short look at other works, including the *Laozi, Zhuangzi, Guanzi, Han Fei, Tanzi*,[27] and the *Huainan Honglie.* If one read geography books, only the *Comprehensive Record of the Great Ming* (*Da Ming yitongzhi*) and the *Complete Account of the World* (*Huanyu tongji*) thoroughly examined the conditions, population, money, and materials of commanderies and districts, and one should complete one's investigations by reading them. There were other geography works (which Li named), but in the end they did not measure up to the *Comprehensive Record of the Great Ming.* Li advised people not to read them and thereby dissipate their strength.

"The Complete Learning of Essence and Application" ("Tiyong quan-xue"). Li's second reading list addressed the fourth bibliographic category, the philosophers. Here, Li was referring not to the entire spectrum of philosophical thinking, but only to what he regarded as genuine Confucian learning (*ruxue*) since the Song period. As noted above, Li most often called it the "sages' learning" or the "learning of comprehending the essence and extending it to practice."

In his preface to this list, Zhang Er, a student of Li Yong's, pointed out that although later in life Li did turn to practices of contemplation and meditation, earlier he had focused his teachings on the ideas proposed here. Summarizing Li's position, Zhang said that someone who comprehends the essence but does not practice it is a pedant. Someone who practices the essence but does not comprehend it is an opportunist. "Pedantry and opportunism are not that whereby one talks of learning" (EQQJ, 7.1a–b, preface).

Divided into the two main categories "Comprehending the Essence" ("Mingti") and "Practical Application" ("Shiyong"), Li's list of books was concerned with the kinds of knowledge necessary for a Confucian to fulfill his responsibilities — moral thought and behavior, social relations and governmental matters, and the cultural tradition as a whole. The contents reflect Li's fundamental assumptions that values must be put into practice and that one's actions must be guided by the unchanging values of the sages. The list shows how he viewed the contemporary split between the Cheng-Zhu and the Lu-Wang branches of neo-Confucianism. Unlike many others who saw these branches as antagonistic, Li viewed their positions in terms of a difference between applied and theoretical moral philosophy (EQQJ,

7.6a–b). Both still belonged to the category of comprehending the essence. By aiming the category of practical application at officials and those concerned with official matters, Li affirmed the political realm as an important aspect of Confucian thought and action.

I have included most of Li's comments on the books listed below in order to show the ethical standards that governed Confucian philosophical thinking. Li made his comments in the traditional style, employing stock phrases and sometimes making overly elaborate claims. His comments were not systematic in the sense of presenting a uniform evaluation of each work, but he did have a set of standards upon which his evaluations were based. As shall be seen, the criteria were closely related.

Several questions shaped Li's thinking:

What relationship does this work have to the classics and their ideas concerning the heart-mind, the Way, and other important concepts, such as reverential seriousness?

Does this work acknowledge the dual focus of the Way — of cultivating the self and governing others?

Does this work distinguish between the genuine Way of the Confucians and other, "deviant" ways?

Does this work promote ideas and values that have long-term relevance, and does it oppose a narrow focus on the limited and self-centered "ego" self?

Does this work stress the values of order and harmony, as opposed to turmoil?

Does this work stress both values and practice, with the former guiding the latter and the latter realizing the former?

Does this work emphasize everyday, practical affairs and those things nearby and close at hand, while opposing lofty and far-off interests and empty doctrines?

Does this work recognize differences in people and urge people to work at a pace that is possible and appropriate for them?

Does this work ask that people be critical in their reading and thinking?

Does this work address, and acknowledge the importance of, practical and concrete aspects of governmental administration, such as agricultural affairs, water control, military matters, the salt administration, and laws and regulations?

Does this work recognize that the purpose of government is to give aid to the world?

CATEGORY OF COMPREHENDING THE ESSENCE (*Mingti lei*),
PART I, COMPREHENDING THE ESSENCE (*Mingti*; EQQJ, 7.2A–3B)

The Collected Works of Lu Xiangshan (Jiuyuan, 1139–93). *Xiangshan ji.* Lu Xiangshan extravagantly spread the idea of directly pointing to wash away the Song Confucians' vulgar theories. His incisive discussions helped people comprehend their heart-mind immediately, easily, and directly, and there has rarely been such a person since Mencius. Lu's writings all exist today, but it is acceptable for the learner to read only his chronological biography, recorded conversations, and correspondence.

The Collected Works of Wang Yangming (Shouren, 1472–1529). *Yangming ji.* Although Lu Xiangshan discussed the single transmission and directly pointing, there were still things left unsaid about the basic essence until Wang Yangming began to spread his teaching of extending one's moral knowledge, thereby divulging the secret that had not been transmitted for a thousand years. This teaching enabled people to comprehend thoroughly their original face, and even the ignorant could follow it to enter the Way. This teaching is the kind of effort that appears only once in ten thousand generations. Every phrase, every word, in Wang's works is incisive, including his chronological biography, *Instructions for Practical Living*, *Account of Respecting-the-Classics Pavilion* (*Zunjingge ji*), his theory of broadening and restraining, his various prefaces, and his letters discussing learning. His works should be viewed as necessary as eating and drinking, summer and winter clothing, the compass and the square, and the level and the plumb line.

The Collected Works of Wang Longxi (Wang Ji, 1498–1583). *Longxi ji.* This collection of twenty chapters elucidates the theory of moral knowledge. It is extensive and penetrating, explaining things completely. There were no works like it before it appreared and there have been none like it since, and future writers will not be able to surpass it. And yet in reading it, as well as his correspondence and other works, one still must draw out its essentials. Although one should read it every day to broaden one's understanding, it has some lifeless and incomplete parts.

The Collected Works of Luo Jinxi (Luo Rufang, 1515–88). *Jinxi ji.* Luo's learning is genuine and sincere, and one will daily become more refined and advanced if one follows it. It may be called great and transforming. He truly is the first person in recent times to complete things. His writings explain the central points of the classics, and he actively rejects the narrow path of contemporary Confucians. His works are difficult for beginners, and so it is acceptable to examine a summary of them.

The Collected Works of Yang Cihu (Yang Jian, 1140–1226). *Cihu ji.* Yang's learning directly records the teachings of the mind, and he experienced the great enlightenment eighteen times and the lesser enlightenment countless times. He certainly can be considered eminent among Song Confucians. Although people have attacked him for being close to Chan Buddhism, how is the Master's learning true Chan? People ought to differentiate clearly these two things.

The Collected Works of Chen Baisha (Chen Xianzhang, 1428–1500). *Baisha ji.* Chen's learning takes the natural as primary and rejects the irrelevant uses of sense knowledge. His learning helps one complete the empty, immeasurable spirit. One truly can see his cultivation from his writings and appearance, and he can be described as retiring, distant, and humble. Reading his works enables one to make one's mind and spirit harmonious, just as when a person sits in the spring breeze and his disposition is silently transformed without his realizing it.

CATEGORY OF COMPREHENDING THE ESSENCE,
PART II, EFFORT (*Gongfu*; EQQJ, 7.4A–6A)

The Complete Works of the Two Chengs (Cheng Hao [Mingdao], 1032–85; Cheng Yi [Yichuan], 1033–1107). *Er Cheng quanshu.* The two Chengs revitalized our Way, and so their effort is not less than that of Yu. Their book was edited by Zhu Xi and is very fine and subtle. They represent the genuine branch of Confucius and Mencius.

The Great Compendium of the Conversations of Master Zhu, Arranged Topically (Zhu Xi, 1130–1200). *Zhuzi yulei daquan.* This work collates what is biased and harmful, and it judges the large and small, fine and coarse, of a hundred intellectuals without neglecting a single thing. It brings together the great achievements of the Confucians as the teachers of ten thousand generations. Reading this book and tasting this learning truly are the "weight and beam" of investigating things and thoroughly examining principles. More than 900 chapters are difficult for a learner, however, and so it is acceptable to peruse it, reading the essentials first, and then gradually attain more of it.

The Great Compendium of the Literary Collection of Master Zhu. Zhuzi wenji daquan. Mild and pure, refined and elegant, his discussions are fine and subtle, and in his numerous memorials one can especially see the learning of heavenly virtue and the kingly way.

The Collected Works of Wu Kangzhai (Wu Yubi, 1392–1469). *Wu Kangzhai ji.* Wu based himself on the *Doctrine of the Mean*, and his efforts were incisive and arduous. His daily record was written solely for controlling one's passions and restraining one's anger, and his words are relevant to the daily practices of the learner.

The Reading Record of Xue Jingxuan (Xue Xuan, 1389–1464). *Xue Jingxuan dushu lu.* Xue's *Reading Record* imitates the methods of reading of Zhang Zai, in that he recorded ideas wherever they were attained. His learning is nearby, pure, genuine, and bright. While learners who do have understanding cannot bear to let go of it, even learners who absolutely do not believe have achieved things after reading this work.

The Collected Works of Hu Jingzhai (Hu Juren, 1437–84). *Hu Jingzhai ji.* Hu's learning emphasized personally practicing reverential respect. His discussions are sincere and pure without blemish, and they are what the beginner ought to prize.

The Record of Knowledge Painfully Acquired of Luo Zheng'an (Luo Qinshun, 1466–1547). *Luo Zheng'an kunzhi ji.* Luo discriminated between our Way and other paths, true and false, and right and wrong. He exerted all of his strength in weighing the seriousness of our Way, and one can see good effort and a suffering mind in this work.

The Recorded Conversations of Lü Jingye (Lü Nan, 1479–1542). *Lü Jingye yulu.* During the Jia-Long periods (1522–73) those who discussed learning favored either Wang Yangming or Zhan Ruoshui (1466–1560). Among their corrupt later followers, the lofty ones spoke of "not knowing," and the wise ones spoke of "returning to stillness." Those who steadfastly preserved the theories of Cheng-Zhu without change consisted of Luo Qinshun in the south and only Lü Nan in the north. Lü did not engage in vast and lofty discussions. His words were plain and common, and his writings were fresh. This work is divided into 27 chapters, it was edited by Feng Congwu, and it was published by Censor Bi. It is "must reading" for learners. They should copy and explain it, like the works of the two Chengs, Zhang, and Zhu. This work has some especially profound words and good selections for readers.

The Collected Works of Feng Shaoxu (Feng Congwu, 1556–1627). *Feng Shaoxu ji.* Feng, along with Cao Zhenyu, Zou Dongguo, Jiao Ruohou, Gao Panlong, and Yang Fusuo, opened a school to discuss and lead this (Confucian) culture. The older ones among them were penetrating and insightful, although the enlightened ones mixed with Buddhism. Only Feng remained serious and upright, thoroughly following the teachings of Cheng-Zhu. Altogether this work has 22 chapters, including "A Record of Discriminating Learning," which explains the distinctions between Confucianism and Buddhism; "A Record of Doubts," which dissects the Four Books; and "On Discussing Learning," "On Becoming a Person," prefaces, records, letters, and inscriptions. Together these writings are sufficient to strengthen the aim of the learner and to resolve the doubts of later followers. The ordinary person despises what is close and values what is far, and this is how Feng has been treated.

After this statement on Feng's works, Li commented in a more general way that the books on the list from Lu Jiuyuan to Yang Jian explain mind and nature and make everything known. Anyone who reads them thoroughly can penetrate the great origin of the Way. Afterward one should daily examine the records of the Chengs and Zhu, and the collections of Wu Yubi, Xue Xuan, and the others listed in order to exhaust one's efforts in practical learning and to preserve and protect the Way. One should exert effort in order to be in harmony with the basic essence and pursue what is present in order to complete the origin. Lower studies and upper reaching, inner and outer, root and branches—one thread runs through them all, beginning and completing the limits of reality (EQQJ, 7.6a–b).

Li then listed nine more works but without individual comments. He said that these combined the pure and the mixed together. Therefore, one needed to get rid of the "short" and keep the "long" in order to complete one's investigations (EQQJ, 7.6b).

The Collected Works of Zou Dongguo (Zou Nangao, Yuanbiao, 1551–1624). *Zou Dongguo ji*

The Collected Works of Wang Xinzhai (Wang Gen, 1483–1540). *Wang Xinzhai ji*

The Collected Works of Qian Xushan (Qian Dehong, 1497–1574). *Qian Xushan ji*

The Collected Works of Xue Zhongli (Xue Kan, Shangqian, d. 1545). *Xue Zhongli ji*

The Collected Works of Geng Tiantai (Geng Dingxiang, 1524–96). *Geng Tiantai ji*

The Groaning Words of Mr. Lü Kun (Lü Xinwu, 1536–1618). *Lüshi shenyinyu*

The Collected Works of Xin Fuyuan (Xin Quan, 1588–1636). *Xin Fuyuan ji*

The Collected Works of Wei Zhuangqu (Wei Jiao, 1483–1543). *Wei Zhuangqu ji*

The Collected Works of Zhou Haimen (Zhou Rudeng, 1547–1629). *Zhou Haimen ji*

CATEGORY OF PRACTICAL APPLICATION
(*Shiyong lei*; EQQJ, 7.7A–10A)

The Amplified Meaning of the Great Learning (Zhen Dexiu, 1178–1235). *Daxue yanyi*. Zhen Dexiu selected essential phrases from the classics and histories to complete this compilation on cultivating the self and ruling others, and it contains the regulations and standards for ordering the world, the state, and the family. If one bases one's actions on it, there will be order. If one rejects it, there will be turmoil. Everything rests on cultivating the self and regulating the family. Order in the state and in the world will follow if the ruler of the people can cultivate the self and regulate his family.

Additions to the Amplified Meaning [*of the Great Learning*] (Qiu Jun, 1418–95). *Yanyi bu*. Qiu Jun collected the essentials of the classics and the regulations of past and present. He judged how they promulgated order, and he examined whether they were dangerous. He looked at every affair and every word. He researched deeply and thoroughly the harm and benefit for the times. It is acceptable for those who aim to regulate the country to hold on to this work.

General History of Institutions and Critical Examination of Documents and Studies (Ma Duanlin, 1254–1325). *Wenxian tongkao*. Ma Duanlin from Jiangxi was a famous Yuan Confucian. During the Yuan, virtuous men did not carelessly come forward. Ma made judgments on past and present court records to complete this book. Its subjects are high officials, geography, rites and music, troops, farmers, taxes, the selection of officials, the calendar, and officers and soldiers. Everything is included.

Mr. Lü's Veritable Government Records (Lü Kun, 1536–1618). *Lüshi shizhenglu*. This work was written by Lü Kun of Ningling, who was very knowledgeable about and skilled in the practical learning (*shixue*) of managing and regulating the country. It is very useful to Confucians now. All his veritable government records are what he experienced. If a learner has no aspirations for the world, there is nothing more to say, but if he has aspirations to aid the world, he cannot lack this book for a day.

Gifts from a Simple Home (*Hengmen qin*) and *Stone Carvings on Statecraft* (*Jingshi shihua*). Both were edited by Xin Quan. They contain reliable discussions, all of which can be used.

Essentials of Statecraft. Jingshi qieyao. This work discusses military colonies, water control projects, the salt administration, and national plans to select leaders, drill troops, and control fires. There is no one who does not recommend the necessity of this work.

Record of Military Preparations. Wubei zhi. Eighty volumes altogether, this work is a complete compilation of the tactics of past and present battles, and it must be examined very carefully if one is looking to advance in the examinations. *Sunzi*, *Wuzi*, and others are especially necessary for military studies.

Zhang Er, the recorder of this book list, added that among the methods of governing nothing was more difficult than employing troops, for the difference between victory and defeat lay in a split second. Thus this subject cannot be neglected. Moreover, the admirable strategies of Wu Hou and the military accomplishments of Wang Yangming have shown that it is false to think that military matters are not the concern of the Confucians. Thus, learners must deeply and carefully examine the subject so that they can be prepared when emergencies arise. [28]

The Eight Principles of Statecraft. Jingshi bagang. Altogether it has twenty volumes, but only Feng Yingjing's *Compilation on Practical Use (Shiyong bian)* and Deng Yuanxi's *Complete History, Part II (Hanshi, xiabian)* need to be completely examined. Do not read the remainder.

Complete Summary of the Comprehensive Mirror for Aid in Government. Zizhi tongjian gangmu daquan. In twenty volumes; it is the source for investigating things, and it is a complete record of flourishing and decline, order and turmoil. It consists of discussions that one continually ought to examine.

Collected Statutes of the Ming. Da Ming huidian. The Ming is gone, but its records still exist. Although the times are different and the world is not the same, the subjects of the work are the concerns of government and the lessons of ancient affairs. How can a learner not know them?

Memorials of Famous Officials Through the Ages. Lidai mingchen zouyi. Learners value understanding historical affairs, and memorials and petitions are the things by which one understands such affairs. One ought to examine this work thoroughly and regard it as an aid to memorials and records.

Zhang Er commented here that all the books in this category, from the *Amplified Meaning* to the *Memorials*, are of practical use. The Way is not empty talk. A person should be ashamed if in learning he values the practical and earnestly studies but still cannot begin and complete affairs or give aid when the times are difficult.

Code and Commandment. Lü ling. It is essential to know the code and commandment, and yet there are those among today's learners who have never heard about them.[29] From literate commoners who do not read the regulations to the rulers Yao and Shun, there is ultimately no other method.

Complete Treatise on Agricultural Administration. Nongzheng quanshu

Complete Treatise on Water Control. Shuili quanshu

Western [European] Hydraulics. Taixi shuifa

Essentials of Geographical Dangers. Dili xianyao

These four books are the concerns of governing, and one ought to examine them one by one. And yet, to read books is easy, but to make changes is hard. People hasten to embrace the ability to read ancient writings, but what aid can they actually give to the real world and the existence of what is spiritual and bright? Those who understand the affairs of the times are the brave and heroic. How are students of old books able to analyze such matters? (Three of these four books contain translations of materials from the West.[30] The *Complete Treatise on Agricultural Administration* contains translations of European works on hydraulics, and both the treatise on water control and that on Western hydraulics Li mentioned are sections in this large compilation. The *Complete Treatise* was compiled by Xu Guangqi, a late Ming official who was a scientist, an agronomist, a friend of the Jesuits, and a convert. Chen Zilong edited and published it in 1639 after Xu died. *Western Hydraulics*, which concerns European irrigation methods, was written by Sabatino de Ursis and was first published in Beijing in 1612.)

Li thus ended his annotated list of books with a final jab at those concerned with ancient texts and with a continued plea for action. Li's remarks indicate that his argument was not with the activity of reading per se. He valued books, and he saw them as carriers of Confucian culture. He prized the past and its potential usefulness for the present, and he seems to have accepted historians' presentations and conceptions of the past. His quarrel was thus not with the accepted view of what happened. Rather, his concern was how to conceive the social and political role of Confucians.

Li did not accept that the Confucians were simply descendants of earlier worthies, sometimes transmitting their messages better than at other times. For Li, the Confucians were certainly teachers, but they also were like doctors, with the tasks of diagnosing and treating illnesses. Reading about old prescriptions (former teachings) could be helpful, but it did not take the place of practical action that gave aid to the world. Before one could aid the world, however, one had to learn, and reading was a requirement for learning.

Li's approach to learning thus had many facets that together addressed the varied aspects of learning. His perspective incorporated the ideas of the Song neo-Confucians as well as the Ming thinkers closer to his own time. The "great learning" began with the establishment of one's aim and continued to advance as one obtained appropriate prescriptions, maintained an attitude of reverential seriousness, practiced tranquillity, read and studied certain approved texts, implemented the appropriate teachings, and constantly examined and corrected one's thoughts and actions. Tremendous effort was required, but the goal was equally tremendous—to become a great Confucian, perhaps even a teacher of ten thousand generations.

6   *Concluding Observations*

In this study I have attempted to analyze Confucian philosophy from a perspective designed to contribute to the development of comparative philosophy. I have been concerned with Confucian philosophy as a philosophical system, with the views of one particular philosopher as an illustration of how that system was appropriated, and with the field of comparative philosophy as a tool for analyzing such systems. My approach to Confucian philosophy, as a system and as a position exemplified in the ideas of a particular thinker, has been primarily "metaphilosophical" in that I have been most interested in pursuing questions about theoretical aspects of the system itself. With respect to comparative philosophy, these efforts have aimed at searching for productive questions to ask and for methods to evaluate such questions. I have not, however, proceeded to the next step of producing a study in comparative philosophy; nor has that been my intention here.

My work has focused on certain characteristics of Confucian thought and certain contexts of thought and has slighted others. My plan of analysis has made this kind of bias both unavoidable and obvious. Since I have aimed at reconstructing the Confucian tradition from a specific perspective, my methodological framework has openly shaped the ensuing picture. I hope, however, that I have been sufficiently explicit about my approach so that the reader is able to evaluate this view of Confucian philosophy.

I have assumed that one way to uncover the unstated rules of a system of philosophical thinking is to examine one thinker's appropriation of that tradition. I have focused on Li Yong, who was anxious to defend the tradition (the learning of the sages) and who, in doing so, especially drew on the broader cultural complex of ideas and values that emphasized situational thinking, or thinking in contexts. The issues he addressed reveal many of the tensions within the system. For instance, one source of tension was the disagreement over the behavior proper to a "genuine" Confucian. Li Yong's perspective had its biases, of course, and did not embrace the full spectrum of Confucian interests. Nonetheless, his thinking reflects some of the outstanding strengths of Confucian philosophy, not the least of which was the responsibility to teach and to learn, not just for the present, but for the past and for the future.

I am suggesting that the task of comparative philosophy is to examine ideas in light of certain kinds of questions. Above all, we must recognize that ideas exist within a system of thought (and behavior) and the assumptions — stated or unstated — of that system are relevant to its ideas. Ideas are not isomorphic with particular terms whose "meaning" can be looked up in a dictionary or derived from a statement that says "x" means (or is) "y." Rather, ideas must be reconstructed, and this reconstruction involves a certain amount of decoding of the implicit "rules" of the philosophical system.

I call the representation of ideas a "reconstruction," because all the aspects of any idea cannot be stated; indeed, they are not even known. "Clarifications" and "explanations" of ideas are in fact descriptions. We as scholars and "translators" of ideas focus on certain aspects of ideas and ignore others. However, we can have control over our analyses and comparisons to the extent that we can be aware of our perspectives. Thus, I assume that representations or descriptions of ideas are much like maps — they enable a person to become acquainted with an area from a particular perspective, but they are not that area and they omit many features.

The questions that comparative philosophy needs to consider include What are the fundamental premises about the world and about thought? How are ideas verified? What issues and interests are most important? If we ask these kinds of questions about ideas in different philosophical systems, we will have a basis for comparison that is not simply a matter of personal preferences, idiosyncratic interpretations, or superficial similarities. In other words, I am suggesting that we can compare ideas by applying a set of specific questions that take into account "the surround" of the idea. The answers to these questions will in turn indicate the varying shapes of the ideas.

One way this study addressed the first of these questions was to consider the notion of social time and, in particular, the differing time frames of the tradition, society, and the individual person. Recognition of these time frames is critical to understanding the pragmatic aspect of Confucian ideas about teaching and learning. Since the Confucian teacher-scholar-official was responsible for maintaining the tradition and the society, he engaged in tasks much larger than his own lifetime. Confucian thinkers examined, reviewed, tested, revised, and judged ideas and actions against a time frame of generations, rather than years or months. From a social perspective, this long-term view justified the complex education and preparation for becoming an official, and it served as a bulwark against opportunism and scholasticism.

The existence of multiple paradigmatic contexts pointed out in this study is revealing of fundamental premises about the world and about thought. This phenomenon is in contrast to epistemological frameworks, like that of Descartes, that accept only one foundation for establishing truth. When Chinese philosophers thought in terms of such images as a mirror, a stream, or a family, they were saying, in effect, that the implications of these paradigmatic images best represent the characteristics of the world as they understand it, but not all situations have the same kind of characteristics. An epistemological system characterized by multiple paradigmatic contexts (that determine the logic of thinking) does not exhibit "epistemological chaos" or claim that "everything is relative." Such a system does suggest, however, that it is possible not to think in terms of "either-or," that is, the excluded middle, to use a Western philosophical concept. In Confucian thought, things were thought about from a variety of perspectives, which were recognized as both different and non-contradictory. This characteristic of philosophical thought is also reflected in Confucian philosophers' lack of sympathy for efforts, like those of Shao Yong, to emphasize numbers and so quantify certain kinds of ideas. The abstraction entailed in quantification would perhaps have demanded the use of a single perspective, an unacceptable situation given other philosophical assumptions.

The concept of an ethical standard presented in this study relates to the question of how ideas are verified. A system based on an ethical standard for determining the validity of ideas is opposed most clearly to a logical standard, but it is not characterized by illogical thinking. Rather, the ultimate appeal is to standards outside the process of thinking itself. These standards are attached to actions that result from the ideas. The "rules" that verify ideas thus differ between an ethical system and a logical system. The logical system is concerned more about the relationship between premises and conclusions; the ethical type is concerned more about ideas, the actions they lead to, and, most important, the ethical values of such actions.

Teaching and learning constitute two of the more important issues and interests in Confucian philosophy, and even their brief treatment in this study suggests, it is hoped, the complex and critical nature of these issues. In the case of learning, for instance, the varying conceptions of "what happens" when a person learns should confirm that the term "learning" refers to a number of quite different processes that occur in reference to different levels of social organization. Unless one closely designates the specific context and so the particular reference of the term, the comparison of one philosophical system's view of learning with that of another will be undermined from the start.

And finally, if we are to bring Li Yong's ideas themselves to bear on the matter of comparative philosophy, we must acknowledge his concern for the importance of context. In engaging in comparative philosophy, we must take this concern into account both in terms of our methods and perspectives and in terms of the subjects studied. The world to which ideas apply has many dimensions, and our understanding is potentially richer for recognizing more of those dimensions. Examining ideas from different philosophical systems provides a way to search for things we do not know and questions we have not asked. A critical premise of comparative philosophy thus must be that any universal position about the nature of truth is heuristic, and, in that vein, I stress that the statements made here about Confucian thought, with full appreciation for much within that tradition, are also heuristic.

Reference Matter

Notes

For complete author names, titles, and publication data for the works cited here in short form, see the Works Cited, pp. 249–65.

Chapter 1

1. As Moser and Mulder point out (2), metaphilosophy is the philosophy of philosophy and so entails a second-order, rather than first-order, inquiry. For instance, whereas epistemology is concerned directly with the nature of knowledge, metaphilosophy inquires about the nature of epistemology. I characterize my efforts here as metaphilosophy since my underlying concern is the nature of the Confucian philosophical system.

2. Western scholars have long acknowledged the difficulty (and impossibility) of translating into English, on a strict one-to-one basis, key concepts in Chinese culture. Although some scholars attempt to adapt the translation to the context (for example, by rendering *li* variously as "principle," "pattern," "reasons," "conditions"), others follow the common practice of using the same English term regardless of context. For some recent discussions on the term "Neo-Confucian" in particular, see Jensen; and Tillman, "New Direction" and "Reply." I would also like to say that in this study my use of the term "he," rather than the more inclusive "he or she," is deliberate, because the Chinese thinkers mentioned here were, I believe, referring to men rather than to men and women.

3. The extent to which Confucian learning entailed action as well as thought is clearly revealed in the essays in Tu, *Way*. In other contexts, a more appropriate translation of *ru* may be scholar, classicist, or teacher. For Li, *ru* referred to someone who followed the learning of the sages, or

Confucian learning (see Chapter 2). For the most part I use conventional terminology because the Chinese terms provide a degree of specificity that is unnecessary for the kind of comparative study of concern here.

4. To quote from Gellner (55), "A concept is, of course, far more than a 'mere' concept: it encapsulates and communicates and authorizes a shared way of classifying, valuing, a shared range of social and natural expectations and obligations."

5. With obvious modification, this phrase derives from Nagel's title.

6. For discussions of this issue, see Graham, "Conceptual Schemes"; Solomon; Edwards; Lakoff and Johnson; and Davidson.

7. I have drawn my theoretical position, with its idea of implicit rules that function as a code, from the theory of social communication of Ray L. Birdwhistell and from readings in anthropology and related fields. For readings concerned with this topic, see Sapir, "Unconscious Patterning," and "Language"; G. H. Mead, *Mind*, and *Movements*; R. L. Birdwhistell; D. Hymes; E. Hall; Scheflen; Mead and Byers; Winkin; Berger and Luckmann; Burke; and Douglas, *Implicit Meanings*, and *Natural Symbols*. More recently, Gellner (56) has reaffirmed that "it was Emile Durkheim's central insight to see that concepts are *binding*, and that it was this which really constituted the original unwritten social contract, the distinguishing mark of human sociability." The concept of an unwritten code or set of implicit rules is similar to Thomas Kuhn's widely used concept of "paradigm."

8. Studies such as Ames, *The Art*; D. Hall and Ames; and Graham, *Disputers*, do address the theoretical system. Although the following examples are extremely different and there are no absolute lines of separation between these two kinds of historical studies, examples (in English) of studies focusing on the historical development of ideas are Chan, "Evolution"; and Fung. For examples of studies focusing on the historical context of ideas, see Schwartz; Elman, *Classicism*; and Tillman, *Confucian Discourse*.

9. Both approaches are found, for instance, in Fung. Hansen, *Language and Logic*, "Chinese Language," and "Ancient Masters"; and Graham, *Disputers*, are examples of approaches that do not make such universalistic assumptions.

10. Based on Li Yong's own sense of identity, I refer to him as a Confucian, rather than a neo-Confucian. Li did not differentiate, in a philosophically significant way, between the earlier, classical thinkers and the later Song-Ming thinkers. For Li, they were all *ru* (Confucians) and all engaged in Confucian learning.

11. Li's ideas concerning these four aspects, the corners of his system, incorporated the thought of many philosophers and texts, both those usually regarded as Confucian as well as those seen as non-Confucian, from the ancient period to his own lifetime. My discussion in

the following chapters includes references to earlier adherents and textual sources of the ideas.

12. Rorty (9) makes this accusation against traditional Western philosophy.

13. Many studies have been done on these subjects; examples of works that address a variety of topics, and not limited to the seventeenth century, are Chaffee; de Bary and Chaffee; Ho; Lee; Miyazaki; Walton; Meskill; Busch; H. Wilhelm; Lui; and Elman and Woodside.

14. The quoted phrase is borrowed from Whitehead, *Modes*, 105.

15. A. D. Birdwhistell, *Transition*, 7–10.

16. Confucius, for instance, expressed great confidence that his role was to carry on the culture of King Wen and the Zhou (*Lunyu*, 9.5). As another example, the concept of the eremite (or scholar-in-retirement) was important throughout history and reflected the importance of the imperative to act (morally), even when the political situation suggested that positive action would be immoral.

17. This expression is borrowed from Mead, *Mind*, 217.

18. For example, Liang Qichao emphasized Li as a follower of Wang Yangming; Xu Shichang as a Cheng-Zhu and Lu-Wang eclectic; Qian Mu and more recently Chen Junmin as the last major figure in the tradition; and Lin Jiping as a participant in the historical stream of Song-Ming ontological and self-cultivation thought.

19. Sources for this view include Wu Huaiqing, 4.32a–b; and EQQJ, preface to *juan* 1, 1a–2b; first preface to *juan* 4, 1a; and 25.19a. See Chen Guying et al. for a discussion of Li's thought in the contemporary context of practical learning.

20. See Kai-wing Chow, especially chaps. 1 and 2.

21. On the concreteness of Chinese moral concepts, see Ames, "Mencian Conception."

22. See, e.g., James, 31–32, 97, 169, and 278 (for misinterpretations of his ideas) regarding "cash value," and ibid., 100, regarding "credit system." See also Max Black for a discussion of metaphors from the perspective of logic; and Turner for a similar discussion from an anthropological perspective.

23. For a concise and helpful discussion on rationalism and how its method contrasts with that of pragmatism, a philosophical position with certain features in common with the Chinese approach, see Aune.

24. I am not suggesting that the Chinese defined "living entities" or "life" in the same way(s) as modern scientific thought. Relevant aspects of the Chinese view are discussed further below.

25. Munro discusses these in detail in *Images*, and I discuss others in *Transition*. See also the discussions in Wilson; and Levey, "Clan."

26. As critical as the metaphor of the way (or road, path) and used by probably all Chinese philosophers, water was also extremely impor-

tant as a paradigmatic example. See Teiser for a discussion on the relation of water to ideas about order (the "path of morality") and disorder (the "path of immorality").

27. I discuss how medicine is used as a "theoretical tool" in the pragmatic aspects of Li's thought in my article "Medicine." That is, Li applied to Confucian philosophy the general kinds of questions and problems characteristic of a medical context.

28. Rejecting notions of truth as "timeless," Buddhist thought also emphasized the application of different perspectives and standards. See Kalupahana; and King.

29. The use of medicine as a cultural metaphor is discussed further in Chapter 2. Ideas of pain and suffering, especially in late-Ming thought, are addressed in Taylor, *Sagehood*; Tu, *Way*; and Wu Pei-yi. Medical terms can be found in the thought of many if not most philosophers, including Mencius, Zhu Xi, and Wang Yangming. Song thinkers such as Su Xun, Cheng Yi, and Zhu Xi used the ideas of illness and prescriptions in a way similar to that of Li Yong. On Su, see Hatch, 67; on Cheng Yi, see Schirokauer, "Chu Hsi's Sense," 197*n*20; and on Zhu Xi, see Schirokauer and Hymes, 32, and Schirokauer, "Chu Hsi's Sense," 198 and 218, all in Hymes and Schirokauer. For some comments by Yan Yuan, Li Yong's contemporary, see, e.g., Yan's *Xizhai yuyao, shang*:2b and 4b. For other, particularly political, applications of medical paradigmatic thinking, see Porkert; Leslie; Sivin, "Body"; Unschuld, *Medicine*; K. C. Chang; Tse-tsung Chow; and Bol, *This Culture*, 261. For a discussion of medical education and the Confucian education of some doctors, see Wu Yiyi.

30. In their exchange of letters on *ti* and *yong* (essence and application), Gu and Li used different paradigmatic frames, and thus they were arguing from different theoretical positions. Although both used this bipolar pair as tools of thought, the significance of *ti* and *yong* differed because their paradigmatic frames established different standards of relevance. Gu was using a generative frame, whereas Li was using a medical frame.

31. See Elman, *Classicism*, chaps. 4–8.

32. If the aim is to understand the system of thought (as it is here), the point is not to condemn the written word, as the Daoist philosopher Zhuangzi sometimes did, but to bring into awareness the various elements that went into forming the ideas but were not written down—a point also recognized by Zhuangzi, as indicated by his comment about the area surrounding the footprint—not walked on but still necessary (Watson, *Chuang Tzu*, 299). Thinking usually, however, of unseen principles, or patterns, or of certain kinds of knowledge, the Chinese recognized a type of "meaning beyond words." This is evident not only in the Daoist tradition based on such works as the *Zhuangzi* and *Laozi*, but also

in the Confucian tradition based on the *Chunqiu* (Spring and autumn annals, hereafter the *Annals*), the classic that was regarded as making manifest the "hidden" principles of the *Yijing* (Book of change). I use the term "principle(s)" here and elsewhere in the sense of "regularities that define certain kinds of order," not in the sense of a metaphysical substance.

33. Kalupahana (80) points out that Buddhism also "does not recognize time as a category separable from the events experienced."

34. This brief overview of the various conditions (not confined to the seventeenth century) that contributed in some way to Li's environment is based on various works, including Eastman; Parsons; Tong; Spence and Wills; Leung; Dunstan; Sivin, *Medicine*; Porkert; Leslie; Unschuld; R. P. Hymes; Hucker; Clunas; and the works by Wakeman listed in the Works Cited.

35. Quoted in Leung, 152; this saying is attributed to Fan, a famous official of the Song.

36. Studies in English relating to intellectual developments include Carsun Chang; Ch'ien; Kai-wing Chow; Alison Harley Black; Brokaw; de Bary et al., *Self and Society*, and *Unfolding*; de Bary and Bloom, *Principle and Practicality*; Elman, *From Philology*, and *Classicism*; Handlin-Smith; Peterson, *Bitter Gourd*; Wakeman, "Price of Autonomy"; and Wilson.

37. See Tu, "Yen Yuan"; Chung-ying Cheng: and Freeman. Li's position had many similarities with that of Yan Yuan.

38. Relevant studies include Gernet, *China* and "Christian"; Peterson, "Western Natural Philosophy"; Bray; and Reynolds.

39. Although no translation is satisfactory, *qi* may be translated as "matter-energy" if we recognize that we are not using these terms in a technical twentieth-century sense. See Gernet, "Christian," especially for a discussion of the view of the world during the seventeenth century. The translation of *li* also provides difficulties because of its varied meanings and lack of equivalence to any one Western concept. These two fundamental neo-Confucian concepts, *qi* and *li* (discussed further below), were the subject of continual dispute.

40. Earlier historical materials on Li's life can be found in EQQJ, *juan* 23–26; Wu Huaiqing; Hui et al.; and Li's writings and recorded conversations; more recent accounts include Liang; Xu; Qian; Hou; Chen Junmin; Lin; Chen Guying et al.; Ng; and Araki. Since this is not a biographical and historical study of Li Yong, I do not cite all the available Qing and twentieth-century accounts of Li's life and thought. The year of Li's death is unclear. Lin Jiping follows Hui Longsi in giving Li's date of death as 1703, but I have followed the fuller account of Wu Huaiqing in assigning it to 1705. No events are recorded for the last two years, however.

41. The taboo against using words in an emperor's personal name

led later writers to replace Yong with Rong. In Li Yong's case the taboo involved the name of the Jiaqing emperor (reigned 1796–1821), whose name was Yongyan.

42. Wu Huaiqing, 4.32a.

43. See *Guanzhong san Li nianpu*, in *Guanzhong congshu*.

44. Quan, 12.151.

45. Wu Huaiqing, 4.37b–38a.

46. In my article "Cultural Patterns," I discuss how particular patterns of thought and culture contribute to viewing events from certain perspectives. E.g., the assumption that events and things have beginnings and completions helps establish the view that a son's accomplishments are not due to his efforts alone but begin with the mother's efforts. Thus it was recognized that mother and son together participated in an event (the son's success) that was larger than the actions of either one of them.

47. As discussed below, Confucian philosophy entailed social elements, such as a sense of community, along with its intellectual emphases. Li's relations with educational officials may be found in his letters, in EQQJ, *juan* 17 and 18.

48. On this reaffirmation of traditional morality, see Kai-wing Chow, especially chaps. 1 and 2.

49. For discussions of the "person" in Chinese society that examine some of the issues alluded to here in relation to Li Yong as a person, see the chapters by Tu, Ames, D. Hall, David Wu, and Wolf, in Ames et al., 177–267.

50. Many of the biographies in Huang Zongxi's *Mingru xue'an* (Records of Ming scholars) mention transformation experiences. See Ching and Fang; Tu, *Neo-Confucian Thought*; and de Bary, *Neo-Confucian Orthodoxy*, 6–13, and *Message*, 29–30. Li himself wrote about the transformation experiences of other people; see EQQJ, *juan* 1 and 22. The role of suffering and sickness (in Confucian and neo-Confucian thought) in relation to a person's assuming responsibility for the Way, or to experiencing a transformation in thought, is discussed in Taylor, *Sagehood*; Tu, *Way*; and Wu Pei-yi (see note 29 above). All Chinese traditions of thought applied, in some way, the metaphor of illness to thought.

Chapter 2

1. "Epistemological imperatives" is my own term, but there is a large body of literature on the subject of implicit cultural assumptions that establish rules or codes for social behavior. See Chapter 1, note 7, for selected readings.

2. Specifically in reference to medicine but also as indicative of a related characteristic of Chinese thought, Porkert, 55–106, discusses how the "Chinese use qualitative standards of value to express relationships"

(60). Porkert discusses the standards of *yin* and *yang*, the five (evolutive) phases, and the emblems formed by combining the ten celestial stems and twelve earthly branches in a cycle of 60. In other words, the Chinese often used qualitative standards in situations in which contemporary Westerners would use quantitative standards.

3. For examples of Li's ultimate appeal to an ethical standard, see EQQJ, 1.4a, 11.5a, 15.5a, and *fu* 15.2a.

4. For instance, the Ming philosopher Hu Juren (*Juye lu* [Account of rest and activity], 110) distinguished adaptation from expedience and opportunism, in reference to *jing* and *quan* (the standard and the adaptive). This bipolar concept was mentioned by most, if not all, thinkers since Confucius, and was central, for instance, to the disagreements between Zhu Xi and Chen Liang during the Southern Song. See Tillman, *Utilitarian Confucianism*. For other discussions, see Wei; and Schirokauer, "Chu Hsi's Sense." The concept of *jing* and *quan* is related to that of timeliness (*shi*), which is important to the discussion in Chapter 4 below.

5. James, 28–32, and *passim.*

6. Dewey, from *Democracy and Education* and *Experience and Education*, excerpted in Park, 73.

7. Issues ranged from problems of social and political order to human knowledge, cultural preservation, and personal development. Cf., e.g., the chapter topics of *Xunzi* (trans. by Knoblock and by Watson) from the third century B.C.E. and of Zhu Xi's *Jinsi lu* (trans. Chan, *Reflections*) from the Song. See also Wilson on the topic of anthologies.

8. Wm. Theodore de Bary briefly reviews some of these terms in his *Neo-Confucian Orthodoxy*, xiv–xvi. Although *zhengxue* is often translated "orthodoxy" and *yiduan* "heterodoxy" or "deviant learning," I do not use these translations for reasons indicated in the discussion below.

9. The organization of neo-Confucian intellectual history reflects this phenomenon, as in Huang Zongxi's *Mingru xue'an* (Records of Ming scholars) and *Song-Yuan xue'an* (Records of Sung and Yuan scholars). For discussion on different aspects, see, e.g., Wilson; Elman, "Ch'ing Dynasty 'Schools' of Scholarship," and *Classicism*; Chen Junmin; and Komoguchi. Even the disciples of Confucius apparently specialized in different aspects of his thought; see Hughes, 12; Eno, *passim*; and Schwartz, 130–34. A very early example is Xunzi's "Fei shi'er zi," in which he lists followers of Confucius who went astray.

10. Credited with introducing Wang Yangming's learning into Guanzhong, Nan Daji is one of the few Guanxue philosophers included (EQQJ, 1.13b–14a) in Li's account (EQQJ, 1.8b–18a) of thinkers who experienced profound intellectual-spiritual transformations, as he himself did. Zhou Hui was the only Guanxue philosopher whom Li included (EQQJ, 22.16b–18b) in his *Guan'gan lu* (Record of observations and impressions; EQQJ, 22), an account of thinkers who made extraordinary changes in

their lives. Feng and Zhang were Li's most immediate philosophical predecessors in Guanzhong.

11. Gellner (57) makes a similar point about the ultimate inseparability of the prescriptive and descriptive in reference to Western thought, although he phrases it slightly differently: "Men are not free to think as they wish; they are in thrall to their ideas, and their ideas are socially shared. Like Kant, Durkheim supposed that moral and logical compulsion had the same root, though he differed from Kant as to what that root was. The primary function of ritual, according to Durkheim, was the imprinting of concepts, and hence of the compulsions and obligations built into them, onto our minds and feelings." Durkheim's view thus appears to be quite relevant to the function of *li* (ritual, code of ritual action) in Chinese society.

12. For general discussions (not focusing on Guanxue) of these and other aspects of the social context, see Handlin-Smith; Elman, *From Philology* and *Classicism*; and Neskar (regarding the Song). Additional aspects, such as family traditions of learning, are also present in some degree in Guanxue, but further discussion of the topic is beyond the scope of this study. For Li's activities, see EQQJ, *juan* 9–10 and 16–22.

13. Nakayama, 3–16. See also Henderson on the importance of the classics.

14. See D. K. Gardner, "Modes."

15. Quoted in D. Hall, *Civilization*, 3.

16. Dewey, from *Democracy and Education*, excerpted in Park, 102–3.

17. Rousseau, 168 and 170–71; also excerpted in Price, 382.

18. Rousseau, 172; excerpted in Price, 383.

19. Although he does not use this specific term, Dardess talks about the idea of social time (from a slightly different perspective) in his discussion of Confucianism as a profession and the Confucian community. He refers to the "unbounded unity in both space and time" (82); see also 74–84 and 90.

20. Whitehead, *Aims*, 3.

21. EQQJ, 14.6b; SSFSL, *Lunyu*, pt. 1, 22–23, 34, and 63; *Mengzi*, pt. 1, 12. See Zhang Zai, 292. This passage is referred to again in discussions below.

22. EQQJ, 2.3a, preface by Wang Sifu.

23. Discussed in D. Hall and Ames; and Eno. See Eno, 280–82n3, for a listing of textual references.

24. A phrasing adopted with minor changes from Ross Lee Finney, excerpted in Park, 23.

25. For ancient China, this search is discussed in Graham, *Disputers*; and Schwartz. The Chinese placed little value on absolute certainty in knowledge or on originality in ideas, both concerns of Western thinkers, in part because these concerns were not relevant to the task of the Con-

fucians. Many Western philosophers have of course been concerned with action.

26. This phrasing is borrowed from G. H. Mead, *Mind*, 261.

27. See note 4 to this chapter.

28. Zhang Shundian, a late Ming Guanxue philosopher, provided a statement of this view in a colophon to Feng Congwu's *Guanxue bian*; see Feng, 20.53b–54b.

29. Tillman, "Divergent Philosophic Orientations," and *Utilitarian Confucianism*.

30. Li's predecessor in Guanzhong, Feng Congwu (13.1a–2a), phrased the separation between *dao* and *wen* as a separation between *lixue* (the learning of principle) and *wenzhang* (literature), and he blamed this separation on the fact that the philosophers no longer engaged in the practice of discussing learning (*jiangxue*). He claimed that this failure occurred as early as the Qin and Han dynasties.

31. Many neo-Confucians held this view, which had political as well as philosophical overtones. See, e.g., Cheng Hao and Cheng Yi, *Yishu*, 25.3b, in *Er Cheng quanshu*; and EQQJ, 11.3a and 16.20b–21a.

32. For discussion of conflicts during the Song, a period of fundamental change in many areas, see Bol, "Chu Hsi's Redefinition" and *This Culture*; and Hymes and Schirokauer.

33. Durkheim, *Elementary Forms*, 466.

34. Ibid., 463–64.

35. Numerous works discuss Confucian views on education; see, e.g., Chen Qingzhi; Wang Yunwu; de Bary and Chaffee; and Elman and Woodside.

36. Zhang Zai, 265. Of the seven creators, the first six are usually regarded as mythological, not historical, figures.

37. At various times in history, Confucians faced the fact that any widespread acceptance of teaching to the masses the privileged knowledge of the elite classes would entail changes in the conceptions of knowledge and society; see, e.g., Ebrey, "Education," particularly 279–82; and Handlin-Smith. In Western thought, the pragmatists were particularly concerned about the relationship between the type of education and the type of society; see Finney, excerpted in Park, 17–18; and Dewey.

38. A phrase borrowed from Whitehead, *Aims*, 1–2.

39. Dewey, *Democracy and Education*, excerpted in Park, 103–4.

40. Ames, *The Art*, 158.

41. Feng, 2.29ff; and Yang, *Xiuqi zhizhi ping*, 9a–11b and 36a.

42. Feng, 20.26a. According to Gardner, "Modes," teachers gained in authority as the conversational mode began to take over much of the former importance of the commentarial mode in terms of how ideas were discussed during the Song. In addition, there was historically in

the conception of the Way a separation between the government and rulers, e.g., Yao and Shun, and teaching and teachers, e.g., Confucius and Mencius.

43. *Shangshu* (Book of documents), introduction by Kong Anguo, 2a.

44. See Bol, "Culture and the Way," 84, for examples.

45. See Walton, "Education," 136–53 and 58–61 (respectively), and "Institutional Context," on the Four Masters of Siming: Yang Jian (1141–1226), Yuan Xie (1144–1224), Shen Huan (1139–91), and Shu Lin (1136–99); and on the Five Masters of the Qingli period (1041–48): Lou Yu (*jinshi* 1053), Du Chun (11th c.), Yang Shi (11th c.), Wang Zhi (985–1054), and Wang Shuo (1010–85). The former had national fame and the latter local.

46. See, e.g., Chaffee, 90 and 152; and Walton, "Education," 58–61 and 136–53.

47. On the use of models in education in modern China, see Munro, *Contemporary China*.

48. See D. Hall and Ames, 44.

49. See also Fung, 1: 107–8.

50. Ibid., 2: 407–8; and Wechsler.

51. Hartman; see also Chan, *Source Book*, 451–56, for a translation of Han Yu's essays on the Way and on human nature.

52. See Wilson on the broadened conception of the transmission of the Way.

53. It is interesting to note that although Lu Jiuyuan was later to be seen, along with Wang Yangming, as especially linked to the thought of Mencius, Wu did not include Lu in this list.

54. Although not stated explicitly, the Song proscription refers to the late twelfth-century *weixue* (false learning) prohibition against Zhu Xi and followers of the learning of the Way; see Schirokauer, "Neo-Confucians."

55. "Those who apprehended first" (*xianjue*) is a term found in the *Lunyu*, 14.33, and in *Mencius*, 5A.7.5 and 5B.1.2. It is also a Buddhist term, but Li is using it here in a Confucian context.

56. Translation from de Bary, *Message*, 9. Also translated in Legge, *Shoo King*, 61–62.

57. Xue, 40.

58. Excerpted in Price, 154–56.

59. For discussions that address in different ways how values are spread through the culture and transmitted over time, see Bush and Murck; Bush; Cahill; and Ebrey, *Confucianism and Family Rituals* and *Chu Hsi's Family Rituals*.

60. Yang, *Xiuqi zhizhi ping*, general introduction by Liu Guyu, 1b; and Tu, *Neo-Confucian Thought*, 88–89.

61. See Sivin, *Medicine*, especially 4 and 95.

62. Kleinman, 428.

63. See Porkert for a detailed analysis of the theoretical premises. There are numerous works on medicine in China; see especially Bowers and Purcell; Hymes; Leslie; Needham, "Medicine"; Porkert; Sivin, *Medicine*; Topley, and Unschuld.

64. See Needham et al., vol. 5, pt. 4, 242–79; and Sivin, "Chinese Alchemy."

65. See Needham et al., vol. 5, pt. 5, 67–129.

66. The *Suwen* is a section of the *Huangdi neijing* (Inner canon of the Yellow Sovereign), the important medical text compiled during the Han dynasty. *Qingnang* probably refers to the *Qingnang aozhi* (Mysterious principles of the blue bag), a text attributed to Yang Yunsong, a geomancer during the Tang, but it was also used more broadly as the arts of healing, from its association with the famous Han doctor Hua Tuo. Eclectic in his medical practices, Hua was associated with Indian practices of healing; see Needham et al., 2: 360; and DeWoskin, 188*n*127 and 140–53. See Handlin-Smith and Brokaw for selected uses of the medical framework and imagery, and P. A. Kuhn and Topley on relations between medicine and society.

67. Li's position regarding faults and the analogy to medicine is similar to that of Wang Yangming; see. e.g., Chan, *Instructions*, 68 and 107. Confucian and other philosophers have paid attention to faults or errors in thought (and action) since the time of Confucius himself; see, e.g., *Lunyu*, 1.8, 4.7, 5.27, and 12.4. *Lüshi chunqiu*, section 16, is entitled "Huiguo" (Regretting and criticizing [one's] faults), and the *Huainanzi*, j. 13, p. 226, mentions the faults of the sages, Yao, Shun, Tang, and Wu, as well as those of the five hegemons. The topic of faults is also important throughout the *Book of Change*; see, e.g., the *Great Commentary*, 1.B.3, in R. Wilhelm and Baynes, 291–92. This topic is discussed in Chapter 4 below, on Li's teachings.

68. For Lu's comment, see *Xiangshan quanji*, 34.1b; for Wang's, see *Chuanxi lu* (Instructions for practical living), conversations recorded by Huang Mianzhi, section 313, in Chan, *Instructions*, 239. This idea is expressed in various other passages; see, e.g., Chan, *Instructions*, 68–69 and 193–94.

69. Similar ideas are also found in EQQJ, *fu* 15.2b.

70. *Lüshi chunqiu*, 15.33b–34a.

71. Needham et al., vol. 6, pt. 1, 237.

72. Ibid., 2: 71.

73. See Chow Tse-tsung; and K. C. Chang. Unschuld (*Medicine*, 17–28) claims that the king was not only a ruler and a father but also a "physician," in the sense that he had the responsibility to treat and prevent illnesses, which were seen as arising from the displeasure of the ancestors.

74. See Schipper, "Taoist Body," 355, on the five senses; and Lü Buwei, 7.6a and 20.16b–17a, for instances using these elements with the

medical metaphor. See Sivin, "Body, Cosmos, State"; and Schipper, *Taoist Body*, for further discussion.

75. Correlations were made from various philosophical perspectives; see, e.g., discussions in Sivin, "Body, Cosmos, State"; Kohn; and Queen.

76. See Eberhard for an interesting discussion relating to these associations.

77. See note 29 to Chapter 1 for references.

78. The analogy between medical-type thinking and Buddhist thinking, with its emphasis on "skillful means" (*upaya*), has long been recognized; see, e.g., Birnbaum, *Healing Buddha*. The result in Buddhism is a "spiritual pragmatism," to use a phrase from Buswell and Gimello, 4, and this position has some similarities with that of Li Yong. Li's writings indicate that he was familiar with Buddhism and its texts; see, e.g., his exchange of letters with Gu Yanwu, EQQJ, 16.15a–21a.

79. For some of the historical background relevant to Li's position, see de Bary, *Liberal Tradition*, 13–20. As discussed in de Bary, *Message*, the Cheng-Zhu and Lu-Wang split developed during the late Ming and was not an opposition between two similarly organized "sides" that had existed from the time of Zhu and Lu in the twelfth century. Wang based much of his thinking on Zhu's thought and only late in life began to promote Lu. In his claims, Li Yong used Lu and Wang interchangeably, even in contexts in which only Wang's thought made sense historically.

80. Yang, *Xiuqi zhizhi ping* (Commentary on cultivating [the self], regulating [the family], and directly pointing [to the heart-mind]).

81. Two early passages with this idea are *Mencius*, 4B.20, which mentions the Duke of Zhou's concern that actions be suited to the time, and 4A.17, which allows a man to touch his sister-in-law's hand in certain circumstances, such as to save her from drowning. *Lunyu*, 4.10, also can be interpreted as expressing this notion.

82. See the essays by Rosemont and Graham in Rosemont, 227–63 and 308–21, respectively; and Aboulafia for discussions on the problem of "I."

83. See *Mencius*, 6A. Li compares "we Confucians" and other paths with the sage and the madman; see SSFSL, *Mengzi*, pt. 2, 9.

84. See Ch'ien for a discussion on the unity of the three teachings.

85. See Munro, *Early China*, 96–112, and *Contemporary China*, 135–57.

86. Both the *Biographies of Virtuous Women* (*Lienü zhuan*) and *Elementary Learning* (*Xiaoxue*) have accounts of exemplary persons; see O'Hara; and Kelleher, respectively.

87. See discussion in de Bary et al., *Self and Society*, 145–247.

88. Gerth and Mills, 52–55 and 245–52.

89. EQQJ, 1.4a and 22.1b, self preface; see also de Bary et al., *Self and Society*, 170. The concept of the hero, *da zhangfu* (great man), appears in

Mencius, 3B.2. The hero was associated with visionary thinkers, especially Wang Yangming and Wang Gen. Li used various terms for the hero, including *da zhangfu, haojie, yingxiong*, and even just *ru*; see, respectively, EQQJ, 12.3a, 12.6a and 11.8a, 11.8a, 14.2b, and *passim*.

90. Although Naquin and Rawski discuss conditions of society and social classes during the eighteenth century, the seventeenth-century conditions with which Li was familiar could only have been more oppressive for the masses.

91. It is interesting that Li Yong's mother had originally set for him the goal of becoming a "great Confucian"; see A. D. Birdwhistell, "Cultural Patterns."

92. Lowenthal offers a fast-paced historian's discussion of this subject, and it has long been a focus of anthropologists; see, e.g., M. Mead; and Benedict.

Chapter 3

1. Mencius (7A.14) went so far as to claim that good teaching was more effective than good government. The importance of teaching as well as governing is also expressed in non-Confucian works, e.g., the *Lüshi chunqiu*, 4.4b–8a and *passim*, a text containing Daoist and Huang-Lao thought.

2. See, e.g., Ayala and Dobzhansky; and Whitehead, *Essays*.

3. See K. C. Chang.

4. These are standard terms in neo-Confucian thought. For examples applying to Li Yong, see SSFSL, prefaces by Xu Sunquan, Ma Yushi, Wang Xinjing, and Li Yanmao; Li's own prefatory essay on reading the Four Books; and supplement to *Mengzi*, pt. 1, 7, where Li distinguishes learning that stresses the (moral) root (*ben*) and "real" affairs (*shi*), both ongoing aspects of the tradition, from learning for individual gain.

5. A common phrase in neo-Confucian thought, from the *Lunyu*, 19.12, and used by Zhu Xi in his *Elementary Learning* to refer to the elementary stages of learning.

6. Wang Xinjing, *Qutian fa*, in *Fengchuan zazhu*; and Yang, *Binfeng guangyi*. Yang's work is prefaced with mythological and historical material, citing previous agricultural works.

7. As mentioned above, Li often quoted this teaching of Zhang or some variation of it. Li used it, for instance, in commenting on *Lunyu*, 3.24; see SSFSL, *Lunyu*, pt. 1, 22–23.

8. I am not suggesting, however, that there are only these two conceptions of the self or that Li's position was limited to the implications of these two concepts of the self. For different views about the self (mostly in non-Chinese contexts), see Carrithers et al. Although Wu Pei-yi's study concerns the historical development of Chinese autobiographical

writings, which reached their highest state of development during the sixteenth and seventeenth centuries, his discussion also relates to ideas of the self. On other Chinese views, see Elvin; the essays in Ames et al.; as well as those in Munro, *Individualism*, especially Bloom, "Mind."

9. See Ames, "Chinese Rationality," 100.

10. Feng, 7.24a.

11. See Levey, "Chu Hsi," for a careful discussion addressing some of the problems of the relationship of *li* and *qi*.

12. See Levey, "Clan," for a discussion relating to some of the resulting difficulties in Zhu Xi's thought.

13. Zhang Shundian, *Mingde ji*, 1b–3b, in *Jishan yuyao*.

14. All from earlier texts, these terms appear in numerous passages in Li's works. For Li's views on extrasensory reality, see especially EQQJ, *juan* 2.

15. Li's description of human nature (*xing*) is similar to the description of the sage in the Han dynasty work *Comprehensive Discussions at the White Tiger Hall*; see the passage translated in D. Hall and Ames, 258.

16. If we wanted to apply here G. H. Mead's distinction between the "I" and the "me" as two aspects of the personality, the *shenxin* would be somewhat comparable to, but not quite the same as, Mead's "I," and the *shen* or *xingfen* to Mead's "me." See Aboulafia, 17–18.

17. Feng, 8.4a, "Shanli tu" (Chart of goodness and selfishness).

18. Even the principles of the military sphere, for instance, were not seen as different from those of the political or social sphere. When authors of military treatises during the Warring States period proposed a separation of the military and civil spheres, contemporary Confucians rejected this view. Many later Confucians, including Li Yong, acknowledged military knowledge as a necessity for Confucians. See Lewis, 127–33; and Li's reading list (in Chapter 5 below).

19. For useful anthologies of Western philosophical views on teaching, see Park; and Price.

20. See de Bary's comments in de Bary and Chaffee, 186–218.

21. See, e.g., Lynd; and Znaniecki.

22. See, e.g., Bush; Cahill; and Bush and Murck. For more on Li's views on the place of art and literature, see Chapter 4.

23. "Paper learning" (*zhishang daoxue*) and "useful learning" (*youyong daoxue*) are from Lin Jiping, 118.

24. Li said that prose writing was empty talk (i.e., no action involved), full of just "paper" worries, and so of no help to the Way (SSFSL, *Lunyu*, pt. 2, 2).

25. For a translation of Zhu Xi's remarks, from his *Classified Conversations*, see D. K. Gardner, *Sage*, 88.

26. See Knoblock, *Xunzi, passim*; and *Mencius*, 1A.7.

27. See, e.g., Wu Ching-tzu's *The Scholars*.

28. Translated in de Bary et al., 374–75.

29. See Li Guangdi, *juan* 8, for a selection of relevant comments.

30. See EQQJ, 2.3a, where it is stated that Li had no teacher. The implication is that somehow there was "completion" even without the proper kind of "beginning." This of course was praise for Li.

31. Gu, 304.

32. Regarding a yamen clerkship as low-level and as an obstacle to becoming educated and to becoming a "great Confucian," Li's mother refused to let him become one; see my article "Cultural Patterns."

33. Li's relationships with educational officials can be seen in his correspondence with them; see EQQJ, *juan* 17 and 18.

34. See Handlin-Smith.

35. See Ron-Guey Chu, in de Bary and Chaffee, 270.

36. See Ebrey, "Education," 297.

37. Ibid., 277–82.

38. See Handlin-Smith.

39. The historian Sima Qian is an example of one who wished to establish a name; see his letter, trans. in Birch, 95–102.

40. See comments by Chan, *Chu Hsi: Life and Thought*, 9–10.

41. Raphals, 5. As Raphals (4) suggests, metic intelligence is similar to the Buddhist concept of *upaya*, or "skill in means."

42. Trans. Watson, *Chuang Tzu*, 153.

43. Trans. Legge, *Mencius*, *The Chinese Classics*, 480.

44. *Lienü zhuan*, 1.4a–b. The references to meat and mats are from the *Lunyu*, 10.8–9.

45. See especially the "Records of Learning" and "Regulations Inside [the Home]" chapters in the *Book of Rites*.

46. Referring to different (but related) activities, the term *jiangxue* has been translated in other ways, such as "intellectual discussions," "lecturing," and "learning through discussing." The context makes some interpretations of this phenomenon more plausible than others.

47. "Parting Words," in Li Yong, *Erqu ji*, 10.34a.

48. Human emotions were not in themselves bad in Li's view, and he even claimed that the kingly way was originally based on the seven emotions; see SSFSL, supplement to *Mengzi*, pt. 1, 8.

49. See Chan, *Chu Hsi: Life and Thought*, 58–61; Chan, in de Bary and Chaffee, 389–413; and Meskill.

50. See *Mencius*, 3A.4.8; and de Bary, *Liberal Tradition*, 58–66.

Chapter 4

1. See Ames, *The Art*, for a discussion of the concept of timeliness in pre-Qin thought.

2. Feng, 7.10b–11a. The Ming philosopher Hu Juren, whom Li admired, made a similar point; see Hu, 110.

3. See Wagner, 3–9.

4. EQQJ, preface by Zhang Er, 1b, to *juan* 7. All these slogans, or some variation of them, were common in neo-Confucian thought.

5. There were many variations of these beliefs: e.g., for some contemporary ideas about heroic action in relation to the masses, see Metzger; on the masses and loose sand, see Nathan; and on the development toward intellectual understanding away from heroic action during the Warring States period, see Lewis.

6. In early history, military knowledge underwent a transformation leading to a similar position, as it shifted its emphasis from fighting to analysis; see Lewis on the shift in military thinking and the issue of knowing and doing.

7. Feng, 1.59a–60b.

8. Xu Sunquan, preface to Zhang Shundian, *Jishan yuyao. Jishan yuyao* contains two works by Zhang, *Zhiqu yan* and *Mingde ji*. Xu Sunquan and Li Yong recovered these writings in manuscript form, edited them, and arranged for their printing.

9. Xin Quan, preface to Zhang Shundian, *Jishan yuyao.*

10. As Kusumoto points out (see especially 376–85), Li Yong's teaching of *mingti shiyong* is in the tradition of Zhu Xi's teaching of *quanti dayong* (complete essence and great application; based on the *Great Learning*) and closely follows that of Wang Yangming.

11. For a related discussion, see Yü, *Lishi*, and "Observations."

12. See *Lunyu*, 6.25, 9.10.2, 12.1.1. On Zhu Xi, see Gardner, *Sage*, 116–20 and *passim*.

13. All were exemplary models of virtuous ministers or statesmen; Yi Yin was a teacher and chief minister during the Shang, Fu Yue was a chief minister (to King Wuding) during the Shang, the Duke of Zhou and Duke Shao were early Zhou leaders, and the last four were famous statesmen of the Northern Song.

14. Reference to the *Doctrine of the Mean*, chap. 1. See Zhu Xi's comments in Gardner, *Sage*, 181–82.

15. Translation from Chan, *Instructions*, 276.

16. *Lunyu*, 17.8. Other writers also referred to the lesser ways of farming and the like; see, e.g., Zhen, *juan* 35. Yang Shen (*Xiuqi zhizhi ping*, 23b) spoke specifically of the four sprouts of the farmer—farming, sericulture, growing trees, and raising animals.

17. See de Bary's discussion of Zhu Xi on this topic, in *Liberal Tradition*, 21–24 and *passim*.

18. See de Bary, *Liberal Tradition*, *passim*; and Hymes and Schirokauer, *passim*.

19. Stated in the *Great Learning*, opening section.

20. See also Lewis, 223.

21. Trans. adapted from Chan, *Source Book*, 45, with my substitution of "rightness" for "righteousness."

22. Legge, *Mencius*, 362; Lau, *Mencius*, 145.

23. de Bary, *Message*, 153.

24. In reference to Yan Hui; see de Bary, *Neo-Confucian Orthodoxy*, 76–77.

25. Although there are numerous possible citations, see, e.g., Cheng Yi's commentary on the *Yijing*; and Zhu Xi's *Zhuzi yulei*, 105.2629. Lu Jiuyuan (11.2b–3a), for instance, spoke about *huiguo* (criticize faults), *wuguo* (have no faults), *gaishan* (correct and reform yourself), and *zixin* (renew yourself). On Liu, see discussion in Tu, *Way*, especially 114–16; and for Yan Yuan, see his *Xizhai yuyao, xia*:4b.

26. See discussions in Handlin-Smith; Taylor, *Cultivation*; and Wu Pei-yi.

27. Reference to Yu is from the "Jundao" chapter of the *Shuo yuan*, a Han dynasty work compiled by Liu Xiang. Reference to Tang is from the *Book of Documents*, 4.2.1. Reference to King Wen is from *Mencius*, 4B.20. Reference to King Wu is from the "Wu wang jianzuo" chapter of the *Record of Rites of the Elder Dai* (*Da Dai Liji*). Reference to the Duke of Zhou is from the poem "Youfeng puofu" in the *Book of Poetry*, 1.15.4. Reference to Confucius is to *Lunyu*, 7.16.

28. Li is referring here to the Great Commentary, 2.5.11–12, to the *Book of Change*, which contains a quote of Confucius about Yan Hui.

29. See *Chengshi waishu*, j. 12, in *Er Cheng quanshu*; also Chan, *Reflections*, chap. 4, *passim*.

30. The reference to upper- and middle-level people follows a distinction made by Wang Yangming, who classified Wang Ji (Longxi) as sharper than Qian Dehong (Xushan) in regard to endowment and cultivation efforts; see Chan, *Instructions*, 243–44, the Tianquan bridge conversation.

31. Confucius spoke of upward reaching in the *Lunyu*, 14.24. The passage on principle, nature, and destiny is found in *Shuo gua* (On selected trigrams), j. 1, in the *Book of Change*.

32. See the passage on daily renewal in the *Great Learning*, j. 2, of Zengzi's commentary; and the Great Commentary, I.5, in the *Book of Change*. The ideas of not being ashamed before heaven and men, etc., can be found in *Mencius*, 7A.20.

33. Zhu Xi (118) had articulated a similar idea, that the sages used different words, but their meaning was the same.

34. These teachings are associated respectively with (among others) Zhu Xi, continuing Cheng Yi; Lu Jiuyuan, from Mencius; Yang Jian; Chen Xianzhang; Xue Xuan; Wang Yangming; Zhan Ruoshui; Gao Panlong and Wang Yangming, from the *Great Learning*; Gao Panlong and Luo Nian'an; and Zhang Shundian, from the *Great Learning*.

35. Specific references are to the *Book of Documents*, 4.2.1; *Lunyu*, 1.8.4, 9.24; *Great Learning*, commentary of Zengzi, 6.3; *Doctrine of the Mean*, 29.1; and *Mencius*, 2A.2.

36. This account can be found in many sources. Zhang Zai is re-

garded as one of the five founders of neo-Confucianism, or the learning of the Way. For biographical accounts of Zhang Zai, see the *Song shi*, 427.15a–17b; *Yi-Luo yuanyuan lu* (hereafter YLYYL), comp. by Zhu Xi; and Huang and Quan , j. 17 and 18. Okada, chap. 7, 340–86, provides useful information on all these historical figures and is the source of much of the bibliographical information given in the following notes. Although I follow Li Yong's text fairly closely in giving the accounts of these historical figures, I regard my text here as more a paraphrase than a translation and so have not used quotation marks.

37. Xie Liangzuo was one of the four primary disciples of the Cheng brothers. The phrase, "trifling with things and losing one's aim," often used by Song thinkers, derives from the *Book of Documents*, 5.5.6, and is paired with the phrase, "trifling with men and losing one's virtue." It appears, for example, in *Chengshi yishu*, j. 3, and *Chengshi waishu*, j. 12, both in *Er Cheng yishu*. See also Zhu Xi, *Zhuzi yulei*, j. 5, and *Jinsi lu*, j. 2, both of which quote from *Chengshi yishu*; and Chan, *Reflections*, 52–53 and 151. Cheng's phrase describing Xie as a learner comes from *Lunyu*, 19.7.6. For accounts of Xie, see the *Song shi*, 428.1b–2a; Huang and Quan, j. 24; and YLYYL, j. 9.

38. For Zhu's encounter with Li Tong (Yanping), see *Zhuzi yulei*, j. 104. There are numerous accounts of Zhu Xi; see, e.g., those in the *Song shi*, 429; and Huang and Quan, j. 48 and 49.

39. Wu Cheng was a major neo-Confucian thinker during the Yuan period.

40. Chen Chun was a disciple of Zhu Xi. Rao Lu was a disciple of Huang Gan (1152–1221), a disciple of Zhu Xi. See Chan, *Neo-Confucian Terms Explained*.

41. Xue Xuan was an important early Ming thinker. For Xue's biography, see Goodrich and Fang, 1: 616–9; and Huang, trans. in Ching and Fang, 90–96.

42. Luo Rufang was a major thinker of the so-called left-wing branch of Wang Yangming's school of thought. Yan Jun was an important late Ming thinker. For Luo's biography, see Huang, j. 16, trans. Ching and Fang, 185–91; and Goodrich and Fang, 1: 975–78. For Yan's biography, see Huang, trans. Ching and Fang, 165–66; and under He Xinyin's biography in Goodrich and Fang, 1: 513–15. Illness of the mind and of the body is a common distinction in Buddhism. See, e.g., Burtt, 98–100.

43. For selected works on Wang, see Chan, *Instructions*; Ching, *To Acquire Wisdom*; Tu, *Neo-Confucian Thought*; Goodrich and Fang, 2: 1408–16; and Huang, trans. Ching and Fang, 100–107.

44. A follower of Wang Yangming, Nan Daji helped to edit Wang's *Instructions for Practical Living* and was very important in spreading Wang's ideas. He is regarded as the person who introduced Wang's learning into Guanzhong, Li Yong's home region. For Nan's biography,

see Huang, 29.1a–b, 11a–b; and Feng Congwu's *Guanxue Register* (*Guanxue bian*), in *Shaoxu ji*, from which Li Yong's account was taken.

45. Yang Tingxian was the father of the Song philosopher Yang Jian (Cihu, 1140–1225), the most prominent follower of Lu Jiuyuan; see Balazs, 425. Lu wrote Yang Tianxian's epitaph, which contains this account.

46. Qiu Lan (Xiang, Later Han). This passage appears in Fan Hua's biography in the *History of the Later Han* (*Hou Han shu*), *lie zhuan* 66.

47. Xu Shu (Yuanzhi) recommended Zhuge Liang to Liu Bei and himself served Liu Bei. This passage appears in the commentary to the biography of Zhuge Liang in the *Account of the Three Kingdoms* (*Sanguo zhi*), j. 35 (*Shu shu*, 5), and is drawn from the *Wei lüe*.

48. Zhou Chu (Ziyin) was from the Western Jin. He served as an official in Wu during the Three Dynasties period, and when Wu was defeated, he served in Jin. This account is based on his biography in the *History of the Jin* (*Jin shu*), j. 58.

49. This passage, beginning with Zizhang and excluding the last sentence, is quoted from "Meng Xia Ji," "Zun shi" (Respecting Teachers) in the *Spring and Autumn Annals of Mr. Lü*, 4.3.8b–9b. The preceding passage in Lü's text identifies the early sages and worthies and their teachers and emphasizes the importance of teachers and of learning. Many sections in this text contain views similar to Li Yong's.

Chapter 5

1. Durkheim, *Suicide*, 246–54, on anomie.

2. See Bruer, "Mind's Journey," and *Schools for Thought*.

3. Bateson, 279–308.

4. See discussions in de Bary and Chaffee; and in Miyazaki.

5. See Chan, *Instructions*, 272; and EQQJ, 25.14b–15b, for the role of Li's mother in encouraging him to become a "great Confucian."

6. See Cahill.

7. Other images used for analogical purposes included the road, way, family, music, holy rite, and sacred ceremony; see Ames, "Chinese Rationality," 106–7 (e. g., reference to *Lunyu*, 7.1); and Fingarette, 1–17.

8. Graham ("Conceptual Schemes") touches on this subject, but his analysis is only introductory.

9. Li's position follows that of the Duke of Zhou, in *Mencius*, 4B.20. For King Wen, see the *Book of Poetry*, 3.1.6. This series appears in the discussion above.

10. Wang Yangming held a similar view; see Chan, *Instructions*, 271–80.

11. For the similarity with Wang Yangming, see ibid.

12. Excerpted in Li Guangdi, 7.15b.

13. Translated in full in Chapter 2 above.

14. Lu, 23.1a–b.

15. Li also claimed, however, that his own teaching of *huiguo zixin* could be substituted for all those of the classics and past philosophers; see especially Chapter 2 above.

16. Munro, *Contemporary China*.

17. These prescriptions are mentioned in many passages; see, e.g., EQQJ, 11.3a. See also Chapter 3 and earlier in Chapter 5.

18. See discussion in Kai-wing Chow.

19. See Chan, *Neo-Confucian Terms Explained*, 104. This was also Zhang Zai's view.

20. Li Yong quoted not only from standard Confucian sources such as the Great Commentary to the *Book of Change*, *Book of Documents* (the "Great Plan" chapter), *Lunyu*, and *Doctrine of the Mean*, but also from the *Guanzi*.

21. On Wang Ji, see de Bary, *Self and Society*, 136. "Letting everything go" (*yiqie fangxia*) was a favorite expression of Wang's.

22. The early twentieth-century revolutionaries who led the New Culture movement certainly understood the point that texts convey both implicit and explicit ideas, and thus they advocated such measures as the use of the vernacular in writing and new literary forms.

23. That is, Li lists Sima Guang's *Zizhi tongjian* in one list and Zhu Xi's summary of it, *Zizhi tongjian gangmu*, in other lists. I thank Conrad Schirokauer for his comments on this.

24. See Kelleher.

25. As pointed out by Conrad Schirokauer, the discussion of the *Annals* with analogies to law goes back at least to Cheng Yi during the Song. See also Schirokauer, "Chu Hsi's Sense," 197*n*20.

26. See Smith et al. for a discussion of this classic in Song thought.

27. Not the name of any well-known thinker, Tanzi may be a copyist's error for Yangzi (Yang Zhu) or perhaps even refers to Tan Gong, a ritual specialist from Lu whose name is the title of chapter 2 of the *Book of Rites*, a classic to which Li often referred.

28. The *Sunzi* and *Wuzi* are two ancient military classics. Wu Hou probably refers to Sun Wu (sixth c. B.C.E.), traditionally considered the author of the *Sunzi* (*bingfa*). It is now thought that perhaps this work was begun by Sun Wu but finished by Sun Bin. See Raphals, 101–66, for a discussion of military thought, particularly that relating to strategy. Li Yong's practical and contextual emphases (along with the fact that his father was greatly interested in military studies) suggest he drew from the complex of military ideas. See also Sawyer on these military works.

29. "Code" and "Commandment" are probably a reference to the Great Ming code (*Da Ming lü*) and Great Ming commandment (*Da Ming ling*). See discussion in Farmer.

30. See discussion in Bray (Needham), 64–70 and *passim*.

Works Cited

Aboulafia, Mitchell. *The Mediating Self: Mead, Sartre, and Self-Determination*. New Haven: Yale University Press, 1986.

Ames, Roger T. *The Art of Rulership: A Study in Ancient Chinese Political Thought*. Honolulu: University of Hawaii Press, 1983.

——. "Chinese Rationality: An Oxymoron?" *Journal of Indian Council of Philosophical Research* 9: 2 (Jan.–Apr. 1992): 95–119.

——. "The Focus-Field Self in Classical Confucianism." In Ames et al., pp. 187–212.

——. "The Mencian Conception of *ren xing*: Does It Mean 'Human Nature'?" In Rosemont, pp. 143–75.

Ames, Roger T., ed., with Wimal Dissanayake and Thomas P. Kasulis. *Self as Person in Asian Theory and Practice*. Albany: SUNY Press, 1994.

Araki, Kengo 荒木見悟. *Ri Nikyoku* 李二曲 (Li Erqu). Tokyo: Meitoku shuppansha, 1989.

Aune, Bruce. *Rationalism, Empiricism, and Pragmatism: An Introduction*. New York: Random House, 1970.

Ayala, Francisco José, and Theodosius Dobzhansky. *Studies in the Philosophy of Biology: Reduction and Related Problems*. Berkeley: University of California Press, 1974.

Balazs, Etienne. *A Sung Bibliography*. Ed. Yves Hervouet. Hong Kong: Chinese University Press, 1978.

Bateson, Gregory. *Steps to an Ecology of Mind: Collected Essays in Anthropology, Psychiatry, Evolution, and Epistemology*. Northvale, N.J.: Jason Aronson, 1972; rev. ed. 1987.

Benedict, Ruth. *Patterns of Culture*. Boston: Houghton Mifflin, 1934.

Berger, Peter L., and Thomas Luckmann. *The Social Construction of Reality: A Treatise in the Sociology of Knowledge*. Garden City, N.Y.: Doubleday, 1966.

Birch, Cyril, comp. and ed. *Anthology of Chinese Literature: From Early Times to the Fourteenth Century.* New York: Grove Press, 1965.

Birdwhistell, Anne D. "Cultural Patterns and the Way of Mother and Son: An Early Qing Case." *Philosophy East and West* 42: 3 (July 1992): 503–16.

———. "Medicine and History as Theoretical Tools in a Confucian Pragmatism." *Philosophy East and West* 45: 1 (Jan. 1995): 1–28.

———. *Transition to Neo-Confucianism: Shao Yung on Knowledge and Symbols of Reality.* Stanford: Stanford University Press, 1989.

Birdwhistell, Ray L. *Kinesics and Context: Essays in Body Motion Communication.* Philadelphia: University of Pennsylvania Press, 1972.

Birnbaum, Raoul. *The Healing Buddha.* Boulder, Colo.: Shambhala, 1979.

———. "Seeking Longevity in Chinese Buddhism: Long Life Deities and Their Symbolism." *Journal of Chinese Religions* 13–14 (Fall 1985–86): 143–76.

Black, Alison Harley. *Man and Nature in the Philosophical Thought of Wang Fu-chih.* Seattle: University of Washington Press, 1989.

Black, Max. *Models and Metaphors: Studies in Language and Philosophy.* Ithaca, N.Y.: Cornell University Press, 1962.

Bloom, Irene. "On the Matter of the Mind: The Metaphysical Basis of the Expanded Self." In Munro, *Individualism,* pp. 293–330.

Bloom, Irene, trans., ed., and with an introduction by. *Knowledge Painfully Acquired: The "K'un-chih chi" by Lo Ch'in-shun.* New York: Columbia University Press, 1987.

Blount, Ben G., ed. *Language, Culture, and Society: A Book of Readings.* Cambridge, Mass.: Winthrop Publishers, 1974.

Bol, Peter K. "Chu Hsi's Redefinition of Literati Learning." In de Bary and Chaffee, pp. 151–85.

———. "Culture and the Way in Eleventh Century China." Ph.D. diss., Princeton University, 1982.

———. *"This Culture of Ours": Intellectual Transitions in T'ang and Sung China.* Stanford: Stanford University Press, 1992.

Bowers, John Z., and Elizabeth F. Purcell. *Medicine and Society in China.* New York: Josiah Macy, Jr., Foundation, 1974.

Bray, Francesca, *see* Needham et al.

Brokaw, Cynthia J. *The Ledgers of Merit and Demerit: Social Change and Moral Order in Late Imperial China.* Princeton: Princeton University Press, 1991.

Bruer, John T. "The Mind's Journey from Novice to Expert." *American Educator* 17: 2 (Summer 1993): 6–15, 38–46.

———. *Schools for Thought: A Science of Learning in the Classroom.* Cambridge, Mass.: MIT Press, 1993.

Burke, Peter. *History and Social Theory.* Ithaca, N.Y.: Cornell University Press, 1993.

Burtt, E. A., ed. *The Teachings of the Compassionate Buddha*. Rev. ed. New York: Penguin (Mentor), 1982.

Busch, Heinrich. "The Tung-lin Academy and Its Political and Philosophical Significance." *Monumenta Serica* 14 (1949–55): 1–163.

Bush, Susan. *The Chinese Literati on Painting: Su Shih (1037–1101) to Tung Ch'i-ch'ang (1555–1636)*. Cambridge, Mass.: Harvard University Press, 1971.

Bush, Susan, and Christian Murck, eds. *Theories of the Arts in China*. Princeton: Princeton University Press, 1983.

Buswell, Robert E., Jr., and Robert M. Gimello. *Paths to Liberation: The Marga and Its Transformations in Buddhist Thought*. Honolulu: University of Hawaii Press, 1992.

Cahill, James F. "Confucian Elements in the Theory of Painting." In Arthur F. Wright, ed., *The Confucian Persuasion*, pp. 115–40. Stanford: Stanford University Press, 1960.

Carlitz, Katherine. "The Social Uses of Female Virtue in Late Ming Editions of *Lienü zhuan*." *Late Imperial China* 12: 2 (Dec. 1991): 117–52.

Carrithers, Michael, Steven Collins, and Steven Lukes, eds. *The Category of the Person: Anthropology, Philosophy, History*. Cambridge, Eng.: Cambridge University Press, 1985.

Chaffee, John W. *The Thorny Gates of Learning in Sung China: A Social History of Examinations*. Cambridge, Eng.: Cambridge University Press, 1985.

Chan, Wing-tsit. *Chu Hsi: Life and Thought*. Hong Kong: Chinese University Press, 1987.

———. "The Evolution of the Confucian Concept *Jen*." *Philosophy East and West* 4 (1954–55): 295–319.

Chan, Wing-tsit, ed. *Chu Hsi and Neo-Confucianism*. Honolulu: University of Hawaii Press, 1986.

———, trans., with notes. *Instructions for Practical Living and Other Neo-Confucian Writings by Wang Yang-ming*. New York: Columbia University Press, 1963.

———, trans., ed., and Introduction by. *Neo-Confucian Terms Explained (The "Pei-hsi tzu-i") by Ch'en Ch'un, 1159–1223*. New York: Columbia University Press, 1986.

———, trans., with notes. *Reflections on Things at Hand: The Neo-Confucian Anthology*. Comp. Chu Hsi and Lü Tsu-ch'ien. New York: Columbia University Press, 1967.

———, trans. and comp. *A Source Book in Chinese Philosophy*. Princeton: Princeton University Press, 1963.

Chang, Carsun. *The Development of Neo-Confucian Thought*, vol. 2. New York: Bookman Associates, 1962.

Chang, K. C. *Art, Myth, and Ritual: The Path to Political Authority in Ancient China*. Cambridge, Mass.: Harvard University Press, 1983.

Chang, Y. Z. "China and the English Civil Service Reform." *American Historical Review* 47: 3 (Apr. 1942): 539–44.

Chen Guying 陳鼓應, Xin Guanjie 辛冠潔, and Ge Rongjin 葛榮晉, eds. *Ming-Qing shixue sichao shi* 明清實學思潮史 (History of the Ming-Qing trend of practical learning). Jinan: Qilu shushe, 1989.

Chen Junmin 陳俊民. *Zhang Zai zhexue sixiang ji Guanxue xuepai* 張載哲學思想及關學學派 (The philosophy of Zhang Zai and the Guanxue school). Beijing: Renmin chubanshe, 1986.

Chen Qingzhi 陳青之. *Zhongguo jiaoyu shi* 中國教育史 (History of Chinese education). Shanghai: Shangwu yinshuguan, 1936.

Cheng, Chung-ying. "Practical Learning in Yen Yuan, Chu Hsi, and Wang Yang-ming." In de Bary and Bloom, pp. 37–67.

Cheng Hao 程顥 and Cheng Yi 程頤. *Er Cheng quanshu* 二程全書 (Complete works of the two Chengs). *Sibu beiyao* 四部備要 ed.

Ch'ien, Edward T. *Chiao Hung and the Restructuring of Neo-Confucianism in the Late Ming.* New York: Columbia University Press, 1986.

Ching, Julia. *To Acquire Wisdom: The Way of Wang Yang-ming.* New York: Columbia University Press, 1976.

Ching, Julia, ed., with Chaoying Fang. *The Records of Ming Scholars*, by Huang Tsung-hsi. Honolulu: University of Hawaii Press, 1987.

Chow, Kai-wing. *The Rise of Confucian Ritualism in Late Imperial China: Ethics, Classics, and Lineage Discourse.* Stanford: Stanford University Press, 1994.

Chow, Tse-tsung 周策縱. "Zhongguo gudai de wuyi yu jisi, lishi, yuewu, ji shi di guanxi" 中國古代的巫醫與祭祀, 歷史, 樂舞, 及詩的關係; "Guwu dui yuewu ji shige fazhan de gongxian" 古巫對樂舞及詩歌發展的貢獻 (Ancient Chinese *wu* shamanism and its relationship to sacrifices, history, dance-music, and poetry). *Tsing Hua Journal of Chinese Studies*, n.s. 12 (Dec. 1979): 1–59; n.s. 13 (Dec. 1981): 1–25.

Clunas, Craig. *Superfluous Things: Material Culture and Social Status in Early Modern China.* Urbana: University of Illinois Press, 1991.

Dardess, John W. *Confucianism and Autocracy: Professional Elites in the Founding of the Ming Dynasty.* Berkeley: University of California Press, 1983.

Davidson, Donald. "On the Very Idea of a Conceptual Scheme." *Proceedings and Addresses of the American Philosophical Association* 67 (1973–74): 5–20.

de Bary, Wm. Theodore. *The Liberal Tradition in China.* Hong Kong: Chinese University Press, 1983.

——. *The Message of the Mind in Neo-Confucianism.* New York: Columbia University Press, 1989.

——. *Neo-Confucian Orthodoxy and the Learning of the Mind-and-Heart.* New York: Columbia University Press, 1982.

de Bary, Wm. Theodore, and the Conference on Ming Thought. *Self and Society in Ming Thought*. New York: Columbia University Press, 1970.

de Bary, Wm. Theodore, and the Conference on Seventeenth-Century Chinese Thought. *The Unfolding of Neo-Confucianism*. New York: Columbia University Press, 1975.

de Bary, Wm. Theodore, and Irene Bloom, eds. *Principle and Practicality*. New York: Columbia University Press, 1979.

de Bary, Wm. Theodore, and John W. Chaffee, eds. *Neo-Confucian Education: The Formative Stage*. Berkeley: University of California Press, 1989.

de Bary, Wm. Theodore, Wing-tsit Chan, and Burton Watson, comps. *Sources of Chinese Tradition*, vol. 1. New York: Columbia University Press, 1960.

Deutsch, Eliot, ed. *Culture and Modernity: East-West Philosophic Perspectives*. Honolulu: University of Hawaii Press, 1991.

Dewey, John. *Democracy and Education: An Introduction to the Philosophy of Education*. New York: Macmillan, 1916.

DeWoskin, Kenneth J. *Doctors, Diviners, and Magicians of Ancient China: Biographies of Fang-shih*. New York: Columbia University Press, 1983.

Douglas, Mary. *Implicit Meanings: Essays in Anthropology*. London: Routledge and Kegan Paul, 1975.

———. *Natural Symbols: Explorations in Cosmology*. London: Barrie and Rockliff; Cresset Press, 1970.

Dunstan, Helen. "The Late Ming Epidemics: A Preliminary Survey." *Ch'ing-shih wen-t'i* 3: 3 (Nov. 1975): 1–59.

Durkheim, Emile. *The Elementary Forms of the Religious Life*. Trans. Joseph Ward Swain. New York: Free Press, 1915.

———. *Suicide: A Study in Sociology*. Trans. John A. Spaulding and George Simpson. Glencoe, Ill.: Free Press, 1951.

Eastman, Lloyd E. *Family, Fields, and Ancestors: Constancy and Change in China's Social and Economic History, 1550–1949*. New York: Oxford University Press, 1988.

Eberhard, Wolfram. *Guilt and Sin in Traditional China*. Berkeley: University of California Press, 1967.

Ebrey, Patricia Buckley. *Confucianism and Family Rituals in Imperial China: A Social History of Writing About Rites*. Princeton: Princeton University Press, 1991.

———. "Education Through Ritual: Efforts to Formulate Family Rituals During the Sung Period." In de Bary and Chaffee, pp. 277–306.

Ebrey, Patricia Buckley, trans and intro. *Chu Hsi's Family Rituals: A Twelfth-Century Chinese Manual for the Performance of Cappings, Weddings, Funerals, and Ancestral Rites*. Princeton: Princeton University Press, 1991.

Ebrey, Patricia Buckley, and Peter N. Gregory, eds. *Religion and Society in T'ang and Sung China.* Honolulu: University of Hawaii Press, 1993.

Edwards, Steven D. *Relativism, Conceptual Schemes and Categorial Frameworks.* Aldershot, Eng., and Brookfield, Vt.: Avebury, Gower Publishing, 1990.

Elman, Benjamin A. "Ch'ing Dynasty 'Schools' of Scholarship." *Ch'ing-shih wen-t'i* 4: 6 (1981): 1–44.

———. *Classicism, Politics, and Kinship: The Ch'ang-chou School of New Text Confucianism in Late Imperial China.* Berkeley: University of California Press, 1990.

———. *From Philosophy to Philology: Intellectual and Social Aspects of Change in Late Imperial China.* Cambridge, Mass.: Harvard University Press, 1984.

———. "The Hsueh-hai T'ang and the Rise of New Text Scholarship in Canton." *Ch'ing-shih wen-t'i* 4: 2 (Dec. 1979): 51–82.

———. "Imperial Politics and Confucian Societies in Late Imperial China: The Hanlin and Donglin Academies." *Modern China* 15: 4 (Oct. 1989): 379–418.

———. "The Relevance of Sung Learning in the Late Ch'ing: Wei Yuan and the *Huang-ch'ao ching-shih wen-pien.*" *Late Imperial China* 9: 2 (Dec. 1988): 56–85.

Elman, Benjamin A., and Alexander Woodside. *Education and Society in Late Imperial China, 1600–1900.* Berkeley: University of California Press, 1994.

Elvin, Mark. "Between the Earth and Heaven: Conceptions of the Self in China." In Carrithers et al., pp. 156–89.

Eno, Robert. *The Confucian Creation of Heaven: Philosophy and the Defense of Ritual Mastery.* Albany: SUNY Press, 1990.

Farmer, Edward L. "Social Order in Early Ming China: Some Norms Codified in the Hung-wu Period." In McKnight, ed., pp. 1–36.

Feng Congwu 馮從悟. *Shaoxu ji* 少墟集 (Collected works of Shaoxu). *Siku quanshu* 四庫全書 ed., 5th series.

Fingarette, Herbert. *Confucius: The Secular as Sacred.* New York: Harper Torchbooks, 1972.

Freeman, Mansfield. "The Ch'ing Dynasty Criticism of Sung Politico-Philosophy." *Journal of the North China Branch of the Royal Asiatic Society,* n.s. 59 (1928): 78–110.

Fung Yu-lan. *A History of Chinese Philosophy.* 2 vols. Trans. Derk Bodde. Princeton: Princeton University Press, 1952, 1953.

Gardner, Daniel K. "Modes of Thinking and Modes of Discouse in the Sung: Some Thoughts on the *Yü-lu* ("Recorded Conversations") Texts." *Journal of Asian Studies* 50: 3 (Aug. 1991): 574–603.

———. "Transmitting the Way: Chu Hsi and His Program of Learning." *Harvard Journal of Asiatic Studies* 49: 1 (June 1989): 141–72.

Gardner, Daniel K., trans. and comp. *Learning to Be a Sage: Selections from the "Conversations of Master Chu, Arranged Topically."* Berkeley: University of California Press, 1990.

Gardner, Howard. *Multiple Intelligences: The Theory in Practice.* New York: Basic Books, 1993.

Gellner, Ernest. *Plough, Sword and Book: The Structure of Human History.* London: Collins Harvill, 1988.

Gernet, Jacques. *China and the Christian Impact: A Conflict of Cultures.* Trans. Janet Lloyd. Cambridge, Eng.: Cambridge University Press, 1985.

———. "Christian and Chinese Visions of the World in the Seventeenth Century." *Chinese Science* 4 (Sept. 1980): 1–17.

Gerth, H. H., and C. Wright Mills, trans., ed., and with an Introduction by. *From Max Weber: Essays in Sociology.* New York: Oxford University Press, 1946.

Goodrich, L. Carrington, and Chaoying Fang, eds. *Dictionary of Ming Biography, 1368–1644.* 2 vols. New York: Columbia University Press, 1976.

Graham, A. C. "Conceptual Schemes and Linguistic Relativism in Relation to Chinese." In Deutsch, pp. 193–212.

———. *Disputers of the Tao: Philosophical Argument in Ancient China.* La Salle, Ill.: Open Court, 1989.

Gu Yanwu 顧炎武. *Rizhi lu* 日知錄 (A record of daily knowledge). *Guoxue jiben congshu* 國學基本叢書 ed. Taibei: Shangwu yinshuguan, 1968.

———. *Tinglin shiwenji* 亭林詩文集 (Collected essays and poetry of Tinglin). *Guoxue jiben congshu* 國學基本叢書 ed. Taibei: Shangwu yinshuguan, 1968.

Guanzhong congshu 關中叢書 (Encyclopedia of Guanzhong). Comp. Song Liankui 宋聯奎. *Congshu jing hua* 叢書菁華 ed. Photo-offset reproduction of Shaanxi tongzhiguan ed. of 1934–36. 30 vols. Taibei: Yiwen yinshuguan, 1970?

Guy, R. Kent. *The Emperor's Four Treasuries: Scholars and the State in the Late Ch'ien-lung Era.* Cambridge, Mass.: Harvard University Press, 1987.

Haeger, John Winthrop, ed. *Crisis and Prosperity in Sung China.* Tucson: University of Arizona Press, 1975.

Hall, David L. *The Civilization of Experience: A Whiteheadian Theory of Culture.* New York: Fordham University Press, 1973.

———. "To Be or Not to Be: The Postmodern Self and the *Wu*-Forms of Taoism." In Ames et al., pp. 213–34.

Hall, David L., and Roger T. Ames. *Thinking Through Confucius.* Albany: SUNY Press, 1987.

Hall, Edward T. *The Silent Language.* Garden City, N.Y.: Doubleday, 1959.

Handlin-Smith, Joanna F. *Action in Late Ming Thought: The Reorientation of Lü K'un and Other Scholar-Officials.* Berkeley: University of California Press, 1983.

Hansen, Chad. "Chinese Language, Chinese Philosophy, and 'Truth.' " *Journal of Asian Studies* 44: 3 (May 1985): 491–517.

——. *Language and Logic in Ancient China.* Ann Arbor: University of Michigan Press, 1983.

——. "Should the Ancient Masters Value Reason?" In Rosemont, pp. 179–206.

Hartman, Charles. *Han Yü and the T'ang Search for Unity.* Princeton: Princeton University Press, 1986.

Hatch, George. "Su Hsun's Pragmatic Statecraft." In R. P. Hymes and Schirokauer, pp. 59–75.

Henderson, John B. *Scripture, Canon, and Commentary: A Comparison of Confucian and Western Exegesis.* Princeton: Princeton University Press, 1991.

Ho Ping-ti. *The Ladder of Success in Imperial China: Aspects of Social Mobility, 1368–1911.* New York: Columbia University Press, 1962.

Hou Wailu 侯外盧. *Zhongguo sixiang tongshi* 中國思想通史 (Complete history of Chinese thought). 5 vols. Vol. 5: *Zhongguo zaoqi qimeng sixiang shi* 中國早期啓蒙思想史 (History of early enlightened thought in China). Beijing: Renmin chubanshe, 1958.

Hu Juren 胡居仁. *Juye lu* 居業錄 (Account of rest and activity). In *Congshu jicheng jianbian* 叢書集成簡編, vols. 212–13, ed. Wang Yunwu 王雲五. Taibei: Shangwu yinshuguan, 1966.

Huainanzi zhu 淮南子注 (The Huainanzi, with commentary). Taibei: Shijie shuju, 1965.

Huang Zongxi 黃宗羲. *Mingru xue'an* 明儒學案 (Records of Ming scholars). *Sibu beiyao* 四部備要 ed.

Huang Zongxi 黃宗羲 and Quan Zuwang 全祖望. *Song-Yuan xue'an* 宋元學案 (Records of Song and Yuan scholars). *Sibu beiyao* 四部備要 ed.

Huangchao jingshi wenbian 皇朝經世文編 (Qing statecraft essays). Ed. He Zhangling 賀長齡. In *Jindai Zhongguo shiliao congkan* 近代中國史料叢刊, vol. 731, pt. 1, comp. Shen Yunlong 沈雲龍. Taibei: Wenhai chubanshe, 1966.

Hucker, Charles O., ed. *Chinese Government in Ming Times: Seven Studies.* New York: Columbia University Press, 1966.

Hughes, E. R., ed. and trans. *Chinese Philosophy in Classical Times.* London: J. M. Dent & Sons, 1954.

Hui Longsi 惠龗嗣 et al. *Linian jilüe* 歷年紀略 (Chronological outline). In Li Yong 李顒, *Erqu ji* 二曲集, j. 45.

Hummel, Arthur W., ed. *Eminent Chinese of the Ch'ing Period.* 2 vols. Washington, D.C.: U.S. Government Printing Office, 1943.

Hymes, Dell. *Foundations in Sociolinguistics: An Ethnographic Approach.* London: Tavistock Publications, 1977.

Hymes, Robert P. "Not Quite Gentlemen? Doctors in Sung and Yuan." *Chinese Science* 8 (Jan. 1987): 9–76.

Hymes, Robert P., and Conrad Schirokauer, eds. *Ordering the World: Approaches to State and Society in Sung Dynasty China*. Berkeley: University of California Press, 1993.

Idema, Wilt. "Diseases and Doctors, Drugs and Cures: A Very Preliminary List of Passages of Medical Interest in a Number of Traditional Chinese Novels and Related Plays." *Chinese Science* 2 (1977): 37–63.

James, William. *Pragmatism: A New Name for Some Old Ways of Thinking* and *The Meaning of Truth. A Sequel to Pragmatism*. Introduction by A. J. Ayer. Cambridge, Mass.: Harvard University Press, 1978 [1907].

Jensen, Lionel. "Manufacturing 'Confucianism': Chinese and Western Imaginings in the Making of a Tradition." Ph.D. diss., University of California, Berkeley, 1992.

Kalupahana, David J. *A History of Buddhist Philosophy: Continuities and Discontinuities*. Honolulu: University of Hawaii Press, 1992.

Kelleher, M. Theresa. "Back to Basics: Chu Hsi's 'Elementary Learning' (*Hsiao-hsüeh*)." In de Bary and Chaffee, pp. 219–51.

King, Sallie B. *Buddha Nature*. Albany: SUNY Press, 1991.

Kleinman, Arthur. "Indigenous and Traditional Systems of Healing." In Arthur C. Hastings, James Fadiman, and James S. Gordon, eds., *The Complete Guide to Holistic Medicine: Health for the Whole Person*, pp. 427–42. Boulder, Colo.: Westview Press, 1980.

Knoblock, John. *Xunzi. A Translation and Study of the Complete Works*, vol. 1, *Books 1–6*. Stanford: Stanford University Press, 1988.

Kohn, Livia. "Taoist Visions of the Body." *Journal of Chinese Philosophy* 18: 2 (June 1991): 227–52.

Komoguchi Osamu 菰口治. "Kangaku no tokuchô" 关学の特徴 (Characteristics of Guanxue). 2 pts. *Shûkan Tôyôgaku* 18 (Oct. 1967): 28–38; *Bunka* 32: 3 (1969): 47–74.

Kuhn, Philip A. *Soulstealers. The Chinese Sorcery Scare of 1768*. Cambridge, Mass.: Harvard University Press, 1990.

Kuhn, Thomas. *The Structure of Scientific Revolutions*. 2d ed. Chicago: University of Chicago Press, 1970.

Kusumoto Masatsugu 楠本正继. *Chûgoku tetsugaku kenkyû* 中国哲学研究 (Research studies in Chinese philosophy). Tokyo: Kokushikan daigaku toshokan, 1975.

Lakoff, George, and Mark Johnson. *Metaphors We Live By*. Chicago: University of Chicago Press, 1980.

LeBlanc, Charles. "A Re-examination of the Myth of Huangti." *Journal of Chinese Religions* 13–14 (Fall 1985–86): 45–63.

Lee, Thomas. *Government Education and Examination in Sung China*. Hong Kong: Chinese University Press, 1985.

Legge, James, trans. *The Chinese Classics*. 5 vols. Reprinted—Taibei: World Book Company, 1963.

Leslie, Charles, ed. *Asian Medical Systems: A Comparative Study.* Berkeley: University of California Press, 1976.

Leung, Angela Ki Che. "Organized Medicine in Ming-Qing China: State and Private Medical Institutions in the Lower Yangzi Region." *Late Imperial China* 8: 1 (June 1987): 134–66.

Levenson, Joseph R. *Confucian China and Its Modern Fate: A Trilogy*, vol. 1, *The Problem of Intellectual Continuity.* Berkeley: University of California Press, 1972.

Levey, Matthew A. "Chu Hsi as a 'Neo-Confucian': Chu Hsi's Critique of Heterodoxy, Heresy, and the 'Confucian' Tradition." Ph.D. diss., University of Chicago, 1991.

——. "The Clan and the Tree: Inconsistent Images of Human Nature in Chu Hsi's *Settled Discourse.*" *Journal of Sung-Yuan Studies* 24 (1994): 101–43.

Lewis, Mark Edward. *Sanctioned Violence in Early China.* Albany: SUNY Press, 1990.

Li Guangdi 李光地, comp. *Xingli jingyi* 性理精義 (Essential meanings of nature and principle). *Sibu beiyao* 四部備要 ed.

Li Yong 李顒. *Erqu ji* 二曲集 (Collected works of Erqu). 46 *juan.* Shiquan Peng shi ed., 1877.

——. *Li Erqu xiansheng quanji* 李二曲先生全集 (Complete works of Master Li Erqu). Photo-offset of 1828 ed. 2 vols. Taibei: Huawen shuju, 1970.

——. *Sishu fanshen lu* 四書反身錄 (Record of reflections on the Four Books). 1702 ed. n.p. (located in Gest Library, Princeton University).

Liang Ch'i-ch'ao. *Intellectual Trends in the Ch'ing Period.* Trans. Immanuel C. Y. Hsü. Cambridge, Mass.: Harvard University Press, 1959.

Lienü zhuan 列女傳 (Biographies of virtuous women). *Sibu beiyao* 四部備要 ed.

Liji yishu 禮記義疏 (Book of Rites, with commentaries). *Siku quanshu* 四庫全書 ed., 8th series.

Lin Jiping 林繼平. *Li Erqu yanjiu* 李二曲研究 (A study of Li Erqu). Taibei: Shangwu yinshuguan, 1980.

Lowenthal, David. *The Past Is a Foreign Country.* Cambridge, Eng.: Cambridge University Press, 1985.

Lü Buwei 呂不韋. *Lüshi chunqiu jishi* 呂氏春秋集釋 (Annals of Mr. Lü, with collected commentaries). Taibei: Shijie shuju, 1966.

Lu Jiuyuan 陸九淵. *Xiangshan quanji* 象山全集 (Complete works of [Lu] Xiangshan). *Sibu beiyao* 四部備要 ed.

Lui, Adam Yuen-chung. *The Hanlin Academy: Training Ground for the Ambitious, 1644–1850.* Hamden, Conn.: Archon Books, 1981.

Lunyu zhengyi 論語正義 (Analects of Confucius, with commentaries). *Sibu beiyao* 四部備要 ed.

Lynd, Robert S. *Knowledge for What?* Princeton: Princeton University Press, 1939.

Major, John S. *Heaven and Earth in Early Han Thought: Chapters Three, Four, and Five of the Huainanzi.* Albany: SUNY Press, 1993.

McKnight, Brian E., ed. *Law and the State in Traditional East Asia: Six Studies on the Sources of East Asian Law.* Honolulu: University of Hawaii, 1987.

Mead, George H. *Mind, Self and Society: From the Standpoint of a Social Behaviorist.* Ed. Charles W. Morris. Chicago: University of Chicago Press, 1934.

——. *Movements of Thought in the Nineteenth Century.* Ed. Merritt H. Moore. Chicago: University of Chicago Press, 1936.

Mead, Margaret. *Continuities in Cultural Evolution.* New Haven: Yale University Press, 1964.

Mead, Margaret, and Paul Byers. *The Small Conference: An Innovation in Communication.* Paris: Mouton, 1968.

Mencius. Trans. D. C. Lau. New York: Penguin Books, 1970.

Mengzi zhengyi 孟子正義 (The Mencius, with commentaries). *Sibu beiyao* 四部備要 ed.

Meskill, John. *Academies in Ming China: A Historical Essay.* Tucson: University of Arizona Press, 1982.

Metzger, Thomas A. *Escape from Predicament: Neo-Confucianism and China's Evolving Political Culture.* New York: Columbia University Press, 1977.

Miyazaki, Ichisada. *China's Examination Hell: The Civil Service Examinations of Imperial China.* Trans. Conrad Schirokauer. New York: John Weatherhill, 1976.

Moser, Paul, and Dwayne Mulder. *Contemporary Approaches to Philosophy.* New York: Macmillan, 1994.

Mungello, D. E. *Curious Land: Jesuit Accommodation and the Origins of Sinology.* Honolulu: University of Hawaii Press, 1985; reprinted 1989.

Munro, Donald J. *The Concept of Man in Contemporary China.* Ann Arbor: University of Michigan Press, 1977.

——. *The Concept of Man in Early China.* Stanford: Stanford University Press, 1969.

——. *Images of Human Nature: A Sung Portrait.* Princeton: Princeton University Press, 1988.

Munro, Donald J., ed. *Individualism and Holism: Studies in Confucian and Taoist Values.* Ann Arbor: University of Michigan Press, 1985.

Nagel, Thomas. *The View from Nowhere.* Oxford: Oxford University Press, 1986.

Nakayama, Shigeru. *Academic and Scientific Traditions in China, Japan, and the West.* Trans. Jerry Dusenbury. Tokyo: University of Tokyo Press, 1984.

Naquin, Susan, and Evelyn S. Rawski. *Chinese Society in the Eighteenth Century.* New Haven: Yale University Press, 1987.

Nathan, Andrew J. *Chinese Democracy*. Berkeley: University of California Press, 1985.

Needham, Joseph. "Medicine and Culture." In idem, *Clerks and Craftsmen in China and the West*, pp. 263-93. Cambridge, Eng.: Cambridge University Press, 1970.

Needham, Joseph, et al. *Science and Civilisation in China*, vol. 2 (1956); vol. 5 (1976-83); vol. 6, pt. 2 (1984): *Biology and Biological Technology*, Part II, *Agriculture*, by Francesca Bray. Cambridge, Eng.: Cambridge University Press.

Neskar, Ellen. "The Cult of Worthies: A Study of Shrines Honoring Local Confucian Worthies in the Sung Dynasty (960-1279)." Ph.D. diss., Columbia University, 1993.

Ng, On-cho. "Mystical Oneness and Meditational Praxis in Li Yong's Confucian Thought." *Journal of Chinese Religions* 22 (Fall 1994): 75-102.

O'Hara, Albert Richard. *The Position of Women in Early China According to the Lieh Nü Chuan, "The Biographies of Chinese Women."* Taibei: Mei Ya Publications, 1971.

Okada Takehiko 岡田武彦. *Ōmeigaku taikei* 陽明學大系 (An outline of the learning of Wang Yangming), vol. 7. Tokyo: Meitoku shuppansha, 1974.

Park, Joe, ed. *Selected Readings in the Philosophy of Education*. New York: Macmillan, 1958.

Parsons, James Bunyan. *The Peasant Rebellions of the Late Ming Dynasty*. Tucson: University of Arizona Press, 1970.

Peterson, Willard J. *Bitter Gourd: Fang I-chih and the Impetus for Intellectual Change*. New Haven: Yale University Press, 1979.

———. "Western Natural Philosophy Published in Late Ming China." *Proceedings of the American Philosophical Society* 117: 4 (Aug. 1973): 295-322.

Porkert, Manfred. *The Theoretical Foundations of Chinese Medicine: Systems of Correspondence*. Cambridge, Mass.: MIT Press, 1974.

Price, Kingsley. *Education and Philosophical Thought*. 2d ed. Boston: Allyn and Bacon, 1967.

Qian Mu 錢穆. *Zhongguo jin sanbainian xueshu shi* 中國近三百年學術史 (History of Chinese thought in the past three hundred years). 2 vols. Taibei: Shangwu yinshuguan, 1966 [1937].

Quan Zuwang 全祖望. "Erqu xiansheng bianshi wen" 二曲先生窆石文 (Epitaph of Mr. Erqu). In idem, *Jiqiting ji* 鮚埼亭集 (Collection from the room on Jiqi mountain), 12: 147-51, p. 151. In *Guoxue jiben congshu* 國學基本叢書. Taibei: Shangwu yinshuguan, 1968.

Queen, Sarah. "From Chronicle to Canon: The Hermeneutics of the *Spring and Autumn Annals* According to Tung Chung-shu." Ph.D. diss., Harvard University, 1991.

Raphals, Lisa. *Knowing Words: Wisdom and Cunning in the Classical Traditions of China and Greece*. Ithaca, N.Y.: Cornell University Press, 1992.

Reynolds, David C. "Redrawing China's Intellectual Map: Images of Science in Nineteenth-Century China." *Late Imperial China* 12: 1 (June 1991): 27–71.

Rickett, W. Allyn. *Kuan-tzu: A Repository of Early Chinese Thought: A Translation and Study of Twelve Chapters*. Hong Kong: Hong Kong University Press, 1965.

Rorty, Richard. *Philosophy and the Mirror of Nature*. Princeton: Princeton University Press, 1979.

Rosemont, Henry, Jr., ed. *Chinese Texts and Philosophical Contexts: Essays Dedicated to Angus C. Graham*. LaSalle, Ill.: Open Court, 1991.

Rousseau, Jean-Jacques. *Emile or On Education*. Introduction, trans., and notes by Allan Bloom. New York: Basic Books, 1979.

Sapir, Edward. "Language." In Blount, pp. 46–66.

——. "The Unconscious Patterning of Behavior in Society." In Blount, pp. 32–45.

Sawyer, Ralph D., trans., with Mei-chün Sawyer. *The Seven Military Classics of Ancient China*. Boulder, Colo.: Westview Press, 1993.

Scheflen, Albert E. *Communicational Structure: Analysis of a Psychotherapy Transaction*. Bloomington: Indiana University Press, 1973.

Schipper, Kristofer. "The Taoist Body." *History of Religions* 17: 3–4 (Feb.–May 1978): 355–86.

——. *The Taoist Body*. Trans. Karen C. Duval. Berkeley: University of California Press, 1993.

Schirokauer, Conrad. "Chu Hsi's Sense of History." In Hymes and Schirokauer, pp. 193–220.

——. "Neo-Confucians Under Attack: The Condemnation of *Wei-hsueh*." In Haeger, pp. 163–98.

Schwartz, Benjamin. *The World of Thought in Ancient China*. Cambridge, Mass.: Harvard University Press, Belknap Press, 1985.

Shangshu zhengyi 尚書正義 (Book of documents, with commentaries). *Sibu beiyao* 四部備要 ed.

Sirén, Osvald. *The Chinese on the Art of Painting: Translations and Comments*. New York: Schocken Books, 1963.

Sivin, Nathan. "Body, Cosmos, State." Unpublished paper. 2d draft. Nov. 1993.

——. "Chinese Alchemy and the Manipulation of Time." In idem, ed., *Science and Technology in East Asia*, pp. 109–22. New York: Science History Publications, 1977.

——. *Traditional Medicine in Contemporary China*. Ann Arbor: University of Michigan, Center for Chinese Studies, 1987.

Smith, Kidder, Jr., Peter K. Bol, Joseph A. Adler, and Don J. Wyatt. *Sung Dynasty Uses of the I Ching*. Princeton: Princeton University Press, 1990.

Solomon, Robert C. "Recapturing Personal Identity." In Ames et al., pp. 7–34.

Song shi 宋史 (History of the Song). 20 vols. *Sibu beiyao* 四部備要 ed. Taibei: Zhonghua shuju, 1966.

Spence, Jonathan, and John E. Wills, Jr., eds. *From Ming to Ch'ing: Conquest, Region, and Continuity in Seventeenth-Century China*. New Haven: Yale University Press, 1979.

Taylor, Rodney Leon. *The Confucian Way of Contemplation: Okada Takehiko and the Tradition of Quiet-Sitting*. Columbia: University of South Carolina Press, 1988.

——. *The Cultivation of Sagehood as a Religious Goal in Neo-Confucianism: A Study of Selected Writings of Kao P'an-lung (1562–1626)*. Missoula, Mont.: Scholars Press, 1978.

Teiser, S. F. "Engulfing the Bounds of Order: The Myth of the Great Flood in Mencius." *Journal of Chinese Religions* 13–14 (Fall 1985–86): 15–43.

Tillman, Hoyt Cleveland. *Confucian Discourse and Chu Hsi's Ascendancy*. Honolulu: University of Hawaii Press, 1992.

——. "Divergent Philosophic Orientations Toward Values: The Debate Between Chu Hsi (1130–1200) and Ch'en Liang (1143–1194)." *Journal of Chinese Philosophy* 5 (1978): 363–89.

——. "A New Direction in Confucian Scholarship: Approaches to Examining Differences Between Neo-Confucianism and *Tao-hsueh*." *Philosophy East and West* 42: 3 (July 1992): 445–74.

——. "A Reply to Professor de Bary." *Philosophy East and West* 44: 1 (Jan. 1994): 135–42.

——. *Utilitarian Confucianism: Ch'en Liang's Challenge to Chu Hsi*. Cambridge, Mass.: Harvard University Press, 1982.

Tong, James W. *Disorder Under Heaven: Collective Violence in the Ming Dynasty*. Stanford: Stanford University Press, 1991.

Topley, Marjorie. "Chinese Traditional Etiology and Methods of Cure in Hong Kong." In Leslie, pp. 243–65.

Tu Wei-ming. "Embodying the Universe: A Note on Confucian Self-Realization." In Ames et al., pp. 177–86.

——. *Neo-Confucian Thought in Action: Wang Yang-ming's Youth (1472–1509)*. Berkeley: University of California Press, 1976.

——. *Way, Learning, and Politics: Essays on the Confucian Intellectual*. Albany: SUNY Press, 1993.

——. "Yen Yuan: From Inner Experience to Lived Concreteness." In de Bary et al., *Unfolding*, pp. 511–41.

Turner, Victor. *Dramas, Fields, and Metaphors: Symbolic Action in Human Society*. Ithaca, N.Y.: Cornell University Press, 1974.

Unschuld, Paul U. *Medicine in China: A History of Ideas*. Berkeley: University of California Press, 1985.

Unschuld, Paul U., ed. *Approaches to Traditional Chinese Medical Literature.* Dordrecht: Kluwer Academic Publishers, 1989.

Wagner, Roy. *Symbols That Stand for Themselves.* Chicago: University of Chicago Press, 1986.

Wakeman, Frederic E., Jr. "China and the Seventeenth-Century Crisis." *Late Imperial China* 7: 1 (June 1986): 1–26.

———. *The Great Enterprise: The Manchu Reconstruction of Imperial Order in Seventeenth-Century China.* 2 vols. Berkeley: University of California Press, 1985.

———. "The *Huang-ch'ao ching-shih wen-pien.*" *Ch'ing-shih wen-t'i* 1: 10 (1969): 8–22.

———. "The Price of Autonomy: Intellectuals in Ming and Ch'ing Politics." *Daedalus* 101: 2 (Spring 1972): 35–70.

Walton, Linda (Walton-Vargö, Linda Ann). "Education, Social Change, and Neo-Confucianism in Sung-Yuan China: Academies and the Local Elite in Ming Prefecture (Ningpo)." Ph.D. diss., University of Pennsylvania, 1978.

———. "TheInstitutional Context of Neo-Confucianism: Scholars, Schools, and *Shu-yüan* in Sung-Yuan China." In de Bary and Chaffee, pp. 457–92.

———. "Southern Sung Academies as Sacred Places." In Ebrey and Gregory, pp. 335–63.

Wang Xinjing 王心敬. *Fengchuan zazhu* 豐川雜著 (Miscellaneous writings of Fengchuan). In *Guanzhong congshu* 關中叢書, ed. Song Liankui 宋聯奎, vol. 11. N.p.: Yiwen yinshuguan, 1935.

Wang Yunwu 王雲五. *Zhongguo lidai jiaoxue sixiang zonghe yanjiu* 中國歷代教學思想綜合研究 (A general outline of Chinese educational thought). Taibei: Shangwu yinshuguan, 1971.

Watson, Burton, trans. *Basic Writings of Mo Tzu, Hsün Tzu, and Han Fei Tzu.* New York: Columbia University Press, 1967.

———. *The Complete Works of Chuang Tzu.* New York: Columbia University Press, 1968.

Wechsler, Howard J. "The Confucian Teacher Wang T'ung 王通 (584?–617): One Thousand Years of Controversy." *T'oung Pao* 63 (1977): 225–72.

Wei Cheng-t'ung. "Chu Hsi on the Standard and the Expedient." In Chan, *Chu Hsi and Neo-Confucianism,* pp. 255–72.

Whitbeck, Judith. "Kung Tzu-chen and the Redirection of Literati Commitment in Early Nineteenth Century China." *Ch'ing-shih wen-t'i* 4: 10 (Dec. 1983): 1–32.

Whitehead, Alfred North. *The Aims of Education and Other Essays.* New York: Macmillan, 1929.

———. *Essays in Science and Philosophy.* New York: Philosophical Library, 1947.

——. *Modes of Thought*. New York: Free Press, 1968 [1938].

Wilhelm, Helmut. "The Po-hsüeh hung-ju Examination of 1679." *Journal of the American Oriental Society* 71 (1951): 60–76.

Wilhelm, Richard, and Cary F. Baynes, trans. *The I Ching or Book of Changes*. Bollingen Series 19. 3d ed. Princeton: Princeton University Press, 1967.

Wilson, Thomas A. "Genealogy of the Way: Representing the Confucian Tradition in Neo-Confucian Philosophical Anthologies." Ph.D. diss., University of Chicago, 1988.

Winkin, Yves. *La Nouvelle communication*. Paris: Editions du Seuil, 1981.

Wolf, Margery. "Beyond the Patrilineal Self: Constructing Gender in China." In Ames et al., pp. 251–67.

Wu Ching-tzu. *The Scholars*. Trans. Yang Hsien-yi and Gladys Yang. Beijing: Foreign Language Press, 1972.

Wu, David Y. H. "Self and Collectivity: Socialization in Chinese Preschools." In Ames et al., pp. 235–49.

Wu Huaiqing 吳懷清. *Erqu xiansheng nianpu* 二曲先生年譜 (Chronology of Master Erqu). In *Guanzhong san Li nianpu* 關中三李年譜 (Chronology of the three Li of Guanzhong). In *Guanzhong congshu* 關中叢書, ed. Song Liankui 宋聯奎, vol. 15. N.p.: Yiwen yinshuguan, 1935.

Wu, Pei-Yi. *The Confucian's Progress: Autobiographical Writings in Traditional China*. Princeton: Princeton University Press, 1990.

Wu Yiyi. "A Medical Line of Many Masters: A Prosopographical Study of Liu Wansu and His Disciples from the Jin to the Early Ming." *Chinese Science* 11 (1993–94): 36–65.

Xu Shichang 徐世昌. *Qingru xue'an* 清儒學案 (Records of Qing scholars). Tianjin: n.p., 1938.

Xue Xuan 薛瑄. *Xue Wenqing gong dushu lu* 薛文清公讀書錄 (Reading notes of Mr. Xue Wenqing). In *Congshu jicheng jianbian* 叢書集成簡編, vol. 205, ed. Wang Yunwu 王雲五. Taibei: Shangwu yinshuguan, 1965.

Xunzi jijie 荀子集解 (Xunzi, with collected commentaries). Taibei: Shijie shuju, 1966.

Yan Yuan 顏元. *Xizhai yuyao* 習齋語要 (Essentials of the conversations of Xizhai) *xia*:4b–5a. In Xu Shichang 徐世昌, comp. *Yan-Li shicheng ji* 顏李師承記 (Account of the teachings of Yan Yuan and Li Gong). Reprinted—Taibei: Mingwen shuju, 1985.

Yang Shen 楊屾. *Binfeng guangyi* 豳風廣義 (Expanded discussions from Binfeng). In *Guanzhong congshu* 關中叢書, ed. Song Liankui 宋聯奎, vol. 18. N.p.: Yiwen yinshuguan, 1936.

——. *Xiuqi zhizhi ping* 修齊直指評 (Commentary on cultivating, regulating, and directly pointing). Annot. Liu Guyu 劉古愚. In *Guanzhong congshu* 關中叢書, ed. Song Liankui 宋聯奎, vol. 11. N.p.: Yiwen yinshuguan, 1935.

Yijing (Book of Change). See *Zhouyi Cheng-Zhu zhuanyi zhezhong*.

Yü Ying-shih 余英時. *Lishi yu sixiang* 歷史與思想 (History and thought). Taibei: Lianjing chuban shiye gongsi, 1976.

———. "Some Preliminary Observations on the Rise of Ch'ing Confucian Intellectualism." *Tsing-hua Journal of Chinese Studies* 11: 1/2 (Dec. 1975): 105–46.

Zhang Shundian 張舜典. *Jishan yuyao* 雞山語要 (Essentials of the conversations of Jishan). Ed. Li Yong 李顒 and Xu Sunquan 許孫荃. 1688 [1608]. In *Guanzhong congshu* 關中叢書, ed. Song Liankui 宋聯奎, vol. 9. N.p.: Yiwen yinshuguan, 1935.

Zhang Zai 張載. *Zhangzi quanshu* 張子全書 (The complete works of Master Zhang). Annot. Zhu Xi 朱熹. In *Guoxue jiben congshu* 國學基本叢書, vol. 45, ed. Wang Yunwu 王雲五. Taibei: Shangwu yinshuguan, 1968.

Zhen Dexiu 眞德秀. *Xishan dushu ji* 西山讀書記 (Reading notes of Xishan). *Siku quanshu* 四庫全書 ed., 6th series.

Zhouyi Cheng-Zhu zhuanyi zhezhong 周易程朱傳易折衷 (Zhou Change with commentaries by Cheng Yi and Zhu Xi). *Siku quanshu zhenben chuji* 四庫全書珍本初集 ed.

Zhu Xi 朱熹. *Yi-Luo yuanyuan lu* 伊洛淵源錄 (Account of the origins of the school of the two Chengs). *Congshu jicheng* 叢書集成 ed.

———. *Zhuzi yulei* 朱子語類 (Conversations of Master Zhu, arranged topically). Taibei: Zhengzhong shuju, 1973.

Zhu Xi 朱熹 and Lü Zuqian 呂祖謙, comps. *Jinsi lu jizhu* 近思錄集注 (Reflections on things at hand with collected commentaries). *Siku quanshu zhenben* 四庫全書珍本 ed.

Zito, Angela, and Tani E. Barlow, eds. *Body, Subject, and Power in China.* Chicago: University of Chicago Press, 1994.

Znaniecki, Florian. *The Social Role of the Man of Knowledge.* New Brunswick, N.J.: Transaction Books, 1986 [1940].

Character List

an shen 安身

Ba dajia wenchao 八大家文鈔
Bai Huancai 白煥彩
Baisha ji 白沙集
Ban Gu 班固
benti 本體
benzhen 本眞
Bianxue lu 辨學錄
bing 病

Cai Xuzhai 蔡虛齋
canren 慚人
Cao Yuechuan 曹月川
Cao Zhenyu 曹眞予
Chan 禪
Chang'an 長安
Chen Chun (Beixi) 陳淳 (北溪)
cheng 成
Cheng Hao (Mingdao) 程顥 (明道)
Cheng Yi (Yichuan) 程頤 (伊川)
Cheng-Zhu 程朱
Chen Jian 陳建
Chen Liang 陳亮
Chen Shizhi 陳世祉

Chen Xianzhang (Baisha) 陳獻章 (白沙)
Chen Zhensheng (Shengfu) 陳眞晟 (剩夫)
Chen Zilong 陳子龍
Chongzheng bian 崇正辨
Chuanxi lu 傳習錄
chuijiao wanshi 垂教萬世
chuishi lijiao 垂世立教
Chunqiu Danshi zhuan 春秋啖氏傳
Chunqiu daquan 春秋大全
Chunqiu Gongyang zhuan 春秋公羊傳
Chunqiu Guliang zhuan 春秋穀梁傳
Chunqiu Hushi zhuan 春秋胡氏傳
Chunqiu Zuoshi zhuan 春秋左氏傳
Chuyang 滁陽
Cihu ji 慈湖集

Da Dai Liji 大戴禮記
Da Ming huidian 大明會典
Da Ming ling 大明令

Da Ming lü 大明律
Da Ming yitongzhi 大明一統志
Dan (Commentary) 啖
Dang Zhan (Liangyi) 黨湛 (兩一)
dao 道
daode zhi shi 道德之士
daotong 道統
daoxue 道學
daru 大儒
dashi 大師
Daxue 大學
Daxue yanyi 大學衍義
da zhangfu 大丈夫
de 德
Deng Qiangu 鄧潛谷
Deng Xi 鄧析
Deng Yuanxi 鄧元錫
Dili xianyao 地理險要
Dili zhengzong 地理正宗
dixue 帝學
Donglin 東林
Dong Yun (Luoshi) 董雲 (蘿石)
Dong Zhongshu 董仲舒
duan 端
Duan Ganmu 段干木
Du Chun 杜醇
Du Fu 杜甫
Dushu cidi 讀書次第
Dushu lu 讀書錄

Er Cheng quanshu 二程全書

fa 法
fang 方
fanguan moshi 返觀默識
Fan Hua 范嘩
Fan Zhongyan 范仲淹
Feng Congwu (Gongding, Shao-xu) 馮從吾 (恭定,少墟)
Feng Shaoxu ji 馮少墟集
Feng Yingjing 馮應京
Fu Bi 富弼

Fujian 福建
Fu Xi 伏羲
fuxing 復性
Fu Yue 傅說

gaiguo qianshan 改過遷善
gaishan 改善
Gao He 高何
Gao Panlong (Jingyi) 高攀龍 (景逸)
Gaozi 告子
Geng Dingxiang (Tiantai) 耿定向 (天台)
Geng Tiantai ji 耿天台集
gongfu 工夫
Gongming Xuan 公明宣
Gongsun Longzi 公孫龍子
Gongyang (Commentary) 公羊
guan gan 觀感
Guan'gan lu 觀感錄
Guanxue 關學
Guanxue bian 關學編
Guanzhong 關中
Guanzi 管子
Guiyang 貴陽
Guliang (Commentary) 穀梁
guo 過
Gu Xiancheng 顧憲成
Gu Yanwu 顧炎武

Hai Gangfeng 海剛峰
Han Fei 韓非
Han Qi 韓琦
Hanshi shangbian, xiabian 涵史 上編,下編
Han Yu 韓愈
Han Zhen (Lewu) 韓貞 (樂吾)
haojie 豪傑
Hao Jingshan 郝京山
he 和
He[dong] 河東
Hengmen qin 衡門芹

He Xinyin 何心隱
Hong Zong 洪宗
Hou Han shu 後漢書
houshi 後世
Huainan Honglie 淮南鴻烈
Huang Di 黃帝
Huangdi neijing [*suwen*] 黃帝内經 [素聞]
Huang Gan (Mianzhai) 黃榦 (勉齋)
Huang Ming shi dajia wenxuan 皇明十大家文選
Huang Ming tongji 皇明通紀
Huang Ming Xianzhang lu 皇明憲章錄
Hu Anguo 胡安國
Huang Zongxi 黃宗羲
Huanyu tongji 寰宇通紀
Hua Tuo 華佗
huiguo 悔過
huiguo zixin 悔過自新
Hui Neng 惠能
Hu Jingzhai ji 胡敬齋集
Hu Juren (Jingzhai) 胡居仁 (敬齋)
Hu Sanxing 胡三省
Hu Yin (Zhitang) 胡寅 (致堂)
Hu Yuan (Anding) 胡瑗 (安定)

Jiading 嘉定
Jia[jing]-Long[qing] 嘉靖隆慶
jiangshu 講書
Jiangxi 江西
jiangxue 講學
Jiangyou 江右
jiao 教
jiaofa 教法
jiaohua 教化
Jiao Ruohou 焦弱侯
jiaoshu 教書
Jiaqing 嘉慶
Jiayou 嘉祐
jing (quiescence, tranquillity) 靜

jing (reverential seriousness) 敬
jing (standard, constant values, classics) 經
jingshi (classics teacher) 經師
Jingshi bagang 經世八綱
Jingshi qieyao 經世挈要
Jingshi shihua 經世石畫
Jing[ye] 涇野
Jinshan 金山
jinshi 進士
Jin shu 晉書
Jinsi lu 近思錄
Jinxi ji 近溪集
Jiu (River) 九
Jiujing jie 九經解
jiyi zhi ren 技藝之人
juan 卷
jue 覺
juexue 絕學
Jundao 君道

Kaoting 考亭
Kongzi (Confucius) 孔子
kun 坤
Kunzhi ji 困知記

Laozi 老子
li (principle, pattern) 理
li (ritual action, rites) 禮
liangfang 良方
liangneng 良能
liangzhi 良知
Li Bai (Qing scholar) 李柏
Li Bai (Tang poet) 李白
Lidai mingchen zouyi 歷代名臣奏議
Lienü zhuan 列女傳
Liji 禮記
Liji daquan 禮記大全
Liji shu 禮記疏
Li Kecong 李可從
li ming 立命

ling 靈
lingming 靈明
lingyuan 靈原
Lin Na 林訥
Li Shibin 李士璸
Li Tong (Yanping) 李侗 (延平)
Liu Bei 劉備
Liu Guyu 劉古愚
Liu Kuang 劉礦
Liu Xiang 劉向
Liu Zongyuan 柳宗元
Liu Zongzhou 劉宗周
lixue 理學
liyan chuixun 立言垂訓
Li Yanmao 李彥瑁
Li Yindu 李因篤
Li Yong (Zhongfu, Erqu) 李顒 (中孚, 二曲)
Li Zhu 李珠
Li Zicheng 李自成
Li Zufa 李足發
Longxi ji 龍谿集
Lou Yu 樓郁
Lü Buwei 呂不韋
Lu Chun 陸淳
lüe 略
Lu Ji 陸機
Lü Jingye yulu 呂涇野語錄
Lu Jiuyuan (Xiangshan) 陸九淵 (象山)
Lü Kun (Xinwu) 呂坤 (新吾)
Lü ling 律令
Lü Nan (Jingye) 呂柟 (涇野)
Lunyu 論語
Luo Qinshun (Zheng'an) 羅欽順 (整菴)
Luo Rufang (Jinxi) 羅汝芳 (近溪)
Luoxue 洛學
Luoyang 洛陽
Luo Zheng'an Kunzhi ji 羅整菴困知記
Luo Zhonglin 駱鐘麟

Lü shi chunqiu 呂氏春秋
Lu Shikai 陸士楷
Lü shi shenyinyu 呂氏呻吟語
Lü shi shizhenglu 呂氏實政錄
Lu-Wang 陸王
Lu Yun 陸雲
Lü Zujian 呂祖儉

Ma Duanlin 馬端臨
Mao Lumen 茅鹿門
Ma Yushi 馬樲士
"Meng Xia Ji" 孟夏紀
Mengzi (Mencius) 孟子
Min (River) 岷
ming (bright) 明
Ming (dynasty) 明
Mingde ji 明德集
mingti 明體
mingti shiyong 明體適用
Minxue 閩學
ming xueshu 明學術
Mozi (Mo Di) 墨子 (墨翟)

Nan Daji (Ruiquan) 南大吉 (瑞泉)
Ningling 寧陵
Nongzheng quanshu 農政全書

Ouyang Xiu 歐陽修

Peng 彭
Piling 毘陵

qi 氣
Qi 齊
qian 乾
Qian Dehong (Xushan) 錢德洪 (緒山)
qianxin xingming 潛心性命
Qian Xushan ji 錢緒山集
Qin (dynasty) 秦
Qing (dynasty) 清

Qingli 慶歷
Qingnang [*aozhi*] *jing* 青囊 [奧旨] 經
Qin Huali 禽滑黎
Qiu Hongyu 邱宏譽
Qiu Jun (Qiongshan) 邱濬 (瓊山)
Qiu Lan 仇覽
qizhi 氣質
quan 權
quanti dayong 全體大用
Quan Zuwang 全祖望

Rao Lu (Shuangfeng) 饒魯 (雙峰)
rensheng xingfen 人生性分
renshi 人師
renxing 人性
Rilu 日錄
Rong 容
ru 儒
ruxue 儒學

Sanguo zhi 三國志
Shaanxi 陝西
Shang 商
"Shanli tu" 善利圖
Shanxi 山西
Shao Gong (duke) 邵公
Shaoxing 紹興
Shao Yong 邵雍
shen 身
Shen Buhai 申不害
sheng 生
shengchuan 聖傳
shengling 生靈
shengren zhi xue 聖人之學
shenguo 身過
shengxue 聖學
shengzhuan 聖傳
Shen Huan 沈煥
shenjiao 身教
Shen Nong 神農

Shenshi Jia-Long wenjian ji 沈氏嘉隆聞見記
shenxin 身心
shenxin zhi xue 身心之學
Shen Xiu 神秀
shenxue 身學
shi (beginning) 始
shi (reality) 實
shi (scholar, literati) 士
shi (timeliness) 時
shidao 師道
shiji 實際
Shijing daquan 詩經大全
Shijing zhushu 詩經諸疏
shixue 實學
shiyong 適用
Shiyong bian 實用編
shu 術
Shuili quanshu 水利全書
Shujing daquan 書經大全
Shu Lin 舒璘
Shun 舜
Shuo yuan 說苑
Sichuan 四川
Sili yi 四禮翼
Sima Guang 司馬光
Sima Qian 司馬遷
Siming 四明
Sishu mengyin 四書蒙引
Sishu yinwen 四書因問
Sishu yisilu 四書疑思錄
Song (dynasty) 宋
Song-Yuan tongjian 宋元通鑑
Su 蘇
Sun Bin 孫臏
Sun Qifeng 孫奇逢
Sunzi 孫子
Sunzi bingfa 孫子兵法
Suo Lucan 索盧參
Su Shi 蘇軾
Suwen 素問

Su Xun 蘇洵

Taixi shuifa 泰西水法
Taizhou 泰州
Tang (dynasty) 唐
Tang (king) 湯
Tan Gong 檀弓
Tanzi 檀子
ti 體
tiyong quanxue 體用全學
tong 同
Tongzhou 同州

Wang Anshi 王安石
wangdao 王道
Wang Dong 王棟
Wang Fuzhi 王夫之
Wang Gen (Xinzhai) 王艮 (心齋)
Wang Ji (Longxi) 王畿 (龍谿)
Wang Mang 王莽
Wang Shuo 王說
Wang Sigen 王四艮
Wang Suoxi 王所錫
Wang Tong 王通
Wang Xinjing (Fengchuan) 王心敬
 (豐川)
Wang Xinzhai ji 王心齋集
Wang Yangming (Shouren) 王陽
 明 (守人)
Wang Zhi 王致
Wei Boyang 魏伯陽
wei ji 為己
Wei lüe 魏略
weixue 為學
Wei Zhuangqu ji (Jiao) 魏莊渠
 集 (校)
wen 文
Wen (king) 文
Wengong jiali yijie 文公家禮儀節
Wenxian tongkao 文獻通考
wenyi 文義
wenzhang 文章

wenzhang qijie 文章氣節
wo 我
Wu (king) 武
Wu (state) 吳
Wubei zhi 武備志
Wu Cheng (Caolu) 吳澄 (草廬)
Wu Guang 吳光
wuguo 無過
Wu Hou (Sun Wu) 武侯 (孫武)
Wujing yi 五經繹
Wu Kangzhai ji 吳康齋集
"Wu wang jianzuo" 武王踐阼
wuyu 物欲
Wu Yubi (Kangzhai) 吳與弼
 (康齋)
Wuzi 吳子

Xi'an 西安
Xiangshan ji 象山集
xianjue 先覺
Xian Zishi 縣子石
Xiaoxue 小學
Xia Tingmei (Yunfeng) 夏廷美
 (雲峰)
Xie Liangzuo 謝良佐
xi jing (abide in or practice reverential seriousness) 習敬
xi jing (practice tranquillity) 習靜
xin 心
Xin Fuyuan ji 辛復元集
xing 性
xing er shang 性而上
xing er xia 性而下
xingfen 性分
xingling 性靈
xinglixue 性理學
xinguo 心過
[Xin]hui [新]會
Xin Quan (Fuyuan) 辛全 (復元)
xinxue 心學
Xuan (king) 宣
Xu Chao 徐超

xue 學

Xue Fangshan 薛方山

Xue Jingxuan dushu lu 薛敬軒讀書錄

Xue Kan (Shangqian, Zhongli) 薛侃 (尚謙, 中離)

xuesheng 學生

xueshu 學術

Xuexin fu 雪心賦

Xue Xuan (Jingxuan) 薛瑄 (敬軒)

xuezhe 學者

Xue Zhongli ji 薛中離集

Xu Guangqi 徐光啓

Xunzi (Hsün Tzu) 荀子

Xu Shu 徐庶

Xu Sunquan 許孫荃

Xu Xing 許行

yang 陽

Yang Fusuo 楊復所

Yang Jian (Cihu) 楊簡 (慈湖)

Yangming ji 陽明集

Yang Qiu 楊球

Yang Shen 楊甡

Yang Shi 楊適

Yang Tingxian 楊庭顯

Yang Xiong 揚雄

Yang Yu 瑒瑀

Yang Yunsong 楊筠松

Yang Zhu (Yangzi) 楊朱 (楊子)

Yan Hui (Yuan) 顏回 (淵)

yanjiao 言教

Yan Jun (Shannong) 顏鈞 (山農)

Yanyi bu 衍義補

Yan Yuan 顏元

Yan Zhuoju 顏濁聚

Yao 堯

Yao[jiang] 姚 [江]

yi 異

Yi 羿

yiduan 異端

Yijing benyi 易經本義

Yili jingzhuan tongjie 儀禮經傳通解

Yili zhushu 儀禮諸疏

yin 陰

yingxiong 英雄

Yin Tun 尹焞

yixue 異學

Yi Yin 伊尹

yong 用

Yongyan 顒琰

"Youfeng pofu" 幽風破斧

youyong daoxue 有用道學

Yu 禹

Yuan 元

Yuan Xie 遠燮

Yulu 語錄

Yuzhang 豫章

Zeng Nanfeng 曾南豐

Zengzi 曾子

Zhang Daoling 張道陵

Zhang Er 張而

Zhang Junsheng 張濬生

zhangju shusheng 章句書生

Zhang Lüting 張綠汀

Zhang Shundian 張舜典

Zhang Xunshui 張洵水

Zhang Zai 張載

Zhan Ruoshui (Ganquan) 湛箬水 (甘泉)

Zhao Kuang 趙匡

Zhen (River) 鎮

Zhen Dexiu 眞德秀

zheng 正

Zhengde 正德

zhenghua 政化

Zheng Jue 鄭玨

zhengxue 正學

zhen ru 眞儒

zhen shi 眞師

zhenzheng xuewen 眞正學問

zhi (order, rule, cure, treat) 治

zhihua 治化

Zhiqu yan 致曲言

zhishang daoxue 紙上道學

zhishi 知識

zhong (the end, completion) 終

zhong (the mean, centrality) 中

Zhongyong 中庸

Zhou (dynasty) 周

Zhou Chu 周處

Zhou Dunyi (Lianxi) 周敦頤 (濂溪)

Zhou Gong (Duke of Zhou) 周公

Zhou Haimen ji 周海門集

Zhou Hui (Xiaoquan) 周蕙 (小泉)

Zhou Rudeng (Haimen) 周汝登 (海門)

Zhouyi Chengshi zhuan 周易程氏傳

Zhouyi daquan 周易大全

Zhouyi gujinwen quanshu 周易古今文全書

Zhouzhi 盩厔

Zhuangzi (Zhuang Zhou) 莊子 (莊周)

Zhuge Liang 諸葛亮

Zhu Shu (Guangxin) 朱恕 (光信)

Zhu Xi (Ziyang, Hui'an) 朱熹 (紫陽, 晦菴)

Zhu Yunqi 朱蘊奇

Zhuzi wenji daquan 朱子文集大全

Zhuzi yulei daquan 朱子語類大全

Zisi 子思

Zixia 子夏

zixin 自信

Zizhang 子張

Zizhi tongjian gangmu daquan 資治通鑑綱目大全

Zizhi tongjian Hushi zhu 資治通鑑胡氏註

Zou Dongguo (Nangao, Yuabiao) 鄒東郭 (南皋, 元標)

Zou Dongguo ji 鄒東郭集

Zou Yan 鄒衍

zuiren 罪人

Zunjingge j 尊經閣記

"Zunshi" 尊師

Zuo (Commentary) 左

zuo ren 作人

Index

In this index an "f" after a number indicates a separate reference on the next page, and an "ff" indicates separate references on the next two pages. A continuous discussion over two or more pages is indicated by a span of page numbers, e.g., "57–59." *Passim* is used for a cluster of references in close but not consecutive sequence. Entries are alphabetized letter by letter, ignoring word breaks, hyphens, and accents.

Library of Congress Cataloging-in-Publication data

Birdwhistell, Anne D.
    Li Yong (1627–1705) and epistemological dimensions of Confucian
philosophy / Anne D. Birdwhistell.
        p.   cm.
    Includes bibliographical references and index.
    ISBN 0-8047-2605-1
    1. Li, Yung, 1627–1795.   2. Knowledge, Theory of.
3. Confucianism.   I. Title.
B5234.L483B57   1996
181' . 112--dc20   95-31977
                                                        CIP

⊗   This book is printed on acid-free paper

Original printing 1996

Last figure below indicates year of this printing
05   04   03   02   01   00   99   98   97   96